MARGUERITE PATTEN'S

FAMILY

COOKBOOK

MARGUERITE PATTEN'S
FAMILY
COOKBOOK

Bounty
Books

Editor: Nicola Hill
Assistant Editor:
Selina Higgins
Art Editor: Lisa Tai
Designer: Alyson Kyles
Production Controller:
Michelle Thomas

Special Photography:
Amanda Heywood
Home Economist:
Louise Pickford

First published in Great
Britain in 1993 by hamlyn,
a division of Octopus
Publishing Group Ltd

This edition published in
2007 by Bounty Books, a
division of Octopus
Publishing Group Ltd, 2-4
Heron Quays, London
E14 4JP

Copyright © 1993, 2007
Octopus Publishing
Group Ltd

ISBN-13: 978-0-753715-34-5
ISBN-10: 0-7537-1534-1

A CIP catalogue record for
this book is available from
the British Library

Printed and bound in China

Recipe notes

At the top of each recipe you will find a coding. This is to help you select a suitable dish for a particular meal. The symbols denote price and timing.

THE PRICE
The cost of food is important. There will be days when you require an inexpensive dish and other times when you are prepared to spend rather more money. The symbols used are as follows:

▲	▲ ▲	▲ ▲ ▲
is an inexpensive dish	is a moderately priced dish	is a more luxurious dish

THE TIMING
The time a dish takes to prepare, cook and serve is a major consideration. If you are in a hurry look for recipes marked ✪. The symbols are as follows:

✪	✪ ✪	✪ ✪ ✪	✪ ✪ ✪ ✪
Prepared and cooked within 30 minutes	Prepared and cooked within 1 hour	Prepared and cooked within 2 hours	Takes longer than 2 hours

NOTE: Sometimes recipes marked ✪ ✪ to ✪ ✪ ✪ ✪ are speedy to prepare and cook. The reason for the extra time is because the ingredients need to stand for a while, cool, be allowed to set or need to be frozen. These points have been taken into consideration when choosing the coding.

THE INGREDIENTS
In all recipes the quantities of ingredients are given in both metric and imperial weights and measures. Follow one set only.

In a few recipes, there will be slight modifications of the metric weights or measures, e.g. 110 g/4 oz instead of the usual 100 g/ 4 oz. The reason for this is that, in the particular recipe, you achieve a better result using a slightly larger amount. Your scales may not measure 110 g easily, but all you need to do is use just a little extra flour, or butter, etc.

Standard level spoon measurements are used in all recipes:
1 tablespoon = one 15 ml spoon.   1 teaspoon = one 5 ml spoon.

CHOICE OF INGREDIENTS
In some recipes, there is a choice of ingredient or quantity, e.g. butter or margerine, 2 or 3 onions, etc. The first ingredient or amount is my personal choice, but I realise that some people may prefer the second suggestion. The important point is that whichever you select, the recipe has been carefully tested with both sets of ingredients.
Eggs: In some recipes, it simply states 2 eggs; this means the size is unimportant for that particular dish. In other recipes, you will find the exact size is given, e.g. 2 eggs, size 3. This means that, in the particular recipe, the size of eggs makes a difference to the consistency or balance of ingredients and it is important to use the size given.
Fruit rinds: It is always important to grate the rind of citrus fruits carefully, so you do not use too much bitter white pith.

In some recipes, it simply states 'grated fruit rinds'; in others it specifies 'zest', i.e. the very outer, coloured part of the peel. Where the word 'zest' is used, it means you must not have any tough rind.

CONTENTS

INTRODUCTION

The aim of this book is to give cooks, of whatever experience, the greatest confidence and pleasure. This comes from knowing you are shopping wisely, and then cooking with skill, so that your family, friends, and you yourself, can enjoy interesting, appetizing and nourishing meals. During the many years I have written and talked about the exciting world of food and cookery I have had the opportunity to work with experts in many fields. This has given me the chance to learn about and assess the important part food plays in creating and maintaining good health. I have been fortunate enough to use the latest gadgets and appliances, both in my own kitchen and when I give demonstrations, and this enables me to help people make a good selection of these.

On my travels abroad, both for work and pleasure, I have been able to acquire knowledge at first hand about the cuisine of many countries. All these points are combined in this book.

The first chapter deals with the wise choice of foods and planning healthy meals. All too often, theories regarding the importance of certain foods cause the misconception that you must choose between eating foods that 'are good for you' and those you enjoy. This is, of course, quite wrong. Eating a wide variety of foods in well-planned meals will provide enjoyment and satisfaction, as well as good nutrition.

The second chapter gives information about shopping, the wise selection of foods and the correct way to store them. Shopping may be a task you find both time-consuming and troublesome – I hope I can help to make it easier. The wide range of fresh, chilled and frozen foods available today enables us to eat in a much more interesting and varied manner than in the past. If you shop well, you will save both time and money.

The processes of food preparation and cooking can be helped by a sensible choice and the correct use of cooking equipment and appliances. I have often heard people say they feel some of the equipment in their kitchen is not used to its full potential, simply because they do not know how and when it is most valuable. That is a pity, for the right use of good appliances can make food preparation and cooking less time-consuming and more successful.

In addition to the information on pages 40 to 47, you will find tips in recipes about the use of specialist equipment – where this is relevant.

Mealtimes should be pleasurable occasions; a tradition of happy family meals helps children to establish good social habits and they, in their turn, may well become accomplished cooks and lovers of good food.

The many recipes in this book include a number that are suitable for today's more informal way of living. There are recipes for parties of all kinds and for all ages, for barbecues and picnics, for vegetarians, for anyone trying to lose weight, as well as a variety of family meals. Some recipes come from other countries, but most ingredients needed to make these dishes are easily obtainable today.

To assist in your choice of dish, methods of coding are used with all the recipes to indicate the approximate cost of the dishes and the time needed for preparation and cooking. These, together with other information about the recipes, are on page 4.

Every part of this book is based on my own experience in running a home and teaching people the art of good cooking. I hope you will agree that it really is a FAMILY COOKBOOK and that you enjoy using it.

GOOD NUTRITION

I am sure we all appreciate the fact that we eat food for three very important reasons. The first is to stop the pangs of hunger, the second is to enjoy interesting tastes and textures in appetizing dishes and the third is to provide the essential nourishment (often called 'the fuel') for establishing and maintaining good health. The right kind of food is essential to promote satisfactory growth in babies, children and young adults, ensuring that they develop strong bones and bodies and have plenty of energy. A wise choice of food will help to maintain good health, strength and vitality throughout our adult lives.

People worry, about the various theories on nutrition put forward by different experts. They seem to suggest so many ways of changing our diet to fit in with modern research. It is wise to listen to or read about these and weigh up the different facts, then consider how they could affect the way you choose and cook food. The advice might suggest certain changes you should make, which would give more enjoyable and healthier meals. It is unwise to change all established eating habits after hearing one broadcast or reading an article, when the viewpoint expressed might well be contradicted within a short time.

As a general guideline if you and your family eat a varied selection of fresh foods, you will be having a reasonably well-balanced and healthy diet. A basic knowledge about the function of various foods, together with an idea of why we need certain nutrients, is useful when selecting ingredients and planning meals. That is the purpose of the information that follows.

Convenience foods

Some nutritionists criticize the popularity of convenience foods and condemn their consumption. It is far too sweeping a statement to say 'all convenience foods are bad for you'. Just what is meant by the term 'convenience foods'? Fresh fruit, cheese and dairy produce are some examples of natural convenience foods, for they need little if any preparation before consumption. Frozen vegetables and fish retain the health-giving value of fresh vegetables and fish; they may even be better in quality, as they have been harvested when in peak condition. They can be called convenience foods as much of the initial preparation has been done before freezing and packaging

The criticisms have arisen mainly because of fear that in some of the wide range of ready-prepared dishes available in vacuum-packed, frozen and cook-chill forms, there may be too much fat or sugar. These prepared dishes can be invaluable to busy people with little time to prepare fresh food during a working week, but we need to assess their health value when buying them. Make a point of reading the labels to find out the ingredients in the pack. You can then judge whether you and your family are getting the best value in terms of healthy food. It could be that by augmenting a convenience dish with something fresh, you create a well-balanced meal.

Fish is an excellent source of animal protein

KNOW ABOUT FOOD VALUES

This brief synopsis will give you an easy guide to the work of nutrients in various foods and the reason they are so important. Foods are divided into three energy-giving groups – proteins, carbohydrates and fats. Very often, a food provides more than one type of nutrient, e.g. beef is a source of both protein and fat; it also contains certain minerals and vitamins, see page 9.

Proteins: It is essential to eat foods that provide protein to build new tissue and maintain existing tissue in the body. The importance of protein has been appreciated for a long time, but advice about the choice of foods containing it has changed during the past years. One modern reassurance is the fact that people in the Western world have a more than adequate intake of foods that provide protein.

Protein is found in a wide range of foods. There are the animal proteins and the vegetable proteins. The situation has altered and we are now urged to reduce our intake of animal proteins, especially those that are high in fat, and concentrate on eating more vegetable proteins, which do not contain fat. This is, of course, very satisfactory for vegetarians. One point to remember, though, is that whereas meat (animal protein) is an excellent source of iron, vegetable proteins do not include this mineral, so other foods rich in iron should be eaten, (see Iron – under Minerals).

Pulses such as beans, peas and lentils are high in vegetable protein

Animal proteins – in all meats, poultry, fish, cheese, eggs and milk.

Vegetable proteins – particularly high in the pulses, i.e. beans, peas and lentils. Also present in grains like rice and wheat (products such as bread and pasta, made from wheat, provide protein). Nuts are a good source of protein and so are seeds, such as sunflower and sesame. Avocados are a fruit that supplies protein and there is some in Brussels sprouts.

A few people are allergic to some proteins, especially eggs, and suggestions for replacing these are given on pages 13 to 15.

Carbohydrates: These are divided into starches and sugars. Starches are considered of great importance and we are urged to eat more of them, for they provide energy and satisfy the appetite.

Starch is found in flour and products made with flour, like pasta, and all cereals such as lentils, rice and oatmeal. It is present in vegetables such as potatoes and peas.

Often people are afraid to eat many starchy foods, as they have a reputation of being fattening. Research has shown that it is not the starch that adds so many calories, but fatty spreads put on to bread, the fat used in frying potatoes, the creamy sauces added to pasta, that are far more likely to be the reason for excess weight.

Sugars are found in sugar itself and foods like honey, syrup and treacle. There is great criticism of the high

Pasta is a typical carbohydrate – a filling and energy-providing food which contains starch

quantities of sweet foods eaten in the Western world and it is considered wise to cut down sugar where possible. If you feel you are eating too much sugar, try to use less in sweetening fruit, in beverages and between meal snacks.

Fats: These are important foods, providing a concentrated form of energy; this is why they are so high in calories. It is important to have a reasonable amount of fat in the diet, unless you are recommended to follow a fat-free diet for a certain ailment, or to reduce your calorie intake. Modern nutritionists recommend that the ideal proportion of daily energy (total calories per day) given by fat is a maximum of 30 per cent. This is counting the fat on meat, oil from fish, butter, margarine, etc. Many people's diets consist of appreciably more fat than that.

Hints on reducing the fat content of some dishes are given in the individual recipes. You will find information about the value of the particular oil found in some fish on page 22, and ways of cooking meat and other foods with the minimum of fat throughout the book.

The choice of oils and fats are covered in the next chapter, on pages 20 to 21, so you may see which ones are ideal if you are anxious to follow a low-cholesterol diet.

Minerals: There are many mineral salts in foods and these play an important part in keeping us fit. Below are some of the most valuable.

Calcium – this helps to build and maintain strong bones and teeth and aids the circulation. It is present in cheese, milk and milk products. Do not worry if you choose low-fat cheese or skimmed milk, you still have the calcium content. There is calcium in fish, meat, poultry, soya beans, nuts, grains and some vegetables – potatoes, Brussels sprouts and broccoli in particular. It is also found in honey and treacle. Vitamin D helps the body absorb calcium.

Fish and poultry both contain calcium, one of the mineral salts important for good health

Iodine – relieves nervous tension and controls proper functioning of the thyroid gland. We need very little but a small amount is important. It is present in certain fish, such as cod, lobster and salmon; also in milk and milk products and some vegetables – onions in particular. Edible seaweed, such as in laverbread, provides iodine.

Iron – ensures healthy red blood. A severe lack of iron can cause anaemia and a tired listless feeling. Iron helps to produce healthy shining hair, gums and finger nails. Iron is present in meat, particularly beef, turkey, liver, kidneys and heart. It is in egg yolk, grains, wheatgerm, cocoa powder, honey and black treacle and in dried fruits, such as apricots and prunes. You also obtain iron from dark green vegetables such as parsley, spinach and watercress. Peanuts are another source. Vitamin C helps the body absorb iron.

Phosphorus – like calcium, helps the healthy formation of bones and teeth. It assists in the digestion of carbohydrates and fat. It is present in egg yolk, fish and meat, particularly liver and kidney. It is to be found in cheese, milk and nuts and in most vegetables and fruits. Cranberries are particularly high in this mineral. Vitamin D helps the body absorb phosphorus, as well as calcium.

Sodium chloride – common salt – is a valuable mineral. It helps to prevent cramp; but it is important to use only a reasonable amount of salt, for this helps to prevent hypertension (high blood pressure). If you want to cut down on salt, flavour food with herbs, lemon juice and spices instead. They do not take the place of salt, but they do give an interesting taste, so the reduction or lack of salt is less apparent. The correct use of a small amount of salt in cooking enhances the taste of many foods and may well prevent people adding too much at the table. Relatively little salt added when cooking food penetrates it much more efficiently than sprinkling it over the cooked dish.

If you are following a low-salt diet, check labels on snacks like potato crisps to ensure you are buying a salt-free variety; also omit salted meat and fish from your meals.

Vitamins: These are not foods, but protective elements found in food. If you are healthy and eat a good balance of various foods, vitamin supplements are quite unnecessary.

Vitamin A – this helps to keep the skin, the lining of the nose, the mouth, ears and eyes healthy; it also aids digestion. This vitamin is found in oily fish, such as herrings, fish liver oil, liver, egg yolk, cheese, unskimmed milk, soya beans, carrots, green vegetables and some fruits. Margarine is another good source for this vitamin.

Vitamin B – a complex group of vitamins. These maintain energy, help to prevent muscular diseases, nervous disorders and anaemia. The main sources are wheatgerm (wholemeal bread and pasta contain more than the white variety), brewer's yeast, yeast extract, liver, heart and brains. To a lesser extent, you can obtain these vitamins from beans, peas, nuts, egg yolk, unskimmed milk and yogurt.

Vitamin C – this is known as ascorbic acid. It is an essential vitamin for it builds up resistance to illness, helps the body absorb iron and keeps the skin and gums healthy. The body cannot store it, so foods rich in vitamin C should be eaten each day. One large orange will supply the basic daily needs of one person, although you would be wise to eat more foods containing vitamin C. This vitamin is found in citrus and berry fruits, in raw and lightly cooked green vegetables. Prolonged soaking before cooking and over-cooking destroys the vitamin. Potatoes also supply this vitamin.

Vitamin D – this enables the body to absorb calcium, which keeps bones and teeth healthy. Vitamin D is present in oily fish, fish liver oil, egg yolk, butter, milk and margarine. It is added to some breakfast cereals. The main source is not, in fact, food because the body manufactures its own vitamin D under the action of sunlight.

Vitamin E – helps to maintain healthy muscles. It is obtainable from wheatgerm, green vegetables and seeds.

Vitamin F – another vitamin that helps the body absorb calcium as well as other vitamins. It is present in oils, grains and vegetables.

Vitamin K – aids calcium to ensure the healthy clotting of blood. It is in leafy green vegetables, such as kale and broccoli.

Fibre: This term has been extensively used during the past few years. It was generally referred to under the term 'roughage'. The importance of dietary fibre is its role in helping to prevent many diseases, such as constipation, ailments of the bowel, coronary heart disease, diverticulitis and obesity.

Cereals, particularly the bran in them, and oats, fruits and vegetables supply fibre. That is why so many breakfast foods, especially porridge and muesli, are good. If your cereal has added fruit, it is even better. Wholemeal bread has three times as much fibre

Dried fruits contain iron and are especially important for vegetarians who eat no animal protein

as white bread because of the larger amount of bran in the flour. If you do not like wholemeal bread, you might like to try one of the modern white breads to which cereal grains have been added.

The term 'soluble fibre' is given on certain food labels particularly those containing oats. Many medical authorities recommend these foods for people suffering from diabetes and to aid the reduction of cholesterol in the body. It is important, though, not to eat vast quantities of high-fibre foods without a doctor's advice.

Assessing your meals

It is not suggested that you should calculate the food value of every dish you prepare, but that it helps to keep a sensible perspective on your mode of eating if you simply consider whether they form part of a well-balanced daily, or even weekly eating plan. If you are aware that a certain meal is somewhat deficient in vitamins or protein, then you can ensure that the next few meals have a more generous quantity than usual.

A selection of main and light meals is given, but the day starts with the most problematical meal of all – breakfast. People differ widely in the way they regard the first meal of the day. Some state 'they couldn't eat a thing'; others 'that they could not face the day without a good breakfast'.

The latter statement leads to the next question, just what is a good breakfast? Three illustrations are given on page 13, the first is for an uncooked meal and the second and third for cooked ones. All are excellent; the reasons are given beside the menus.

Is it wise to leave home without eating a meal? Medical opinions seem fairly unanimous on this subject; they state quite firmly that it is not. If you do not eat anything first thing in the morning, your energy-level drops badly by mid-morning and you are then inclined to droop and consequently, require some form of nourishment, generally in the form of less health-giving confectionery and/or biscuits.

If you do not eat breakfast because there is not enough time to prepare it first thing in the morning, why not make a habit of putting out china and simple ingredients last thing at night? Then you can have a ready-prepared cereal with fruit, or drink fruit juice and have crispbread – which comes straight from the packet.

If you or members of the family do not eat breakfast because you find it boring, why not try to 'ring the changes' and serve a variety of different foods, such as muesli flavoured in different ways, see page 13 or porridge, topped with cooked or fresh fruit, or try a platter of various cheeses and/or cold meats, such as salami.

Easily prepared fish dishes, such as fish cakes (these can be heated from the frozen state), smoked fish, fish pâtés on toast or crispbread, old-fashioned kedgeree (this can be prepared the night before and simply reheated in a pan, or microwave cooker, see page 133), bacon – grilled or cooked in the microwave with various accompaniments.

If children or adults are having a meal away from home – it could be a packed lunch or school dinner – then it is doubly important to make certain they have something nourishing at the beginning of the day. The suggestions above could be followed, or you could have some kind of toasted snack. Baked beans on toast are a favourite with many children. Strangely, these used to be somewhat despised before it was found that they are not only a splendid source of protein, but of fibre as well. Canned sardines are an excellent fish, as they contain valuable fish oils, see page 22, and it takes only a moment to heat them. Slices of quiche or pizza may seem unusual for breakfast, but they are extremely satisfying, especially if homemade, when you can include ingredients that are suitable for the first meal of the day.

If you are a parent and do not eat breakfast, it is worthwhile doing do as children take their tone from adults. If you decline food, they are likely to do the same.

Mixed dried fruit salad with muesli and yogurt

Kippers with wholemeal toast

MENU 1   BREAKFAST   ▲ ▲ ✪

Orange juice

**Mixed dried fruit salad
with Muesli,**
see right, or other high fibre
cereal

Yogurt

**Wholemeal toast and
butter or other spread**

NUTRITIONAL VALUE
Protein: A reasonable amount from yogurt and bread.
Carbohydrates: Excellent starch content; natural sugar from
various fruits.
Fat: Will vary according to whether high- or low- fat yogurt is
chosen and the spread on the toast.
Fibre: Very high – from the cereal, toast and dried fruits.
Vitamins and minerals: A good quantity of vitamin C from
orange juice and plenty of iron from dried prunes and
apricots.

MUESLI:
No exact recipe is needed.
Blend rolled oats and/or bran
with chopped nuts, add milk
or yogurt to moisten. You can
add grated apple, raisins or
other dried fruit. For a softer
muesli, moisten rolled oats or
bran with liquid the night
before and refrigerate.

MENU 2   BREAKFAST   ▲ ✪

Orange juice

Kippers,
see methods of cooking on
the right

**Wholemeal toast and
butter or other spread**

NUTRITIONAL VALUE
Protein: A good amount from the fish.
Carbohydrates: Starch content good from the bread; a low-
sugar menu.
Fat: Kippers (from herrings) provide oils that are beneficial in
reducing cholesterol. Other fat content will vary according to
the spread on the toast.
Fibre: Good from the bread; orange juice does not give as
much fibre as eating a whole orange.
Vitamins and minerals: A good quantity of vitamin C from
orange juice and vitamin A, together with calcium, from the
kippers.

WAYS TO COOK KIPPERS:
Kippers can be grilled, baked
or cooked with little or no fat
in a pan. The microwave
cooker is excellent for cooking
fish. Two ways of avoiding the
smell of the fish is to buy the
'boil in the bag' type or to put
the fish in a dish, pour over
boiling water, cover and leave
to stand for 5 minutes.

MENU 3   BREAKFAST   ▲ ✪

Porridge

NUTRITIONAL VALUE
Protein: A reasonable amount if milk is served with the
porridge.
Carbohydrates: A limited amount, depending on how much
sugar (if any) is put on the porridge.
Fat: Depends upon whether full-cream or skimmed milk is
used with the porridge.
Fibre: Excellent amount from the oats.
Vitamins and minerals: This breakfast would be improved if
fresh fruit were included, particularly citrus fruit, or fruit juice.

MAKING PORRIDGE:
Modern rolled oats make it
possible to produce this hot
breakfast dish in a very short
time.
   Follow the directions on the
packet for the proportions of
oats and water.
   A microwave is an ideal way
of cooking this.

Main meals

The cost of a meal does not necessarily affect the nutritional value; this depends upon a good balance of ingredients, which should also provide an interesting combination of flavours and textures. The three menus given below are quite different from the point of view of the kind of dishes selected and the cost of the food. In each case the meal has been well-chosen from the nutritional point of view. Advice on lowering the fat and sugar content of some of the dishes is given in the right hand column. This change would not spoil the flavour of the dishes.

MENU 1

Tarragon Carrot-orange Soup,
page 66

Savoury Haddock,
page 75

Rosti,
page 146

Mixed Salad,
page 152

Coconut Shortcake,
page 181

BASED UPON FISH   ▲ ✿ ✿

NUTRITIONAL VALUE
Protein: Good, from main course and dessert.
Carbohydrates: Starch content good; sugar quantity reasonable.
Fat: The choice of white fish, low-fat stuffing and this shortcake make a low-fat meal.
Fibre: A generous amount from vegetables and fruits.
Vitamins and minerals: Uncooked orange juice in the soup and raw tomato salad make a menu rich in vitamin C; other vitamins and minerals are adequate.

USE OF LOW-FAT SPREADS
IN COOKING:
The use of these in baking is limited. The shortcake recipe on page 181 shows that in certain recipes a low-fat spread can be used.

MENU 2

Stuffed Mushrooms,
page 151

Stilton Chicken,
page 116

Onion and Potato Bake,
page 149

Sweetcorn Risotto,
page 135

Apricot and Raisin Mould,
page 170

FAMILY MEAL   ▲ ▲ ✿ ✿ ✿

NUTRITIONAL VALUE
Protein: Generous – from chicken, cheese and dessert.
Carbohydrates: Even if potatoes are omitted, as suggested below, there is plenty of starch in the meal. The fruits provide natural sugar.
Fat: Very high; to reduce this, see right and omit potato recipe. Serve a green vegetable, such as broccoli, instead.
Fibre: An excellent quantity, especially with the oatmeal in the Stuffed Mushrooms.
Vitamins and minerals: Adequate, but even better if a green vegetable is added, see under Fat.

REDUCING FAT CONTENT:
Low-fat cheese can be used in cooking and it would be a good contrast to the richer cheese in the filling for the chicken. Choose non-stick pans where possible if using skimmed milk in sauces.

MENU 3

Seafood Platter with Avocado Dressing,
page 84

Burgundy Pheasants,
page 119

Pepperonata,
page 150

Potato Salad, and Celery Salad,
page 152

Trio of Ices and Sorbets,
pages 172 and 173

DINNER PARTY MENU   ▲ ▲ ▲ ✿ ✿ ✿ ✿

NUTRITIONAL VALUE
Protein: An excellent amount from all the courses.
Carbohydrates: Starch content high; the desserts contain a lot of sugar, but see right.
Fat: Seafood and pheasants are good low-fat foods.
Fibre: A reasonable amount.
Vitamins and minerals: Diversity of dishes ensure these are adequate.

REDUCING SUGAR CONTENT:
Even if your family is quite happy to eat ice creams that are well sweetened, your guests may be trying to slim, so have alternative desserts of sorbets or use sugar substitute in some recipes.

Light meals

Do not make the mistake of thinking that a light meal or even a snack is necessarily low in nutritional value. If selected wisely, it can be just as valuable and interesting as a heavier main meal. Often people are inclined to think that a meal of sandwiches is lacking in good nutritional value. Bread is a first class food, for it provides protein as well as carbohydrates. The fibre content is very high if wholemeal bread is chosen. The fillings can provide essential vitamins and minerals.

MENU 1

Cottage Cheese Éclairs,
page 142

Tomatoes Provençale,
page 153

VEGETARIAN ▲ ✪ ✪

NUTRITIONAL VALUE
Protein: A good amount from both dishes.
Carbohydrates: Starch content low; little sugar in tomatoes.
Fat: Very low, if choux pastry made as given on right.
Fibre, vitamins and minerals: Relatively low in all these, cooked tomatoes lose vitamin C. Check that other meals contain adequate amounts.

TO REDUCE FAT IN CHOUX PASTRY:
Follow the recipe on page 50 but substitute low-fat spread for butter or margarine. Result is good.

MENU 2

Lobster Soufflé with Asparagus,
see page 141 and page 148

Mango and Passion Fruit Sorbet,
page 173

LUNCHEON OR SUPPER ▲ ▲ ▲ ✪ ✪ ✪

NUTRITIONAL VALUE
Protein: High – from fish and eggs.
Carbohydrates: Fairly low in both starch and sugar.
Fat: High due to the number of egg yolks; see right.
Fibre: A good amount from the asparagus and mango.
Vitamins and minerals: A reasonable quantity; lemon juice in sorbet adds to the vitamin C content.

SOUFFLÉS MADE WITH EGG WHITES ONLY:
Follow the hints given on pages 140 and 141. The flavour is not as rich as when whole eggs are used, but the soufflé sinks less.

MENU 3

Chestnut Terrine,
page 165

Spiced Coleslaw,
page 154

Orange and Celery Salad,
page 155

VEGETARIAN ▲ ▲ ✪ ✪

NUTRITIONAL VALUE
Protein: A generous amount from the terrine.
Carbohydrates: Starch content low; natural sugar in fruits.
Fat: A low-fat menu.
Fibre: A generous amount in all dishes.
Vitamins and minerals: Excellent range from the diversity of ingredients used.

TO ADD MORE STARCH TO VEGETARIAN MENUS:
1 and 2:
Serve crusty rolls or bread.

Tomatoes Provençale;
Cottage Cheese Eclairs

SHOPPING WISELY

Good cooking really begins in the shop or supermarket where we buy all the ingredients. No one can achieve really successful results with poor quality food; stale produce will not only spoil the flavour of the dishes, but it could have serious consequences for the health of the people who eat the food. It is, therefore, up to us to shop wisely. The following pages provide essential information on buying and storing a wide range of produce and ingredients.

BUYING PERISHABLE FOODS

It is essential to see that the surroundings and the staff who handle food are scrupulously clean and that the food they sell is of the highest possible quality. One important thing to watch is that raw and cooked foods are stored in separate places and that the staff do not handle raw, then cooked foods without first washing their hands. These precautions minimize the spread of harmful bacteria.

Perishable foods must have an indication of their shelf life; always check the 'use by', or the 'sell by' dates. It is all too easy for a member of staff to make an occasional mistake and leave one or two containers of older food on show, although it is now illegal for shops to sell food beyond the 'use by' date.

When you buy frozen foods, make certain that the cabinet from which you or the shop staff take the packets is not over-filled. Avoid any damaged packets.

TRANSPORTING PERISHABLE FOODS

Having bought the food, carry it home as quickly as possible and store it correctly in the freezer or refrigerator. It is wise to invest in an insulated cold bag or box so that the food arrives home without its temperature having been raised. This is particularly important if you have bought cook-chilled dishes or frozen or highly perishable fresh foods, such as dairy products, fish and meat.

STORING PERISHABLE FOODS

In the refrigerator: The ideal temperature in the storage compartment of a domestic refrigerator is between 0°C and 5°C, (32°F and 41°F). These are the settings at which certain highly perishable foods are stored in shops and supermarkets.

Cooked and uncooked foods must be put on separate shelves. Uncooked meat, poultry and fish should be wrapped or covered and placed in a dish at the base of the refrigerator. Cooked foods should be placed towards the top. Always remove the giblets from inside fresh poultry as soon as you can. As these tend to deteriorate more rapidly than the bird, it is wise to cook them soon after purchase.

Fresh and cooked meat and poultry can be stored for up to 3 or 4 days in the refrigerator. Use minced meat or offal and fresh fish within 24 hours. These times assume the refrigerator is set at the recommended temperature, see above.

Dairy produce should be stored in the refrigerator. There are comments about storing cheeses on page 142.

It is recommended that eggs are kept in the refrigerator. Buy these at frequent intervals, so they are fresh, and use within the shortest possible time. This minimizes the risk from salmonella.

The storage of vegetables is covered on page 26.

In the freezer: The recommended temperature is below −18°C (0.4°F). Place frozen foods in the cabinet as soon as possible after purchase. Frozen food cabinets in shops should also be at this temperature.

An example of well-displayed and stored fresh poultry in a supermarket

ORGANIC FOODS

Over the past few years, the demand for foods produced without the use of chemical pesticides and drugs has grown enormously. Nowadays, you will find many supermarkets have a section of their greengrocery department in which they sell some organic vegetables and fruits. These are of the kind grown in this country, as overseas products cannot be monitored in the same way. You will also find a few butchers who specialize in organic meat. The price of organic food is generally higher than that of the non-organic.

Ways of shopping

There are really two basic ways in which we can shop for food, each has certain advantages and disadvantages.

FIRST OPTION – BULK BUYING

This means planning all the requirements for a week, or perhaps even a little longer.

Advantages: You will have worked out all the meals for the period, so you have no last minute worrying or indecision about what you will cook.

You will save money on things that you eat regularly, such as larger packets of breakfast cereals; large cartons of cream and yogurt. That is the reason why in recipes, where these foods are used, the measurements are given as '150 ml/$\frac{1}{4}$ pint', '300 ml/$\frac{1}{2}$ pint'. This enables you to take the right amount from a large carton.

You save time and energy and money on fuel or fares. If the weather is bad, you do not need to shop; you will have plenty of food in stock.

Disadvantages: You can become too dependent on non-perishable, canned and frozen foods; green vegetables and some fruits need buying regularly.

SECOND OPTION – SHOPPING VERY REGULARLY

Advantages: You can derive pleasure from looking around food shops and learning about new and unusual foods. You make sure your family has really fresh foods.

Disadvantages: If you buy small amounts of food, you can be left without ingredients to produce a meal for unexpected visitors.

You will spend more money on buying smaller quantities.

Buying Dairy Products

The range of dairy products available today is an extremely large and interesting one. It is important to appreciate the fact that even if we buy dairy products labelled 'low-fat', these still include important nutrients. If you are trying to cut down the amount of fat eaten, choose these. It is advised that young children should be given whole, rather than semi-skimmed or skimmed milk, but check with your doctor or at the health clinic. Always store dairy products carefully and use by the date indicated.

MAIN KINDS OF MILK

All milk sold by dairies and supermarkets is now pasteurized; this means it has been subjected to a high temperature to destroy harmful micro-organisms. This process is helpful in preventing milk from fermenting.

The richest milk is called '**Channel Island**', this has a 4·8 per cent fat content; both **whole milk** and **homogenized** contain 3·8 per cent fat. The advantage of homogenized milk is that the fat is evenly distributed throughout. Many people like to see the cream at the top of the bottle of milk and they use this in coffee, instead of single cream.

The lower-fat milks are **semi-skimmed**, with only 1·8 per cent fat or even a little less, and **skimmed milk** which has virtually no fat content. These make refreshing drinks and are ideal in batters where you need a light texture. If you are using them to make a sauce, use a non-stick pan or a basin in the microwave cooker, see page 159, the reduction in fat means the mixture is more likely to stick in an ordinary saucepan.

Sterilized milk keeps for several weeks and **long-life** (Ultra-heat Treated or U.H.T.) even longer – check the date stamp on this. These milks should be stored in a cool place and, once the container is opened, in the refrigerator, just like fresh milk. **Dried** and **canned evaporated milks** are useful stand-bys in the store-cupboard.

KINDS OF CREAM

It is possible to obtain **extra thick double cream**, but this is not readily available. It is so thick that it does not whip, so it is less useful than double cream. **Clotted cream** has been heat-treated to give that special texture. The process makes it keep rather better than ordinary creams.

When you need to whip cream, buy the richer **double cream**, which has about 48 per cent butterfat or **whipping cream** which has only 35 per cent. Because of its lighter texture you will find that whipping cream produces a slightly greater bulk than double cream; also it is appreciably cheaper. Choose **single cream** for pouring or to add richness to soups, sauces and other dishes. This cannot be whipped.

The less usual creams are **soured cream**, which is ideal for savoury dishes, and **crème fraîche**, which can be whipped and used instead of whipping cream but which has a slightly sharper taste.

YOGURTS

This is made by adding a culture to milk and it has become extremely popular. You can choose from a whole range of products – from very **low-fat yogurt**, made from skimmed milk, to **creamy thick yogurt**. This is not only made from whole milk but may have a little cream added, the label will indicate this. Look for **Greek-style yogurt** when the recipe states 'thick yogurt'. Many yogurts are labelled 'fruit-flavoured'; that does not mean they contain fruit, so you need to check the label to ensure you are buying a product containing whole or puréed fresh fruit.

Yogurt is given as an alternative to cream in many of the recipes in this book; this does not spoil the flavour of the dish in any way, but it does tend to produce a lighter texture and it reduces the fat content.

CHEESES

We are fortunate in having a great tradition of cheese-making in this country and in importing some of the most interesting varieties from abroad. Vegetarians can now obtain special cheeses which are made with a non animal-based rennet. Most cheeses are made from pasteurized milks, although non-pasteurized cheeses are available in some areas.

Some of the soft cheeses are mentioned in recipes.

Fromage frais is, as the name indicates, a cheese, but it has such a mild flavour that it can take the place of cream or yogurt, even in sweet dishes. It is available with various flavourings. The fat and calorie content are very low.

Curd cheese is low in fat and a very good alternative to **cream cheese**, which varies in fat content from about 65 per cent to 29 per cent, so check the labels if you are anxious to reduce the fat content of a dish. **Cottage cheese** is very low in fat, although different kinds vary slightly. It is high in protein, so it is an excellent choice for slimmers. It can be given an unlimited range of flavours if you add spices, herbs or fruits. **Cheese spreads** can take the place of curd cheese in some recipes.

Well-known British cheeses include the world-famous English **Cheddar**, **Cheshire**, **Lancashire**, Wensleydale, Double Gloucester and **Stilton** cheeses, **Dunlop** and **Crowdie** from Scotland, crumbly **Caerphilly** from Wales and many others.

From Holland, we import **Edam**, (a good choice if you are watching your weight) and **Gouda** cheeses; from Italy **Gorganzola** (this also comes from France) and the perfect strong cooking cheese – **Parmesan**. If you use a lot of Parmesan, do buy it in a piece and grate it yourself, rather than buying the small drums. The difference in flavour is unbelievable.

The French produce about 600 different cheeses, probably the most popular being **Camembert**, **Brie** and **Roquefort**, the latter a real luxury blue cheese. There are many others, as shown in the second picture. Swiss **Gruyère** and **Emmenthal** are perfect partners for making Fondue, see page 143.

To choose cheese: Obviously you choose the flavours you like and those suitable for the particular dish. There are, however, a few golden rules you would be wise to follow.

Freshly cut cheeses should look moist, but not wet on the outside. The cut surface must not look hard and dry; this indicates that the cheese has been standing for a considerable time since the last portion was removed.

An extensive selection of French cheeses

Soft cheeses, such as Brie and Camembert, must be soft when pressed to indicate they are ripe, but not so runny or over-soft that they are likely to become over-ripe in too short a time. It is better to buy these in a slightly under-ripe state and allow them to ripen at home, so you enjoy them in perfect condition.

Much of the cheese on sale today is pre-packed. Check dates on this very carefully and inspect the cheese. It must not look wet inside the package.

The storage of cheese and freezing are covered in the section that begins on page 142, together with advice on cooking with cheese.

EGGS

These are a perishable food and so should be purchased and stored carefully, see page 16 and the introduction to the egg section on page 136. You will find a note about the size of eggs to use on page 4.

People who are allergic to eggs will find some recipes that do not need them.

Buying Fats

Butter is one of the traditional fats. It is a dairy product, churned from cream. Butter comes from various countries, each giving a particular flavour. There is a choice of unsalted, slightly salted or salted butter. **Salted** butter tends to keep better than **unsalted**, use by the date on the packet.

Store butter in the refrigerator but bring it into the kitchen for a while if you want it to soften for creaming or spreading. Butter is not an ideal fat for frying as it burns fairly easily. So if you want the flavour of butter, heat a small amount of oil with it.

Margarine is made from oils and fats. Some margarines contain a little milk or whey, so if you are a strict vegetarian, buy **vegetarian margarine**. Basically there are two kinds of margarines, the hard and the softer **polyunsaturated margarine**. The composition of these makes them suitable for anyone wanting to follow a low-cholesterol diet. Both kinds of margarine are good in cooking, but follow the manufacturer's suggestions as to the way in which they should be handled. The one-stage pastry on page 177 is ideal for soft margarines. The calorific value of margarines is approximately 220 calories per 28·35 g/1 oz. Butter is slightly higher at 260 calories per 28·35 g/1 oz, on average. Margarines are not good frying fats, as they tend to splutter rather badly.

There are **spreads** made by churning cream with some oil. The product is softer and it can be taken straight from the refrigerator to spread or cream. Use as butter.

Cooking fats, often called **shortenings**, are made from various oils, and **lard** is an animal product. Both of these can be used in making pastry, either by themselves or mixed with butter or margarine. They are also good for frying, although the emphasis today is upon using oil for this purpose. The calories of both of these is about 240 per 28·35 g/1 oz. You can obtain **polyunsaturated fat**; this has the same properties as polyunsaturated margarines.

Suet comes from around lamb or ox kidneys; it is the traditional fat for many steamed sweet or savoury puddings. Packet suet has a little flour blended with shredded suet to add to the keeping qualities.

If you are cutting down on animal fats, you can replace the suet in recipes with margarine. The flavour of the dish will not be exactly the same, but the result is satisfactory. The calories of suet are the same as for butter.

Low-fat spreads have about half the number of calories as margarine, so they are a wise choice if you are slimming. The use of these spreads in cooking is limited. As you will see, they can be used in Scones, page 177, Choux Pastry page 50, and Herb Dumplings, pages 110 and 111. Low-fat spreads are not necessarily polyunsaturated.

Very low fat spreads should not be used in cooking. They are extremely low in calories.

Buying Oils

There has been a great change in attitude towards the use of cooking oils in this country. Because of a desire to reduce consumption of animal fats and the fact that one can use just a very little oil in many forms of cooking, oil is becoming the accepted fat for many purposes. It must be remembered, however, that if you are trying to cut down your consumption of all fats, then oils, of any kind, must be used sparingly. The average number of calories in oils is about 160 per 28·35 g/1 oz or 100 per standard 15 ml tablespoon. Many ethnic dishes use oil and so do salad dressings. You may be given the choice of buying **unrefined** or **refined** oils. The former have a better flavour and are the more expensive because they have been pressed naturally and left to mellow before being sold.

Olive oil is the classic oil. Olives are grown in many countries and each region produces a different flavoured oil, so you can experiment and find those you like best. You may be a little confused by the labels, which can state 'extra virgin', 'virgin' or simply 'olive oil'. Extra virgin or virgin olive oil are the finest, for they come from the first pressing of the olives. Obviously, it is the most expensive, so use it in special dishes. Olive oil should not be used for deep-frying; it cannot be heated to the high temperatures needed. It is a monounsaturated oil. While not having exactly the same properties as polyunsaturated oils, it is considered to have a beneficial effect in helping to reduce blood cholesterol.

Ground nut also known as **peanut oil** and **arachide oil**, is another monounsaturated oil. It is quite often used in salad dressings and for frying.

Oils that are readily available and highly recommended as being **polyunsaturated**, are **corn**, **grapeseed**, **safflower** and **sunflower**. These can be used in all forms of cooking. Their flavour is not particularly pronounced, so they blend well with other ingredients. As you will see in the salad dressings on page 156 there are suggestions for blending one of these oils with the richer olive oil to produce a lighter dressing.

An oil with a very pronounced flavour is **sesame oil**. This is ideal, if used in small quantities, for giving an interesting flavour to dishes. Chinese recipes often use this oil with another type, such as sunflower.

Almond and **walnut oils** both have distinctive flavours, excellent in salad dressings.

Special **frying oils** are sold. These are generally a combination of various oils, selected to be used for high temperature frying. These may not be polyunsaturated, unless marked to that effect.

Information about using oil or fat in frying is given on page 76.

Store oils in a cool place; never use an oil if it has developed a rancid taste.

A variety of oils are available, each with their own flavour and use

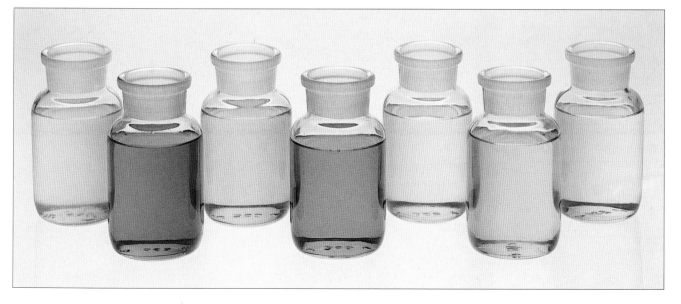

Buying Fish

Try not to have too decided a view as to the exact fish you will purchase. In many recipes you will find a choice; this means you can buy the kind that offers the best value in price and quality on any particular day. Weather affects the catches; many fish have a specific season when they are at their best. You may find some fish labelled 'local caught' or even 'morning's catch'. It would be worthwhile planning the meal to include these, for truly fresh fish is unbeatable.

Fish is highly perishable, so bring fresh fish home quickly and place it in the refrigerator; frozen fish should be stored in the freezer until you are ready to use it. When a can is opened or the contents of a packet defrosted, the fish becomes as perishable as when it is fresh.

How to tell if fish is fresh

Stale fish is not only unpleasant but can be injurious to health. White, freshwater and oily fish can be judged as follows:

Appearance: The fish should look firm, the eyes, scales and skin bright.

Aroma: This should be pleasant, with a suggestion of the smell of the sea, although freshwater fish have little odour. If there is any smell of ammonia, beware! It means the fish is stale.

Shellfish is sold in both uncooked and cooked form. Directions for dealing with uncooked shellfish, such as mussels, will be found in the recipes. Cooked lobsters and prawns should have a pleasantly bright red colour. You can tell if they are freshly cooked by gently pulling out the tail until it is straight. If it springs back easily and quickly, the fish is freshly cooked. Handle crabs before buying if this is possible; if they feel unexpectedly light for their size, they are 'watery' and poor value, as they contain little solid flesh.

Smoked fish varies in appearance. It should look pleasantly moist, not dry and hard, which indicates that it is not 100 per cent fresh. If buying smoked mackerel you may have the choice between fish topped with peppercorns and plain mackerel. If buying pre-packed fish press the pack firmly to ascertain that the mackerel is soft and not dry. Some of the smoked fish sold today is paler in colour. This is because it has not been dyed.

Varieties of fish

Fish are divided into various groups. If you do not have the exact fish suggested in the recipe, try to select another from the same group, so the flavour will be similar.

White fish: These form the biggest group, ranging from everyday cod, fresh haddock and plaice to the less-used skate and more luxurious turbot and halibut. All white fish are low in fat and, therefore, low in calories.

Freshwater fish: This group is well known to anglers, who catch a great variety in rivers and lakes. Many of the fish are considered to lack flavour. Freshwater bream (a member of the carp family) is a different species from the bream caught at sea, which has a much better flavour than freshwater bream.

Both river and sea trout are the same species. This fish used to be quite difficult to obtain, but much of the trout on sale today comes from trout farms and is plentiful and of good value. Trout belongs to the same family as salmon, so it has the qualities of oily fish. Salmon trout is a delicious fish, which is almost as highly prized as salmon. It has a delicate pink colour.

Oily fish: Varieties such as herrings, mackerel, salmon, sardines, sprats, trout and tuna. All fish are valuable foods, but these are considered especially important nutritionally.

Fish and shellfish are all highly perishable and must be stored correctly

APPROXIMATE QUANTITIES TO BUY

Each recipe gives the average amount of fish required per serving. This may vary in recipes, as it is dependent on the other ingredients used in the dish. If you are buying fish without a specific dish in mind, the following is a reasonable guide.
You need to allow per person:

You need to allow per person:

Whole fish (after gutting) and cutlets with large bones	225 g/8 oz per person:
Whole fish, complete with heads and bones	300 to 350 g/10 to 12 oz
Crab or lobster	half if large; whole if small
Mussels in their shells	by volume 750 ml/1¼ pints by weight 450 g/1 lb
Prawns in their shells	175 g/6 oz
Prawns without shells (peeled)	75 g/3 oz
Oysters	6 to 12

The natural oils in the fish help to reduce blood cholesterol. You may be offered the choice of wild or farmed salmon; the latter is generally cheaper but may not have quite such a fine flavour as wild salmon at its best.

Shellfish: There are many different species. As they are so popular, you will find the most common, such as crab, lobster, mussels, oysters, prawns and scallops, as well as some lesser-known varieties, used in recipes for starters and main dishes. These are the most perishable of all fish, so they must be stored with particular care.

The popularity of smoked foods means that many more fish are being treated in this way. **Smoked fish** make excellent pâtés or simple hors d'oeuvre, see pages 56 and 57. The popular varieties include smoked cod and haddock, eel, mackerel, salmon and trout.

PREPARING FISH FOR COOKING

Most fishmongers are helpful and will clean (gut) the fish and cut it into the required portions. If this has not been done, it is not difficult to do it yourself. Place the fish on a firm surface and use a sharp knife.

To remove the intestines: Slit the fish along the stomach and remove the intestines. These may be discarded, although the roe of fish like herrings can be an ingredient in a recipe.

To cut fish into slices (steaks or cutlets): Cut the whole fish downwards, you may need to bang the knife sharply with a small weight to help cut through the backbone.

To bone small fish, like herrings: Remove the intestines. Open the fish out flat. Lay it on a board – skin side uppermost. Run your thumb firmly down the centre of the fish to loosen the bones. Turn the fish over; the backbone, with small bones attached can be lifted from the flesh. The fish can then be cut into two fillets.

To fillet flat fish, like sole: Cut around the edge of the flesh – avoid bones and fins. Insert the tip of the knife under the flesh. Carefully cut the first fillet away from the backbone. Repeat with the second fillet. Turn the fish over. Repeat the process above, so giving four fillets, see page 82. Smaller fish can be cut into two fillets only; in which case do not cut down the backbone but just around the edges.

To skin fish: Dip the knife blade in a little salt. Make a firm cut across the fillet as near the tip as possible. Slowly and gently cut away the skin from the fish.

Buying Vegetables and Fruit

These are some of the most difficult foods to buy, as their quality and price vary so much. This must be expected because most fruits and vegetables are seasonal and their availability, flavour and cost depends upon that. To enjoy fruits and vegetables at their best and cheapest buy them when in season. You may be able to save money by picking your own at farms or fruit orchards; this can make an enjoyable outing for all the family.

GREEN VEGETABLES

It is fairly easy to judge the freshness of green vegetables; the leaves must not be yellow but bright green. **Cabbages** and **lettuces** of various kinds should be firm, crisp and feel heavy for their size, indicating that they have a solid heart. Be adventurous in your choice of lettuce; there are a good number from which to choose. **Chinese cabbage** is an economical buy, it can be served cooked or raw in salads and it keeps well. **Brussels sprouts** must look green and firm and have a pleasant smell.

In this country **endive** is the name given to a curly green type of lettuce, whereas on the continent it is used to describe white chicory or witloof. **Watercress** must have firm stalks as well as bright green leaves. **Cauliflowers** should be very white; never buy **broccoli** or **calabrese** if the green heads are turning yellow, as this gives the vegetable an unpleasant bitter taste.

Spinach deteriorates very quickly, so use as soon as possible after purchase. The leaves must look firm and green. As this vegetable shrinks a great deal in cooking, be generous in the amount you buy. The type known as **spinach beet** gives two vegetables; cook the leaves as ordinary spinach and the stalks like celery. **Chard** is cooked in the same way.

Asparagus must not be wrinkled and the heads should be firm and erect. **Globe artichokes** should be green and firm, avoid any with brown leaves.

OTHER VEGETABLES

Celery can be white or pale green; make sure there are no brown stalks. **Chicory** should have a firm white head with delicate green on the outer leaves; if there is any trace of brown, the vegetable develops a bitter taste. Use raw in salads or cooked. **Florence fennel** is the full name of the white vegetable, to distinguish it from the herb fennel. It is delicious raw in salads or cooked. Do not discard the feathery leaves; add them to sauces or use as a garnish. **Fresh peas** must have firm crisp pods; if they are yellow on the outside, they are stale. **Mangetout peas** may seem expensive, but you need to discard only the stalk tips and you then eat the complete vegetable.

There are a variety of **green beans** available at different times of the year. They range from small haricots verts – these just need 'topping and tailing' and are cooked whole – to the larger types of **French beans** and **runner beans**. Larger beans need the stringy sides removed and slicing before cooking. Never buy beans if they are wrinkled; this means they are stale. When **broad beans** are first in season, it is possible to slice and cook the pods as well as the beans.

Fresh **bean sprouts** are generally sold in a covered container. Look critically at these and check the 'use by' date. The tips should be a delicate greeny-yellow and the stalks white and firm. Never use if stale. Eat raw or cook for a very short time only.

Fresh **sweetcorn** makes a delicious start to the meal, see page 55. The outer leaves must be fresh-looking and the corn kernels bright golden and plump.

A less usual vegetable is **okra** (ladies' fingers). The pods must be firm and green.

There is now a much greater variety of **mushrooms** on sale. If you intend chopping the fungi, then buy the large **open** type, as they have much more flavour. For using whole, buy **button** mushrooms. If really fresh, these are delicious served raw in salads. **Cup** mushrooms are good for stuffing. Look for **oyster mushrooms, ceps, chanterelles, morels** and even other types in good shops. Mushrooms are highly perishable, so look at them critically. They are fresh when plump and smell unpleasantly strong when stale.

ROOT VEGETABLES

These spoil less easily, so they can be bought in larger quantities.

Potatoes are the most important vegetable of all to many families. There is a great variety of potatoes, so experiment and find the flavour you prefer and the type best suited to different methods of cooking. Look for unblemished potatoes. If you intend cooking them whole, then select those of a uniform size. Potatoes are really 'new' if the skin rubs away easily, although many people prefer to cook them in their skins. Never cook potatoes too quickly: they should be simmered steadily.

Sweet potatoes and **yams** are gradually becoming better known. Select them as you would ordinary potatoes.

New **carrots** are often sold in bunches with their leaves, so you can assess their freshness. Avoid old or new carrots that are wrinkled or blemished. **Parsnips, turnips, swedes** and the lesser-known **celeriac** and **kohlrabi** are at their best when fairly small, when they are younger and, therefore, sweeter in flavour. Both celeriac and kohlrabi tend to discolour when peeled, so keep them in water with a little lemon juice. This is also necessary when preparing slim-rooted **salsify**, also known as **oyster plant**, as the flesh tastes a little like that of shellfish.

Most people like to buy ready-cooked **beetroot**. Make sure they are firm, not sweating, which indicates that they have been stored for too long. Raw beetroot should be sold with a little stem; if cut at the top, they may have bled and so lost some of their juices and flavour.

A selection of fresh vegetables, all of which are readily available in most greengrocers and supermarkets

Jerusalem artichokes are quite unlike the globe variety. They are difficult to prepare, so try and select the most evenly-shaped ones. Peel and keep in lemon-flavoured water until ready to cook. Add a little lemon juice to the cooking water.

Onions are to many people, the most important of all flavourings for savoury dishes. Spanish onions are generally large, with a milder taste than the home-grown variety. Shallots are much smaller in size, so they are ideal for using whole. **Spring onions** are available throughout most of the year now. They are perfect in salads or in stir-fry dishes, where you need to retain a crisp texture. At certain times of the year, you can obtain baby pickling onions. These can be used in cooking, see the recipe for Stifado on page 109.

To avoid crying when preparing strong onions: Peel under running water and leave a little of the stalk end in position until the rest of the onion is chopped or sliced.

Garlic is sold in single or several bulbs. Remove just one section, called a clove, at a time, so none is wasted. These keep quite well before they are peeled. Garlic bulbs should feel really firm and hard.

Leeks have a delicate taste which makes them an ideal vegetable to serve with a variety of dishes. These should have bright green tops and firm white roots. They need plenty of washing in cold water. Look for small leeks as they have a particularly good taste. Never over-cook this vegetable, it should retain a certain firmness.

FRUITS – TREATED AS VEGETABLES

Although always classed as vegetables, the following are really fruits.

Aubergines, **courgettes** and the larger members of the same family, **marrows**, **pumpkins** and **squashes** as well as **cucumbers** should look unmarked and feel firm and heavy. This indicates that they are fresh and full of natural juice. **Sweet peppers**, also called **capsicums**, must not be wrinkled. It makes dishes colourful if you use a mixture of red, yellow and green peppers. The smaller **green**, **yellow**, **red** and even blackish **chilli peppers** are used to give a hot flavour to food. Be careful how you handle them; if you get seeds on your lips they really do give an unpleasant burning sensation. Always wash your hands after preparing chilli peppers.

Tomatoes are undoubtedly the most important member of this group. Cherry tomatoes are ideal for cocktail savouries; the flavour of yellow tomatoes is not dissimilar to red ones. You can obtain large **beef tomatoes** that are not only ideal for stuffing but excellent in salads. **Plum tomatoes** are sold fresh, as well as in cans; these are a perfect tomato for cooking.

Good tomatoes must be bright in colour and free from blemishes.

TO STORE VEGETABLES

Vegetables lose flavour and texture if they become stale; **green vegetables** also lose some of their vitamin content. Some vegetables can taste really unpleasant if they are not eaten soon after purchase – or picking if you grow your own or can obtain them from farms.

It is best to store most vegetables in racks in a cool place, even out-of-doors in a garage or shed, providing the weather does not become frosty. They need a good circulation of air between and around the racks.

Salad vegetables, like watercress, lettuce, celery, etc. can be stored in the salad container of the refrigerator, if space permits.

Tomatoes and cucumber and peppers should be stored in this container, but do not put them next to damp lettuce or watercress, as these soften the firmer ingredients. To prevent this, simply place them in half-opened bags or wrappings, so they can breathe but are kept dry.

If you have no salad container, then use bags in the refrigerator. Do not store too near the freezing compartment.

Fruit will last longer if stored in a cool place

CITRUS FRUITS

These fruits eaten raw provide essential vitamin C; more details about this on page 11. **Oranges**, **grapefruit** and **lemons** are plentiful throughout the year. **Pink grapefruit** is no longer a rarity; it is a good ingredient in savoury, as well as sweet dishes. Buy **limes** when you can; their individual flavour makes a pleasant change from lemon. Try **pomelo** – like an ultra large grapefruit; **mineola** – a cross between tangerine and orange; and **ugli fruit** – a cross between grapefruit, orange and tangerine.

Citrus fruits ripen on the tree, so they should be in perfect condition when sold. They dry out if kept for too long. Each fruit should feel heavy for its size; if it feels very light, then the flesh inside is dry. Small **kumquats**, with their rather bitter taste, are eaten as a whole fruit, complete with skins. They, like most citrus fruits, make good marmalade, although the traditional fruit for this purpose is **Seville oranges**. Marmalade recipes are on page 186.

FAMILIAR FRUITS

Both cooking and eating **apples** are favourite fruits in this country. Try to taste some of the lesser-known varieties as they come into shops. Some supermarkets are making a special feature of selling these. Often apples are picked when not quite ripe; if you find this is the case, spread them out on a flat surface so they ripen. Never leave a bruised apple touching others, as it will affect them. When buying apples, look for unblemished fruit. If you grow or buy large quantities, store them in trays or on racks in a cool dry place.

Pears are a very fickle fruit; they can appear hard one day and ripen in a warm place within 24 hours. Do not buy too many at one time.

Bananas have more flavour and are easier to digest when they are really ripe, but in warm houses they ripen very quickly, so it is sensible to buy a few ripe ones for immediate consumption, and some that are slightly green and under-ripe to use a few days ahead.

All the **plum** family of fruits are seasonal, so buy plums, greengages and damsons when you first see them. Choose a dessert plum, like a Victoria, to eat raw. Other plums are excellent in cooking. These fruits should be really full of colour when you buy them.

Peaches and **nectarines** are luxury fruits, delicious as desserts. They should feel soft when handled, but never exert too much pressure for they bruise easily. Choose **morello cherries** for cooking. There are many varieties of home-produced and imported **cherries**. Make sure these look bright, are firm and not wet and sticky.

Most **apricots** on sale are better cooked than eaten raw.

Rhubarb is classed as a fruit, but it is actually a leaf stalk. Forced rhubarb is ideal for making ices and cold desserts. Never cook and eat rhubarb leaves, as they are poisonous.

Soft fruits

Raspberries, strawberries, black, red and **white currants** with **loganberries** and the lesser-known **boysenberries** (a cross between raspberries, loganberries and blackberries) and **tayberries** make desserts with the minimum of effort. Look critically before buying; soft fruits spoil within hours.

Dessert **gooseberries**, known as levellers, have almost as much flavour as passion fruit.

Cranberries should be bright red in colour and very firm. **Blueberries**, are now cultivated and becoming more plentiful. They make wonderful fillings in pies.

More exotic fruits

Most of these are imported and this is reflected in their price.

Avocados are equally good in savoury or sweet dishes. The problem when buying this fruit is to assess its ripeness. Never press it hard at one end, as this bruises the fruit and turns the flesh black. Cradle it in your hands and it should feel soft and buttery. If under-ripe, put in a warm place and check progress daily.

Melons come from various countries and there are many varieties. If the seeds rattle, that is a sign that the melon is past its best. **Watermelon** has a texture and taste unlike the golden type. It has a bright green skin and red flesh.

Grapes are an all-year-round fruit; there are periods when they are quite inexpensive. Choose seedless grapes, when available, to encourage children to eat them.

Pineapples are among the most refreshing fruits. A ripe pineapple has a fragrant smell; if there is no odour, it is not yet ripe.

The pulp of **passion fruits** or **grenadillas** gives a wonderful flavour to many dishes. The outside should look slightly crinkled. This means it is ripe. If it is very crinkled, it has become over-ripe and the flesh has dried.

A large selection of imported exotic fruit is now widely available in many shops

Fruits seen occasionally are **figs**, **guavas**, **mangoes** and **persimmons**. Judge these as you would peaches; they should feel just soft and be full of colour. **Lychees** have become known through the canned form. The fresh fruit tastes very similar.

Carambola (five-sided star fruit) has little flavour but an eye-catching appearance.

Storing fruits

All fruit is better stored in a cool place if you want to delay its ripening or stop it becoming over-ripe. Although it looks attractive to pile fruits high in a bowl, they bruise less if kept on a flat dish.

Chill fruit salad, melon and other fruits in the refrigerator before serving.

Herbs

These are one of the simplest ways of adding an interesting flavour to dishes. **Fresh herbs** are better, but if you use **dried herbs**, remember to use only half as much.

HERBS

In case you want to grow herbs in the garden or a window box, the letters 'P' and 'A' are given in the following list. 'P' means a perennial and 'A' an annual, so you must sow yearly.

Balm	**(P)**	a lovely lemon flavour; use in puddings and drinks.
Basil	**(A)**	a pungent taste; perfect with tomatoes.
Bay	**(P)**	delicate taste when fresh; strong when dried. Use 1 or 2 leaves in sauces, stews and milk puddings.
Borage	**(A)**	slight cucumber taste; ideal in drinks. Often seeds itself.
Burnet	**(P)**	slight cucumber taste. Add very little to sauces to serve with fish.
Chervil	**(A)**	like a delicate parsley; use as parsley.
Chives	**(A)**	mild onion flavour; use in many savoury dishes.
Coriander	**(A)**	slightly bitter taste; use leaves in savoury dishes.
Dill	**(A)**	slight aniseed flavour; use with fish; seeds in pickles.
Fennel	**(P)**	aniseed taste; excellent in sauces to serve with fish.
Garlic	**(A)**	pungent onion flavour, see page 00.
Horseradish	**(P)**	root very hot; use to make sauce.
Marjoram	**(P)**	slightly sweet taste; use in savoury dishes.
Mint	**(P)**	unmistakeable taste and smell; various kinds, including peppermint; use in sauces, savoury dishes and some drinks.
Oregano	**(P)**	wild marjoram but stronger taste. Use in savoury dishes, especially pizzas.
Parsley	**(A)**	there are two kinds, curly leafed and flat leafed; the latter has the stronger taste. Refreshing flavour; use in all savoury dishes. Considered an annual but really a biennial. Use parsley stalks for stronger flavour; remove before serving.
Rosemary	**(P)**	strong aromatic herb; use sparingly. Excellent with lamb, chicken and in some salads.
Sage	**(P)**	very strong taste. Use in stuffings and stews.
Savory	**(A) and (P)**	summer savory an annual; winter a perennial. Not unlike thyme in taste. Particularly good with beans.
Sorrel	**(P)**	tastes like a more bitter spinach. Excellent in soups and sauces.
Tarragon	**(P)**	Russian tarragon a hardier plant but poorer flavour than French type (which is delicate in winter). Excellent with fish and chicken.
Thyme	**(P)**	a large range of different types. A mild savoury taste. Use in stuffings and many savoury dishes.

Buying Meat

To achieve the best results, it is important to select the right cut, as well as the appropriate kind of meat for a particular dish. It takes a certain amount of experience to recognize the different cuts of meat, so you may find it more helpful to go to a butcher's shop. Most good butchers are only too pleased to give advice and answer questions. If you try and roast the cheaper cuts of meat, you will be disappointed, both by the taste and texture. On the other hand, if you buy an expensive piece of meat for a stew, you could be spending more money than is necessary.

Nowadays, there is great emphasis on lean meat, but when selecting prime joints, look for a slight marbling of the fat on the meat, especially beef. This gives a better flavour and ensures that the flesh keeps moist in cooking.

HOW TO TELL IF MEAT IS FRESH

Meat has to be hung for a certain length of time to allow it to develop flavour and tenderness, so it is not sold when freshly killed. All suppliers of meat understand the importance of this procedure.

Differences in taste and texture make it important to select the right cut, as well as the appropriate kind of meat for a particular recipe

Appearance: This varies according to the kind of meat, so details are given below. All meat should look pleasantly moist, not dry and hard, and the colour described. The points below describe quality as well as freshness.

Aroma: The meat should have only a faint, pleasant smell.

Beef: Varies from a bright red to a reddish-brown after cutting and exposure to the air. The lights in a shop and methods of breeding also affect the colour of meat. The fat on beef should be firm and pale cream in colour. When buying minced beef, check that there is not an undue amount of fat and gristle with the lean. Check also that the meat has not become very dark and dry looking; minced meat deteriorates quickly, due to the many cut surfaces, so this should be carried home and cooked as soon as possible.

Lamb: The flesh of very young lamb should be a light pink colour and the fat very firm and white. In older and larger animals, the lean darkens to be pinkish-red to red; there will be more fat but it should still be white and firm.

Mutton: Once a prime favourite in Britain, is now very scarce. The lean is darker and coarser looking than that of lamb and the flavour of the more mature animal is stronger. The various cuts can be cooked in the same way as lamb, but as the meat is less tender, you will need to allow at least a third longer cooking time.

Pork: The lean of pork should be pale pink and very finely textured. The fat should be white and firm; avoid pork with too much fat.

Veal: Varies in colour; the lean of some veal is almost white in colour as a result of the method of rearing and feeding. Today, this is considered undesirable and the colour of modern veal, reared in a more humane fashion, tends to be a little darker with a pinkish tinge. There is little fat on veal; the small amount should be firm and white.

Venison: Until recently, venison was classed as game and it could not be sold by butchers in the same way as other meats. Today, it is becoming more plentiful and popular. The flesh contains only a small amount of fat; especially if the meat comes from farmed rather than wild deer. The lean is dark red and the fat white and firm.

Venison can be used in any recipe given for beef, but there are several recipes in this book especially for venison. See pages 120, 124 and 125.

Hare and rabbit are covered in recipes on page 125. If buying hare, be sure to ask for the blood and liver.

Bacon: There is always a good choice of bacon available, ranging from rashers to cuts of bacon that can be cooked as a whole joint. When buying bacon, you have a choice of smoked and unsmoked (green) bacon. The latter is milder in taste. The rashers or cuts of bacon should look pleasantly moist, not wet, with a good proportion of leanness. Recommended cuts are given in the recipes.

Offal: There is a very wide choice of offal, ranging from very inexpensive tripe to the truly luxurious calves' liver and calves' sweetbreads. You will find recipes using various kinds of offal – sometimes known as 'variety meats' – in the recipes on pages 111 to 113. All offal is highly perishable, so take great care when buying it and cook it as soon as possible after purchase.

Newer Cuts of Meat. Both private butchers and supermarkets are specialising in new ways of preparing meat, ready for various cooking purposes.

Once only beef was sold as minced meat. Now you can obtain lamb, pork and poultry mince. Tender meat is cut into convenient sized pieces to cook on skewers as **kebabs**. Sausages are made from a variety of meats, including venison. In large shops and supermarkets you will find a very large selection of continental cooked meats and different kinds of salami.

Buy cooked meats from shops where they are displayed well away from raw meat. This means there is less fear of harmful bacteria being present in the meat.

APPROXIMATE QUANTITIES TO BUY

Each recipe gives the approximate amount of meat required per serving. This may appear to vary quite a lot in different recipes, but it will depend on the other ingredients in the dish and the amount of bone in the particular cut of meat recommended.

You need to allow per person:

Beef, pork and veal joints with a large bone	225 to 350 g/8 to 12 oz add extra if you plan to have some left to serve cold
Lamb joints, such as loin and best end	350 to 450 g/12 oz to 1 lb add extra if you plan to have some left to serve cold
Boned and rolled joints	175 to 225 g/6 to 8 oz add extra if you plan to have some left to serve cold
Steaks	varies; but an average of 175 g/6 oz
Chops	2 small or 1 large
Cutlets	3 small or 2 large
Escalopes	100 to 150 g/4 to 5 oz
Meat for stewing	150 to 225 g/5 to 8 oz
Minced meat	100 to 150 g/4 to 5 oz
Bacon rashers	2 to 3

Buying Poultry and Game Birds

The situation with most poultry has changed a great deal in the last few years, for, in addition to whole birds, it is possible to buy individual portions, ranging from thin slices of breast meat (like escalopes) of both chicken and turkey, to breast and leg joints. Duck joints and halved ducks are also available. These are ideal for smaller families or when you need a single portion. They are equally good when you are entertaining, for you can choose a dish that needs all breast or all leg portions and serve these without the bother of carving.

If you buy frozen whole birds, it is essential that these are completely defrosted before cooking, the best place to do this is in the refrigerator. Portions of poultry and game should be defrosted if you intend coating or marinating them; otherwise they can be cooked from the frozen state.

It is now possible to buy many different individual portions of chicken such as legs, quarters, drumsticks and breasts

HOW TO TELL IF POULTRY AND GAME BIRDS ARE FRESH

Appearance: The flesh of **chicken** and **turkey** should be firm and white, with a plump breast. The beak of a fresh bird which has not been trussed should be bright red.

Duck and **goose** should not contain too much fat. Check there is plenty of meat on the breast, for sometimes these birds have large frames which can be deceptive. Modern breeding of ducks in particular has produced much leaner birds with a high proportion of breast meat.

Do not buy poultry if it seems limp and slightly damp.

Game birds will vary in appearance but their flesh should always be firm. There is more about game birds on pages 118 to 120.

Always remove the bag of giblets from inside the birds as soon as possible after purchase and keep them separately from the bird.

The giblets can be simmered in water to give a good flavoured stock, with which to make gravy or a sauce. Before using wash the giblets well and check there is no yellow colour on them. This indicates the gall bladder has been broken in preparing the bird and it gives a bitter taste to the giblets.

Aroma: Really fresh poultry should have a very pleasant smell. If you like game that has been hung for a fairly long period to give a stronger taste, there will be a definite 'gamey' smell about the birds, but this should not be unpleasant in any way.

APPROXIMATE QUANTITIES TO BUY	
This is the oven-ready weight.	
You need to allow per person:	
Turkey and large chickens	350 to 450 g/12 oz to 1 lb add extra if you plan to have some left to serve cold
Goose	at least 450 g/1 lb add extra if you plan to have some left to serve cold
A medium chicken gives	4 portions
A small chicken or duck or guinea fowl or pheasant gives	2 portions
A spring chicken (poussin) or partridge gives	1 portion

Buying Flour

Flour is an essential ingredient in many forms of cooking and the success of recipes sometimes depends upon the wise choice of flour. This is covered in the various recipes. Choose **plain flour** for sauces and pastry and where specified in a recipe. This flour can be used for baking, with the addition of **baking powder**; it is given as an alternative to **self-raising flour** in baking. You may be able to obtain specially **light-textured soft sponge** or **cake flour**. Use this for making sponges, but not for richer cakes.

Where there is no mention of the kind of flour, it is assumed you are using white flour. If you care to substitute **wholemeal flour**, which contains 100 per cent of the wheat grain, or **wheatmeal flour**, which contains 80 per cent of the wheat grain, you may need to adjust the amount of liquid slightly. Both these flours absorb more liquid than **white flour**. A number of recipes mention adjustments.

Both white and wholemeal strong flours have a high gluten content and give a good result in bread-making, see page 178.

To give the effect of **brown flour**, mix equal quantities of white and wholemeal or wheatmeal flours. If you see flour marked 'stone-ground', this simply refers to the method of milling and does not affect cooking results.

STORING FLOUR

Keep flour in a cool dry place. It has a long life, but it is advisable to tip older flour out of the container and use this first before adding fresh flour.

USING CORNFLOUR

This comes from corn or maize and has greater capacity for thickening sauces than wheat flour. If a sauce recipe states that you should use 25 g/1 oz flour, you achieve the same result if you use 15 g/½ oz cornflour. As both flour and cornflour have the same calorie content, this is an advantage if you are trying to lose weight. You can substitute 25 g/1 oz cornflour for the same amount of ordinary flour in baking. It helps to give a crisper texture to biscuits and a finer texture to light cakes. Store as flour.

USING ARROWROOT

This is made from the roots of tropical plants. It contains no gluten, so it can be used by people on a gluten-free diet. It is a good alternative to cornflour and is better for thickening clear liquids. You may find that not all grocers sell it, but chemists do. Use 1 level teaspoon to thicken 150 ml/¼ pint liquid. Blend carefully, then heat until the sauce or glaze for a fruit flan has become thickened and is quite clear.

The choice of flour – plain, self-raising, wholemeal or wheatmeal – may affect the success of a recipe

Buying Tea and Coffee

These are very important to most families and it is worthwhile spending a little time and money trying various blends and brands to find the kind you prefer. One important factor about both tea and coffee is that they should be stored away from strong-smelling ingredients, for they are inclined to pick up the smell. If you take either tea or coffee from their packets, store in airtight containers.

TEA

You can choose between buying packet (loose) tea and tea bags, or keep some of each. If you want an individual cup, you can use a tea bag, but a better pot of tea is made using leaf tea. Always warm the teapot and take the teapot to the kettle, not vice versa, so you make the tea with freshly boiling water.

The various kinds of **Ceylon** and **Indian teas** provide stronger brews; **China teas** have a more delicate flavour. Many of the well-known brands are **blended teas**. You may like to try **herb teas** for a change; there is a range of different flavours. You can also obtain **ordinary teas** flavoured with exotic flowers, such as jasmine.

COFFEE

There are many ways to select the kind of coffee you buy. **Instant coffee** is quick and easy to make, but **ground coffee** gives the true flavour. You can choose between buying coffees from various countries. French coffee has chicory added, which gives a distinctive taste. The finest coffee is made by buying freshly roasted coffee beans, having them ground or grinding them at home, then making the coffee.

Although there are many kinds of coffee-makers on the market, you can make perfectly good ground coffee in a warmed jug. Add water that has just reached boiling point to the coffee and infuse for a few minutes.

DE-CAFFEINATED TEAS AND COFFEES

The demand for these now means you have a choice of buying ordinary teas and coffees and those from which the caffeine has been removed. Many people believe that the stimulant caffeine is harmful.

Ceylon and Indian teas have a stronger flavour than China teas, while herbal teas are becoming increasingly popular

Buying Sugar, Honey and Syrup

These are all classed as sugars and while it is true that most of them add little food value to our diets, they are important ingredients in cooking. As we are urged to cut down on our intake of all sugars, it is wise to use them in moderation and have fewer commercial sweetened drinks and highly sweetened foods.

Sugar acts as a preservative in jams, chutneys and similar products, so when you make or buy these with a lower sugar content, they must be stored in the refrigerator after the jar or bottle has been opened. Use within a short time.

WHITE SUGARS

In many shops there will be a choice of two packets of the same kind of sugar, one marked 'natural' or 'unrefined'. That is because it is untreated. It has the same calorific value as ordinary cane or beet sugars. **Granulated sugar** is the usual kind for general purposes. Choose **caster sugar** when making sponges.

If lumps form in **icing sugar** in storage, put it through a nylon sieve before using. If you run out of icing sugar, you can put some granulated or caster sugar into a liquidizer and grind it finely. The colour is never as white as real icing sugar.

It is wise to buy **preserving sugar** when making jams etc.; see below.

SPECIAL SUGARS – BASED ON WHITE SUGAR

Instant icing sugar is icing sugar combined with dried albumen (egg white). Simply blend with water and flavouring to use as Royal icing.

Special **preserving sugar** which includes pectin may be used when you are making preserves with fruits like dessert cherries and strawberries that lack natural pectin.

Vanilla sugar is made by flavouring sugar with vanilla. It is expensive to buy and you can produce your own by buying vanilla pods, halving one of them and placing it in a jar of sugar.

BROWN SUGARS

Demerara is a sugar with large grains, giving a pleasant gritty texture. **Light and dark soft brown sugars** are used in cooking to give some flavour and a darker colour; both light and dark **Muscovado sugars**, which impart a more distinctive taste, can be used instead. **Molasses sugar** is ideal if you want the taste of black treacle.

HONEY

There is a wonderful range of different flavoured honeys. **Blended honey** is produced from a mixture of flavours. It is easier to use **thin honey** in cooking. It is clear and blends easily with other ingredients. **Thick crystallized honey** is better as a spread.

Use honey in cooking. It imparts a delicious flavour to fruits and because it tastes sweeter, you use less than when sweetening with sugar.

SYRUPS

Golden syrup is a by-product of sugar refining. It gives a soft texture in baking. **Black treacle** and the very similar **molasses** are used in making gingerbreads and other fairly strongly flavoured dishes. As well as giving an interesting flavour and sweetness, these are a source of the valuable mineral iron. **Maple syrup**, as the name implies, comes from the maple tree, not from sugar cane or beet. This is a delicious syrup to use over pancakes. True maple syrup is expensive, so check the quality carefully. It should be light in colour and very clear. Maple-flavoured syrups are cheaper but less good.

You can choose between buying some syrups in cans or jars. The latter is useful if you want to melt syrup in the microwave cooker. Make sure you remove the metal lid.

Storecupboard Extras

A well-planned range of foods in the cupboard enables you to make interesting dishes within a short time. You can cope with unexpected visitors more easily. The following are some of the basic ingredients; recipes may well include some of the lesser-known ingredients, which you can add.

Pasta and **rice** are the basis of many different dishes. You will find details of these foods and recipes on pages 126 to 135.

Cereals are important, especially **rolled oats**, used in various dishes as well as breakfast Muesli and Porridge, see page 13. Check the labels of **breakfast cereals** to see their sugar content if you are trying to cut it down.

Dried pulses – beans, lentils, chick peas and green peas – form the basis of many vegetarian dishes as do **nuts**. Although they keep reasonably well, they do become rancid after a time, so do not buy too large a quantity at one time even though larger quantities generally save money. Store in covered containers. The quality of **nuts** varies, so you may be able to save money by buying less perfect shapes which are quite acceptable if you plan to chop them. **Desiccated** and **creamed coconut** provide two ways of adding this flavour. Desiccated is generally used for baking and creamed for sauces, ice cream etc. Keep opened packets of both products in the refrigerator.

Dried fruits should be stored carefully; they harden if kept uncovered. Some dried fruits, such as **apricots** and **prunes** are sold in two forms: the kind that needs soaking before cooking, and tenderized fruits, which do not require soaking and which can be eaten like a sweetmeat. You may find you are advised to keep the opened packet in a refrigerator. Smaller fruits, such as **raisins, sultanas** and **currants** vary a great deal in quality. Look for those that are plump and juicy. If they have become dry, simply pour cold water over them, spread them out on trays and leave for 48 hours before using in cakes. If they are not required in baking, soften in hot liquid immediately before using. Keep glacé cherries well covered to prevent them becoming over-sticky.

CANNED FOODS

Canned foods keep well, so stock up with a few cans of fish, such as sardines, tuna and salmon (cheaper pink salmon can be used in cooked dishes like Fish cakes, see page 84. Also stock up with canned tomatoes – chopped and whole; sun-dried tomatoes are used in certain dishes.

Choose some soups that could make a sauce in an emergency. Have a small selection of vegetables – select those that are not in the freezer and include various kinds of beans, such as red kidney beans, that take a long time to cook. When buying canned fruits, check the labels; you can choose between fruits in syrup or in natural juices – this means no added sugar. Preserves for storage are covered on page 186.

Sweetened condensed milk is a useful standby; other milks for storage are described on page 18.

VINEGARS

Malt vinegar, traditional in Britain, is brewed from barley. When using this or **white distilled vinegar** in preserving, check labels; make sure you have pure malt and an acetic strength of at least 5 per cent. **Cider vinegar** is considered by many people to have health-giving qualities. It has a strong flavour and can be used for all purposes. **Red** and **white wine vinegars** are produced in a similar manner to wine. Buy the best quality you can afford. The flavour is gentler than malt vinegar. **Sherry vinegar** has a pleasantly sweet taste. **Herb vinegars** are made by infusing fresh herbs in vinegar. These are expensive to buy and easy to make at home. Bruise the leaves of tarragon, rosemary or other herbs, add to bottles of vinegar and leave for some weeks. Spices, such as chilli, can also be added to vinegar.

FLAVOURINGS AND GARNISHES

These are important, as they make foods taste and look more interesting. One of the most useful is **tomato purée**. Buy it in a tube so it is easy to squeeze out the required amount. You may find it useful to buy tubes of garlic and anchovy purée also. **Anchovy sauce**, or the stronger essence, takes the place of the purée, and gives colour and flavour to fish dishes.

Tabasco sauce is an easy way to add a hot flavour to food; add it drop by drop. **Soy sauce** is not only an essential ingredient when preparing dishes from the Far East, but a few drops can liven up a soup or stew. **Light soy sauce** has a more delicate flavour than the more familiar dark sauce. **Worcestershire sauce** adds flavour to many dishes. **Tomato ketchup** is the favourite flavouring for many people. It has real value in sweet and sour and barbecued dishes, giving a sweet as well as a savoury taste. Many people will prefer this in the dressing for prawn cocktail instead of tomato purée. **Mushroom ketchup** is not so well-known, but adds a good flavour to various soups and savoury dishes.

Stock or **bouillon cubes** are a useful substitute for homemade stock. Brands vary, so experiment and find those you like best.

Essences are produced in various flavours, such as almond, vanilla, fruit-flavoured and alcohol-flavoured. Many are now obtainable marked 'natural', which means they have no artificial flavouring. Use these and edible colourings sparingly.

Jars of capers, cocktail onions, gherkins, black, green and stuffed olives are not only used in dishes, but make good garnishes on foods.

Many dishes are enhanced by the addition of flavourings and garnishes which make the food taste and look more interesting

CONDIMENTS AND SPICES

When a recipe states 'season to taste', it means add salt and pepper. These are some of the most important ingredients in savoury cooking. Used carefully, they help to bring out the flavour of foods.

We are urged to cut down the use of **salt** to avoid hypertension (high blood pressure). **Sea salt** and edible **rock salt** tend to have more flavour than ordinary refined salt, so you need less; **block kitchen salt** is now a rarity. **Flavoured salts**, such as celery salt and garlic salt, are useful if you want just a hint of a flavour.

Pepper of any kind is classed as a spice. **White pepper** is produced from the fully ripened dried berries of the pepper vine. **Black pepper** from the berries before they have ripened. White pepper is generally used for serving at the table, although many people prefer black pepper. There is one very important point; you will see that in all recipes the words 'freshly ground black pepper' are used. This is because you do not have anything like the proper taste if you use drums of ready-ground pepper. The dried pepper deteriorates during storage. Invest in pepper-mills for both kitchen and dining room and notice the difference in flavour. A salt-mill, used with sea salt, is as effective.

Fresh green peppercorns are often used in dishes; buy them from specialist shops.

Mustard is made from the seed of the mustard plant. **Traditional English mustard** has a hot flavour, whereas **French mustard** has a savoury taste. There are many kinds of French mustard, the best known being Dijon. Both English and French mustards are obtainable blended with herbs and other flavourings. **Whole grain mustard** has an interesting granular texture.

Used carefully, spices help to enhance the flavour of food

SPICES

These all add an interesting flavour to foods. Remember all spices lose flavour in storage, so buy only small drums. Keep tightly covered. The term 'ground' means in powder form.

Allspice	ground; tastes like mixed spices. Used in sweet and savoury dishes.
Anise	seeds; aniseed taste. Used mostly in sweet dishes..
Caraway	seeds; sweetish flavour. Used in cakes and breads, also added to red cabbage, see page 00.
Cardamom	seeds and ground; hot bitter-sweet taste. Use in curries and some cakes.
Cinnamon	sticks and ground; sweet taste. Used in sweet dishes and drinks in which a piece of the stick is infused.
Cloves	dried flower buds and ground. Strong and pungent taste. Used in many dishes. A particular affinity with apples.
Coriander	also a herb, see page 29, seeds and ground. Slightly bitter taste. Used in Oriental dishes and pickles.
Cumin	seeds and ground. Sweet, not unlike caraway. Used in curries and savoury dishes.
Curry powder	a blending of spices, see page 108.
Garam Masala	another blending of spices, see page 108.
Ginger	fresh root, ground, preserved and crystallized. Hot and spicy. Used in all kinds of dishes.
Juniper	dried berries. Gives special taste to gin. Used also in some pâtés, stews and game dishes.
Mace	blades (outer skin of nutmeg) and ground. Slightly bitter taste. Used in pickles and savoury dishes.
Nutmeg	whole seed (to be freshly grated as desired) and ground. Sweetish-bitter taste. Used in puddings and cakes.
Paprika	ground. Generally mild and sweetish, although there are hotter kinds. Used in savoury dishes, particularly Goulash. Use when fresh; if stale, it develops a musty taste.
Pickling spices	a blending of whole pieces of various spices. The finer these are, the more potent. Used in pickles and chutneys. Tie in muslin; remove before bottling.
Tandoori spices	a blending of spices.
Turmeric	ground. Savoury-sweet taste. Gives bright golden colour as well as flavour to pickles.
Vanilla	dried pod and essence, see page 170. Vanilla is a flavouring used in baking and a wide variety of desserts It must be used judiciously, for too much vanilla taste is very overpowering.

CHOOSING EQUIPMENT

The utensils and equipment in the kitchen can be described as 'the tools of the trade', for they can help to make the preparation and cooking of food much easier and more successful.

When buying small gadgets and equipment, handle them well before buying and ask yourself certain questions, such as:

'is that knife comfortable in my hand?'

'would I be able to lift that saucepan when it was fairly full of food?'

'has that frying-pan the type of handle where the screw might become loose and there could be an accident?'

When buying major appliances, do take the time to inspect various models. Ask your friends about their experiences, but do not necessarily feel you must buy exactly the same appliance. Family needs vary a great deal and what may be perfect for one home could be far from suitable in another. Try and attend a demonstration of the appliance, where you can ask an expert pertinent questions.

A stainless steel steamer that is used on top of a saucepan

POTS AND PANS

Buying: The golden rule is to buy the best quality you can afford; most pans have regular use. The bottoms of cheaper, thinner pans tend to buckle after a time and give uneven heating.

Many pans are 'non-stick'. These have great advantages, as foods like milky sauces and scrambled eggs do not stick to the surface and the pans are much easier to wash up. You can fry foods in a much smaller quantity of fat; even eggs do not stick to a non-stick frying-pan.

Consider carefully, though, before you buy all **non-stick pans**. You cannot use an ordinary metal whisk, spoon or fish slice to handle or remove the food in them; you must use special ones. Is this going to be a problem when cooking certain dishes? If all the family enjoys cooking, are you sure they will take the same care in using and cleaning the special pans that you do yourself? In most homes, it is wiser to have just a few 'non-stick' pans for specific purposes, such as heating milk, cooking pancakes and scrambling eggs.

If you are short of storage space, consider dual-purpose pans. **Deep frying-pans** with lids are excellent as shallow saucepans. **Flameproof** ware is safe to use on top of the cooker, under the grill and in the oven. Never confuse this with **ovenproof** ware – for oven use only. **Casseroles** are obtainable in many materials; consider their versatility and value for a range of uses, including an attractive serving dish.

A **wok** is not only the right utensil for cooking Oriental dishes, but it is splendid for cooking all kinds of foods. You need very little fat or oil in it, the heating is speedy and even and results are excellent. You can steam in most woks, too.

Consider the range of sizes of the pans you buy. You will need at least one large one for cooking joints of bacon and large quantities of stew. If you make only small quantities of home-made preserves, this could double-up as a **preserving pan**, but if you plan to make fairly large batches invest in a proper preserving pan.

Check the diameter of the base of pans in relation to the size of the hotplates on an electric cooker. Most of the pans should cover the entire plate to make the best use of the heat, although there are smaller plates on most cookers.

Most people like to have one or more pans specifically for making omelettes. A **double-saucepan** is useful for cooking egg custards and a **steamer** is an invaluable way of saving fuel. You need a **colander** for draining vegetables; one with a long handle keeps your hands well away from steam. **Strainers** and **sieves** are important for general use; use a nylon one to retain the colour of acid fruits.

The materials from which pans are made varies a great deal. You can choose between aluminium, cast iron, ceramics (these are generally flameproof), copper, enamel, stainless steel or a blending of different metals. Check catalogues and ask in shops about the advantages and disadvantages of each material.

Using: Handle and store pans carefully, so that the lids do not get out of shape. Make certain handles are turned well away from heat so they do not become too hot and difficult to handle. Clean carefully in the manner directed by the manufacturer.

If, over a period of years, lids do become misshapen, you can make them fit perfectly by placing a piece of foil under them. This is important when cooking in a very little liquid or for prolonged cooking, for it can save the pan from boiling dry.

KNIVES ETC.

Cutting tools are very important. You are far more likely to cut yourself on a blunt knife that does the job badly than one that is razor-sharp and cuts efficiently and quickly.

Buying: You need **small knives** and a **potato peeler** for preparing vegetables. It is possible to buy peelers that are equally good for left- as well as right-handed, users. Buy a large, sharp knife, often called a '**cook's knife**', for efficient chopping; handle it well to assess its weight before buying. A slightly **flexible knife** with a thinner blade is ideal for filleting, slicing, etc. A **bread knife** is an essential tool; try to persuade the family to use this for slicing bread only, so it keeps its perfect, serrated edge. A **carving knife** and **fork** are very important. If you entertain a great deal and need to carve large joints, poultry, etc., it is helpful to have two carving knives, as hot flesh blunts the blades during use. **Specialist knives** for cutting grapefruit and other purposes are useful; buy these as you feel the need. A flat-bladed **palette knife** is invaluable for blending ingredients, scraping out bowls, etc., although a plastic scraper does this rather better. Kitchen **scissors** do many jobs quicker than a knife. Buy good quality scissors and also consider the value of poultry scissors for jointing uncooked and cooked poultry.

Using: Keep knives carefully so that their blades are not damaged. Sharpen the blades on a **steel** or **knife sharpener** if necessary. Do not immerse the handles of knives in water; this loosens them. Always keep sharp knives in a place that is inaccessible to small children.

The 'tools of the trade' make life in the kitchen easier

Always choose the correct sized tin that is stated in the recipe

BAKING TINS, SPOONS ETC.

Buying: The picture shows the range of cake-baking ware that you will need if you make a lot of cakes. One interesting piece of equipment is the **spring-form** shape; this is very versatile, for it enables you to make delicate cakes, including cheesecakes, and unlock the side of the tin for easy removal. You have a choice between ordinary and '**non-stick**' baking ware. The latter is more expensive and is not essential if you do not mind using greaseproof paper or parchment in ordinary tins. Non-stick ware tends to brown the surfaces of some cakes more.

When buying **wooden spoons**, choose some with long handles, so that you can stir very hot ingredients without fear of being scalded. You need a large kitchen spoon for handling larger quantities and **measuring tablespoons and teaspoons**, which should be of 15 ml and 5 ml capacity to ensure accuracy in measurements. You also need a good-sized **measuring jug**; choose one with both metric and imperial measurements. A **perforated spoon**, also called a slotted spoon, drains small amounts of food. A **fish slice** lifts food from pans without fear of it breaking; select one on which a large piece of fish will balance perfectly.

Even if you own an **electric whisk**, a **hand balloon** or **flat whisk** is invaluable. Many a lumpy sauce is saved by being briskly whisked. If you do not own an electric whisk, then buy a **rotary whisk** as well; this takes the hard work out of the action.

Chopping boards save marking working surfaces. It is important that cooked and uncooked foods are not chopped or cut on the same board without thorough washing; harmful bacteria could spread.

Handle a **rolling pin** well before buying to make sure it is of the right weight and sufficiently long if you plan to handle large amounts of pastry or sugar-paste icing. You will be fortunate if you can obtain a marble slab for rolling pastry so it keeps cold. You need **pastry cutters** in various sizes.

Using: Wash tins and cutters or wipe them out with soft paper. Make sure they are completely dry before storing. Non-stick tins should be stored with paper between so their surfaces are not scratched.

Wash wooden spoons carefully, dry well and take especial care in cleaning boards or any utensils that have been in contact with uncooked meat, poultry, etc.

BOWLS AND BASINS AND COVERINGS

Choose a range of sizes that can be used for mixing, steaming and in a microwave cooker. If buying special plastic basins, check carefully the maximum temperature to which they can be heated.

There is a range of different types of food bags and coverings. Read labels carefully to make sure that you do not use them for the incorrect purpose. **Aluminium foil** is ideal for covering foods in the oven, in a steamer, etc. Moderate use has a purpose in a microwave but always check this point with the manufacturer's handbook of your particular cooker. Recent investigations show that **cling-film** can be used to cover the tops of containers of food but should not actually touch the food.

ELECTRIC MIXERS AND FOOD PROCESSORS

These appliances have probably done more to relieve the tedium of some of the time-consuming jobs in the kitchen than any other utensils. Many people will find they use both these appliances equally, but if you have neither and want to buy one only, it is wise to consider these points.

An **electric mixer** is of greater value if you make a lot of cakes, bread, etc. Most have the correct attachments, i.e. a whisk, a beater and a dough hook, so you repeat hand processes electrically. While you can prepare cake mixtures in a **food processor**, you do not aerate the mixture as much as when the ingredients are mixed by hand or in an electric mixer. It is excellent for 'all-in-one' mixtures.

A food processor is wonderful for chopping all kinds of foods, from grating cheese, carrots, chocolate, etc. through chopping meat, onions and other foods, to blending all the ingredients in pâtés and stuffings and 'rubbing' fat into flour within seconds. You can have **attachments on a mixer** to do these jobs too. It liquidizes, but see below.

A **liquidizer** (often called a **blender**) is perfect for making mixtures into smooth creamy soups and purées. It is better with highly liquid mixtures than a food processor. It can be used for blending ingredients but only copes with a small quantity at a time.

Buying: There are many makes of these appliances. Consider which would fit on your working surface or in a cupboard for easy withdrawal; people tend not to use appliances if they are difficult to lift out or assemble. Think about the size of bowls in mixers and processors. Even if you are a small family, are there not times when you cook for larger numbers or batch-bake? Prices vary, so make sure you are getting good value and buying from a shop where after-service (if needed) is good.

With **smaller mixers**, you may be able to lift the mixing attachments and blades to use as a portable **whisk** in any basin or pan. **Electric hand whisks** are invaluable for dealing with small amounts for creaming, whipping cream, whisking egg whites and other ingredients. Many people find the combination of a hand whisk and a food processor gives them all the help they need.

Using: Where you have control of speed, as in a mixer and electric hand whisk and with many modern food processors, always use a speed that is similar to that you would use by hand, i.e. slow steady speed for kneading, quicker for creaming, very quick for whisking. Be prepared for the incredible speed with which foods are chopped etc., in a food processor. If not, you will over-chop or over-handle ingredients at first.

Never remove the head from the lid of a liquidizer as you switch on the electricity, even if you are sure the lid is safely in position. Liquid mixtures rise in the goblet with amazing speed and you could have a spill or be scalded by hot liquid splashing. Wash and dry all parts of the appliance well. Have them serviced at recommended intervals or when they do not seem to be as efficient as they should.

Food processors make light work of whisking, beating and blending, chopping and grating

COOKERS

This is the most important choice for most people and it is worth spending time selecting which type you want. First, decide whether you want a **gas** or **electric** cooker. This is a purely personal matter and all recipes in this book are tested on both types.

The next important point is to decide if you want a **free-standing** or **built-in** cooker. The latter is most elegant and it may suit your kitchen lay-out to have the hob at a distance from the oven. A free-standing model enables you to change cookers more easily and cheaply and to take it with you if you move house.

There is a wide choice of both gas and electric automatic cookers; these have a device that enables you to time the switching-on of the heat, plus the start and ending of the cooking process. This may well be a point to consider if you are working away from home and are sometimes delayed from returning on time. It is hygienically important not to leave perishable foods in the oven for too long a period.

Buying: Check the space available and the measurements of the cookers in which you are interested. Check the height of the grill and oven. Imagine yourself lifting the Christmas turkey from the oven – would this be a problem or would one with a slightly higher oven make it easier? Do you like the type of cooker with a cover over the hob? Some cookers have the grill in the top of the oven – would this fit in with your style of cooking. Ask about the costs of installing and availability of service, if required. If possible see the cooker in use, so you can judge the speed of control of heating on the hob. Check how easy the cooker will be to keep clean, especially if liquids boil over.

Using: Be patient when you first use a new cooker; it may vary quite a lot from your previous model. If the oven is of the **fan type**, you will need to reduce the temperature slightly from that given in recipes, i.e. by 10°C or 20°F to 25°F. There will be no need to consider on which shelf to put food with this type of cooker, as the heat is uniform throughout the whole oven.

Try to wipe out the cooker as soon as possible after roasting, especially if the food has not been covered; it is easier to clean a warm rather than a cold oven. Many surfaces may be non-stick; treat these carefully. Be careful, too, with ceramic and enamelled surrounds. Use the cleaner recommended.

MICROWAVE COOKERS

Over half the homes in this country own a microwave because it fits into today's lifestyle. A microwave enables you to defrost frozen foods quickly and heat or cook the special products developed for microwave cookers. You can reheat cooked foods or complete meals. This is ideal if your family come home at various times; if done carefully, the food does not taste reheated.

Many fresh foods and prepared dishes can be cooked in a microwave; there is mention of these throughout this book.

Buying: There is a wide selection of microwaves available. Your first decision will be whether to buy an ordinary microwave cooker or one of the many combination ovens. These have various features.

The simplest combine conventional cooking with the speed of microwave cooking; others include a fan oven so the cooking is done with this added feature, see above for fan ovens. More elaborate models have automatic timing for switching on the power, even if you are not there, others have this, plus a grill.

Not everyone needs a combination oven, but if you feel frustrated by lack of oven space, it will give you a second conventional oven, as well as a microwave cooker.

Other points will concern size, power output and service, if desired.

Do not rush into buying specialist equipment; check what you have in your cupboards first.

Using: Microwave cookers are safe to use; the blind and children can manage to use them quite happily. Do not be concerned about using a microwave cooker. Start by doing simple things, such as heating drinks or an individual cup of soup. Remember the container should not be too full, made of metal or have a gold rim. Stir once during heating, stand for a few seconds in the microwave before taking it out of the cooker. Although dishes do not get as hot in a microwave as an ordinary oven, the food does and this affects the container, so use oven gloves.

Just as you look at the food cooking in a saucepan or in the oven, you should check progress in a microwave, for the size of dish, freshness and maturity of the ingredients will determine the exact cooking time.

There are two important points to remember when using the microwave. The first is that most microwave cookers have cold-spots. The fact they have a turn-table helps to counteract these but even so, it is wise to stir foods once or twice or turn the dish around manually if stirring is not possible. The second important point is that food should be allowed to stand for the time recommended in the microwave instructions, or at least 1 or 2 minutes after cooking. It can stay in the microwave because the timing device has switched off the power. The reason for standing timing is that the cooking process continues during this period.

A microwave is an invaluable asset to a busy working family

Make use of the various settings, for certain dishes are better cooked on DEFROST or other positions. Where microwave cooking is mentioned in this book, the setting is given. Approximate cooking times, where given, are based on a full output, often called HIGH, of 650 watts. If a cooker has a lower output, increase the timing by a few seconds. If a higher output, decrease it accordingly.

When using a combination cooker, follow the manufacturer's instructions about equipment and utensils.

PRESSURE COOKERS

The use of pressure cookers has been largely superseded by microwave cookers. Both appliances shorten cooking times and save fuel, but they do it in different ways and fulfil different functions.

Broadly speaking, a microwave produces the best results when cooking young, tender ingredients. These can be cooked in a pressure cooker, but it also tenderizes elderly vegetables, and stewing steak, ox tongue and ox hearts. Other uses of the cooker are mentioned in recipes in this book. If you are bottling vegetables, you must use a pressure cooker; it is the only safe way to destroy harmful enzymes.

Buying: Choose a pressure cooker that is big enough for the requirements of your family or for when you have visitors, but make sure you do not select a model that is too heavy for you to handle.

Using: Read the manufacturer's instructions carefully and appreciate the fact that there are occasions, as when making steamed puddings, when the initial part of the cooking time has to be done without pressure in order to avoid destroying the raising agent. Follow all recommendations for reducing pressure.

Pressure cookers are ideal for tenderizing tougher cuts of meat

SPECIALIST COOKERS

There are a number of interesting small cookers on the market, such as **electric frying pans** (which double-up as a tiny oven); these provide a chance to have a fun meal by using them at the table.

Fondue cookers enable you to make various kinds of dishes when you entertain, see page 143.

Small **compact cookers** are ideal for people living in limited accommodation, for holiday homes or as a second cooker. It is surprising just how successfully you can boil, grill and bake in these. They help to save fuel.

Electric slow cookers or crock-pots are extremely useful for foods like stews, dried fruits, pulses, etc. that need long periods of slow cooking. It is important that the food is subjected at some period to a short time of high heat to destroy harmful bacteria.

Barbecue cooking is covered on pages 166 and 167.

Although not cookers, the following heat liquids and foods.

A **coffee-maker** enables you to make and serve coffee well. Always select the recommended type of coffee.

Toasters enable the family to enjoy breakfast toast in a relaxed manner. Choose one sufficiently large. **Sandwich toasters** are excellent for making quick snacks; many also double-up as electric griddles.

Kettles should be handled before you buy to make sure you have one that is easy to fill and use.

Buying: These appliances are comparatively expensive, so think carefully and assess the value to you before buying.

Using: Do not expect too much from specialist cookers; they do the limited job for which they were designed well.

Other electrical appliances for use in the kitchen include electric deep fat fryers such as the one pictured above and an ice cream maker which aerates and freezes the ingredients for sorbets and ice creams

Electric Fryers

Frying of any kind can be a dangerous form of cooking. The fat or oil is heated to a very high temperature; if this is greatly exceeded, it could ignite and start a fire. It is all too easy to leave the kitchen to deal with a caller or answer the telephone and forget to turn off the heat under a frying-pan or deep pan of oil – with the result that it very soon becomes over-heated.

Electric fryers have put a stop to that risk. They have thermostats and, even at the highest setting, the temperature cannot be exceeded. When the oil reaches the pre-set temperature, the electricity is automatically switched off.

While frying is not considered the ideal way of cooking, for it encourages us to eat too much fat, it is true that in deep-frying less oil is absorbed by the food. This can be seen by the level of the oil after cooking. You will find it has changed very little from when you began cooking.

Buying: Check the various models. The fryers have a filter to stop the smell of cooking permeating the kitchen – compare these, asking how easy they are to change and at what intervals. Make sure the frying basket is simple to raise and lower.

Using: The thermostat works on the heating point of oil; do not use hard fat, unless the manufacturer gives specific advice about this. The oil may be used several times. This is an advantage of deep-frying; in shallow-frying it must be thrown away after one use. Strain the oil carefully to remove all particles of food. Never use the oil if it has developed a rancid smell. Always drain the fried food on absorbent paper after cooking. The paper absorbs surplus fat or oil.

Keeping food hot

It is all too easy to spoil the look and flavour of cooked food by keeping it hot for too long a period. There are various appliances designed to store cooked foods for a limited period at a temperature sufficiently low to prevent their spoiling. These are particularly useful when you are entertaining and do not want to leave your guests to dish-up the meal at the last minute.

Buying: Check the versatility of the various appliances. Some foods, such as meat, poultry, soups, etc., can be placed on a hotplate, but these are not good for cooked vegetables, as they need less direct heat. If you want to keep a complete meal hot, look at **heated trolleys** or other appliances that have special containers for vegetables as well as the capacity for storing the main dish.

Using: To compensate for the fact that a limited amount of cooking continues when the food is kept hot, it is advisable to undercook vegetables slightly before placing them in the heated containers. Never keep them standing for too long a period.

Specialist equipment

The following appliances are designed to give professional results when you are preparing certain foods or dishes. In order to justify their price, you would need to consider just how often they would be needed.

Ice cream makers aerate and freeze the ingredients for sorbets and ice creams – on the lines of the old-fashioned ice bucket, except there is no manual work involved. While richer ice creams can be made very successfully without one, it is not easy to obtain the very light consistency that produces a perfect sorbet, or a very economical custard-based ice cream, without using this appliance – even if you make the necessary adjustments to the recipes, see pages 52, 53 and 172.

Buying: At this moment there is very little choice of brands, but if demand grows, there may be more on the market.

Using: Follow the manufacturer's advice. Always keep the bowl scrupulously clean, especially after using it with dairy products.

If you eat pasta very regularly, and we are urged to do so, you may like to make your own, see page 127. Although it is both possible and not particularly difficult to roll and cut the dough by hand, it does take an appreciable amount of time. A **pasta maker** does this job for you.

Buying: These are becoming rather more plentiful, so you may be able to choose between various models.

Using: Read the instructions on page 127 about the consistency of the pasta dough; this gives the ideal texture for the machine to handle.

REFRIGERATORS

These are undoubtedly the most important invention for helping to keep the foods we buy and store at home as fresh as possible. They do need to be used wisely and kept at the right temperature, see page 16 for full details.

Buying: Obviously you will select the refrigerator for the best position in your kitchen. It is possible to buy models that fit under the working surface, are part of a built-in unit and are free-standing models. Consider its size for all occasions, like Christmas or when you entertain, not just for everyday storage.

Using: Pack food correctly, details about this are on page 16. When you take food from the refrigerator, close the door at once. It takes only a short time for the temperature in the cabinet to rise, but a surprisingly long time for it to return to the right temperature.

Defrost frequently; the motor works much harder if the ice is thick. Modern models defrost automatically. Wipe out the cabinet frequently and thoroughly. A little vinegar or bicarbonate of soda in the water helps to keep it smelling fresh.

The upright type of freezer occupies less floor space than a chest freezer and may be combined with a refrigerator, as above

FREEZERS

A well-stocked freezer plus a good storecupboard can give you a mini-supermarket in your own home. Some examples of the kinds of foods that can be frozen are listed below.

Buying: Consider the comparative advantages of **chest** and **upright freezers** before buying. The former tend to use less electricity, but it is easier to locate foods in the upright type. It will probably depend upon where you plan to locate your freezer. Some upright models combine a larder refrigerator with a freezer. These are tall, but occupy the floor space of only one cabinet.

Using: The list below and the picture give you some idea of just how helpful a freezer can be.

When freezing vegetables, blanch (very lightly cook) them before freezing to destroy harmful enzymes.

Soft fruits can be frozen raw; many fruits can be made into uncooked or cooked purées or poached lightly in sugar syrup before freezing.

When a recipe states 'open-freeze', it means on flat trays to separate the ingredients and prevent packaging touching the surface. When frozen, wrap or put into boxes.

Some foods that freeze well: Stocks and soups, fish of various kinds, meat and poultry, cooked stews, curries, etc., some sauces, see page 161, vegetables and some vegetable dishes, see page 145, various fruits, iced desserts, some puddings, cakes and breads. Slice cakes and bread before freezing. Separate slices with waxed paper.

Wrap or pack foods carefully.

Defrost your freezer before it is iced up.

BEFORE THE MEAL

One of the pleasures of entertaining is to have the chance to chat with your guests both before and during the meal. You can do this if you have planned the menu carefully. It is wise to work out how you could keep foods hot if your guests are a little late or linger longer than expected over pre-meal drinks and canapés.

To keep food hot: Dish up vegetables and stand in a bain-marie (a deep container of very hot water) over a very low heat. Turn the oven heat very low and cover food with foil. Put buttered damp greaseproof paper over sauces and gravy, so a skin cannot form. An alternative is to dish up most foods and put the cooked vegetables into the microwave for 1 or 2 minutes just before serving.

INTERESTING DIPS

Dolcelatte Dip

These are ideal to serve with a drink, instead of canapés. The crudités, such as sticks of carrot, celery, chicory, florets of cauliflower, spring onions and baby (cherry) tomatoes, have a lovely fresh flavour that does not spoil anyone's appetite.

The consistency of the dip is important. It should be like whipped cream, just thick enough for it to adhere to the crudités.

The dip shown is based upon Dolcelatte cheese, but other cheeses can also be used.
Dolcelatte dip: Blend 300 g/10 oz cheese with 2 tablespoons thick mayonnaise, 2 tablespoons finely chopped chives or spring onions, a good shake of cayenne pepper and approximately 150 ml/¼ pint soured cream or yogurt. Top with chopped chives.
Tuna dip: Blend 225 g/8 oz well-drained and finely flaked canned tuna with 4 tablespoons grated cucumber, 3 tablespoons mayonnaise, a few drops of anchovy sauce or essence, a good squeeze of lemon juice and enough yogurt to give the consistency of whipped cream.

EASY CANAPES

The word 'canapés' is used to describe small pieces of food.
Bases for canapés: You can serve the food on rounds or squares of buttered bread; rye and Pumpernickel are particularly good.

Biscuits can be used if they are topped with firm, rather dry mixtures, such as sliced cheese, but they soften very quickly with a moist topping.

Shapes of fried bread are ideal. Alternatively, you can crisp the shapes in the oven.

The fried bases freeze well; the crisped ones can be stored in an airtight container.
Toppings for canapés: Try to achieve good colour contrasts on the little shapes of food; make sure they really are bite-sized and easy to handle.

Various kinds of fish and shellfish, such as crabmeat, diced lobster and smoked salmon make excellent toppings. Bind with a little mayonnaise.

Cheeses make ideal toppings. Use sliced Gruyère and other hard cheeses; pipe rosettes of cream or curd cheese. Top with pieces of pineapple, halved, seedless grapes, pieces of dessert dates and nuts.

Scrambled and sliced hard-boiled eggs are popular. Top the latter with a little mock caviare (they come from capelin and lumpfish).

Salami, Parma ham and ordinary ham can be used. Garnish with tiny pieces of gherkin, olives and cocktail onions.

Aspic coating for canapés: This is very practical, as it prevents the food from becoming dry. Make the jelly, according to the instructions on the packet. Arrange the canapés on a wire cooling tray with a dish underneath to catch the drips. Allow the jelly to cool until it is like a thick syrup. Brush the toppings with a very little jelly and allow it to set. Brush with a second coat, if necessary.

Many other dishes, such as terrines, savoury moulds etc. can be coated in a similar manner.

Canapés without a base: Serve dishes of nuts, olives and tiny gherkins. Put cocktail sticks around these, so they are easy to pick up.

Spear prawns, baby cooked or raw mushrooms, cubes of cheese and diced pineapple on cocktail sticks. Press them into a loaf, a cabbage or a grapefruit to look like a porcupine.

Fill small lengths of celery with various kinds of cheese blended with mayonnaise or with the Prawn cream on page 84. Fill dessert dates, tenderized prunes or large grapes with cream cheese and chopped nuts.

Savoury Tartlets

▲   ✿ to ✿✿

MAKES 12 TO 15
12 to 15 small slices of bread
40 g/1½ oz butter or
    margarine
For the fillings:
150 ml/¼ pint double cream
2 tablespoons mayonnaise
2 teaspoons lemon juice
1 × 227 g/8 oz can asparagus
    tips
100 g/4 oz peeled prawns
To garnish:
asparagus tips or chopped
    chives

When you have no time to make and bake pastry, use bread as an alternative. You will need to crisp the bread cases, so preheat the oven before making any preparations to 200°C/400°F Gas Mark 6.

Meanwhile, roll the slices of bread with a rolling pin to make them pliable and prevent their breaking. This is successful, even with rather stale bread. Cut the slices into rounds to fit patty tins. Melt the butter or margarine and brush a little over the tins. Press the bread rounds into the tins and coat them with the rest of the melted butter or margarine. Bake for 10 minutes, or until crisp.

Whip the cream, until it just stands in peaks. Mix with the mayonnaise and lemon juice, then divide into 2 portions.

Drain the asparagus, cut off 6 to 8 tips for garnish, chop the remainder and fold into half the cream mixture.

Fold whole or slightly chopped prawns into the rest of the cream mixture.

Fill the hot or cold cases with the two fillings. Garnish.

FRANKFURTER ROLLS:
Remove the crusts from slices of fresh bread and spread with butter and a little mustard. Place a frankfurter on each slice, roll firmly, brush the outsides with melted butter and heat as recipe, left.

Cut into slices before cooking if you are serving as a cocktail snack.

Cooked sausages may be used instead.

USING SHELLFISH:
Flavour the butter with a little lemon juice and roll around shellfish.

Savoury Tartlets

Savoury Profiteroles   ▲ ✪ ✪

MAKES ABOUT 30
150 ml/¼ pint water
50 g/2 oz fat*
65 g/2½ oz plain flour
salt and freshly ground black
     pepper
pinch cayenne pepper
2, size 3 eggs
fillings, see right-hand column

* choose butter, margarine or
     low-fat spread. Do not use
     very low fat spread.

Grease 2 large baking trays or sheets, preheat the oven to 200°C/400°F, Gas Mark 6.

Put the water and the fat into a saucepan and heat until the fat has melted. Sift the flour with the seasonings. Remove the pan from the heat, add the flour and mix well to blend. Stir over a low heat until the mixture forms a firm ball and leaves the sides of the saucepan clean. Allow to cool. Whisk the eggs and gradually beat into the flour mixture. This should be sufficiently firm to stand in soft peaks.

Spoon or pipe tiny balls, the size of a large hazelnut, on to the trays or sheets. Bake for 15 to 20 minutes or until well risen, firm and crisp. Check after 10 minutes; you can lower the heat very slightly but never take choux pastry out of the oven until firm and always cool away from a draught.

Slit the sides with fine kitchen scissors to allow the steam to escape. When cold, fill, see right. You can spoon the filling into the small balls or use a plain, small pipe to insert it.

These cases freeze perfectly. Defrost and crisp for a few minutes in the oven, then cool again before filling.

FILLINGS FOR PROFITEROLES:
Do not fill the choux pastry with soft fillings until just before serving. Try:
Cheese: Blend cream cheese or grated cheese plus whipped cream or mayonnaise with chopped nuts, chopped herbs, sultanas or crushed pineapple.
Pâtés: Such as soft liver or fish pâtés.
Flaked or chopped shellfish.
Minced chicken or ham in mayonnaise.

Cheese Aigrettes   ▲ ✪

MAKES ABOUT 30
ingredients as for Savoury
     profiteroles
50 g/2 oz Parmesan or mature
     Cheddar or Gruyère cheese
For frying:
oil

Make the choux pastry as for Savoury profiteroles. Finely grate the cheese and add to the mixture after incorporating the eggs.

Heat the oil to 190°C/375°F, or when a cube of day-old bread turns golden within ½ minute. Drop teaspoons of the mixture into the very hot oil and cook for 3 minutes or until well puffed up and golden brown. Drain on absorbent paper and serve hot or cold as a cocktail savoury.

NOTE: These also make a good light snack if served with salad and sprinkled with more grated cheese.

FRIED CHEESE MERINGUES:
Whisk egg whites until stiff, add salt and pepper. To each egg white allow 25 g/1 oz grated Parmesan cheese. Fold the cheese into the meringue mixture.

Heat the oil as for Cheese aigrettes and drop teaspoonfuls of the mixture into it. Fry for 2 to 3 minutes, drain and serve.

WAYS TO USE PREPARED PASTRY

The recipe on page 49 uses phyllo pastry. The following suggestions are based upon frozen puff pastry.

Defrost the block of pastry until it is just soft enough to roll out; do not allow it to become too soft. This is just as important when handling the pastry you buy as it is when dealing with homemade pastry.

Always preheat the oven well before baking the pastry. It is a good idea to chill (relax) the cases or fingers before baking – they keep a better shape.

Vol-au-vents: While you can obtain frozen puff pastry vol-au-vents, you may prefer to make a selection of savouries from the one packet of puff pastry.

Roll out the pastry; the thickness will depend upon the diameter of the finished cases. For very small cases, roll out to no more than 1.5 cm/½ inch in thickness; for larger cases it can be from 2 to 2.5 cm/¾ to 1 inch in thickness.

Cut into rounds, tiny cases should be no more than 5 cm/2 inches in diameter; larger ones about 7.5 to 10 cm/3 to 4 inches. Take a smaller cutter and press out a round in the centre, cutting through the pastry to no more than half its thickness.

Brush the tops with a little beaten egg to give a pleasant shine. Chill, then bake for 12 to 15 minutes in a preheated oven, set to 230°C/450°F, Gas Mark 8. Lower the

Vol-au-vents; Cheese and Ham
Fingers

heat after 6 to 8 minutes if the pastry has risen well.

Cool slightly, then carefully remove the centres, giving a good space to fill.

If serving hot, add the filling and serve at once.

If serving cold, put the cold filling into the cold pastry. Do this only a short time before serving. The portions removed can be perched on top of the filling. The last minute adding of the filling prevents the bottom pastry becoming soggy.

Some fillings: Blend chopped ham and chicken or flaked or chopped fish with seasoned, whipped cream, or thick yogurt, or mayonnaise, or thick Béchamel or other sauces, recipes pages 158 to 162. Add herbs or lemon juice to flavour.

Blend chopped, fried mushrooms with finely chopped, cooked fresh tomatoes and lots of chopped parsley and basil.

Blend lightly scrambled egg with finely chopped smoked salmon.

Cocktail mille feuilles: Cut the pastry into small fingers. Bake as the vol-au-vents. Split through the centre and fill with soft cream cheese blended with chopped herbs, or chopped nuts, or tiny pieces of well-drained pineapple. Decorate by spreading or piping a topping of cheese and with small sprigs of herbs, nuts or pieces of fruit.

Cheese and ham fingers: Cut the pastry as above. Bake as for vol-au-vents, until pale golden. Meanwhile, blend finely chopped cooked ham with curd or cream cheese. Carefully spread over the almost baked pastry. Top with finely grated cheese and return to the oven to complete the cooking.

Parmesan twists: Cut fingers of the pastry, about 6 mm/¹/₄ inch in thickness, 1.5 cm/ ¹/₂ inch in width and 5 to 7.5 cm/2 to 3 inches in length. Roll in finely grated Parmesan cheese. Bake as for vol-au-vents, for 10 minutes. Check baking time carefully, as the cheese can burn.

Sausage rolls: Cocktail sausage rolls are always a favourite. Roll out the pastry very thinly and cut into long strips. Roll out sausage meat to just under half the width of the pastry. Place on the pastry moisten the edges, fold over, flake the edges. Cut into small lengths. Make cuts on top, brush with beaten egg. Bake for 10 minutes as for vol-au-vents, reduce heat to 190°C/375°F, Gas Mark 5 for a further 10 to 15 minutes.

A START TO THE MEAL

An interesting start to the meal is probably more important than any other course. It sets the seal on the dinner or lunch and it can turn a meal into something rather special.

On the next few pages, you will find dishes that have been specially chosen for this course; you can also serve some of the pasta, rice, fish and vegetarian dishes from elsewhere in this book. Most of these recipes are planned to serve 4 people as a main course, but it is a fairly safe rule to allow the same quantity to serve 6 or even 8 people as an hors d'oeuvre if the main course is a substantial one.

A modern idea for an hors d'oeuvre is to have a mixture of hot and cold foods, such as hot fish or even warm pâté on a crisp, cold salad. Another up-to-the-minute favourite is a savoury roulade, on page 56.

This section also includes a range of soups to serve either hot or cold. For many people, they are the perfect start to a meal. When serving a more elaborate meal, the soup follows the hors d'oeuvre.

FRUIT HORS D'OEUVRE ▲ ▲ ✿

Fruits of various kinds make delicious hors d'oeuvre. They are refreshing and most people enjoy them.

Grapefruit may sound a little dull, but segments of pink and ordinary grapefruit spooned into glasses or on serving plates look most attractive. Try mixing grapefruit with orange segments or slices of avocado sprinkled with lemon juice.

Hot grapefruit is simple to prepare. Halve the fruit, remove pips and loosen segments. Top with very little butter and oil and brown sugar, or rum and brown sugar, or finely chopped pineapple, sherry, sugar and flaked blanched almonds. Heat under the grill, or in the microwave cooker for just a few minutes.

Melon is the accompaniment to the luxurious Pink champagne sorbet; it is one of the most popular starters to a meal. Serve it with sugar and ground ginger.

Fill halved melons with a selection of fresh fruits moistened with sherry or kirsch.

Sliced melon blends well with fish or meat hors d'oeuvre, see pages 56 and 58.

Some people dislike avocados, so always have an alternative hors d'oeuvre. This fruit is extremely versatile. It can be served cold with various dressings or fillings, such as prawns and crab, or hot.

Pink Champagne Sorbet ▲ ▲ ▲ ✿✿

SERVES 6 TO 8
1 large lemon
150 ml/¼ pint water
75 g/3 oz caster sugar
1 bottle pink champagne or use a sparkling rosé wine
few drops Angostura bitters

Thinly pare the zest from the lemon, squeeze out the juice and strain it carefully. Put the lemon zest into a saucepan with the water, cover the pan and simmer gently for 10 minutes. Strain the liquid, add the sugar while it is still hot and stir to dissolve. Cool, then blend with the lemon juice, champagne and Angostura bitters (add the bitters very sparingly).

Place in an ice cream freezer and freeze.

For the start of a meal, serve with melon balls topped with mint. It is extremely good if surrounded with small rolls of smoked salmon.

To serve as a dessert, it is delicious by itself or with ice cream or with various fruits.

IF YOU DO NOT HAVE AN ICE CREAM FREEZER:
Dissolve 1 teaspoon gelatine in the hot, lemon-flavoured water after straining but before adding the sugar etc.

Freeze the mixture until 'mushy'. Whisk 2 egg whites until stiff, fold in 25 g/1 oz caster sugar; blend with the lightly frozen mixture. Continue freezing.

Grapefruit Sorbet   ▲ ✿ ✿

SERVES 6 TO 8
2 large grapefruit
100 g/4 oz caster sugar or to
   taste
600 ml/1 pint unsweetened
   grapefruit juice
1 to 2 tablespoons lemon juice
2 egg whites
1 teaspoon gelatine (optional)

Cut away the rind from the grapefruit carefully, so you discard all the outer pith; do this over a basin, so no juice is wasted. Cut out the segments of fruit. Put 6 to 8 on one side to decorate the sorbets and sprinkle with just a little of the sugar.

Liquidize the remaining grapefruit segments with the grapefruit and lemon juices and half the sugar.

If using an ice cream freezer: Pour the mixture into the container and switch on until lightly frozen. Whisk the egg whites, fold in the remaining sugar, add to the mixture and continue freezing. This will be ready within about 30 minutes. You can then transfer the mixture to a container and place it in the freezer until required.

In a freezer: Dissolve the gelatine in a little hot grapefruit juice, cool, then add to the other ingredients as page 52 and liquidize. Freeze lightly. Whisk the egg whites until stiff, add the remaining sugar, fold into the partially frozen mixture and freeze until firm.

Serve the sorbet in chilled glasses, decorated with grapefruit segments.

SERVING SORBETS:
These have become very popular and some are equally suitable as a first course, or served in the middle of a formal meal, or as a dessert. You will find more sorbets on pages 52 and 173.

Never serve a sorbet that is too hard. Move it from the freezer into the cabinet of the refrigerator about 20 minutes before serving.

Tomato Ice   ▲ ✿ ✿ ✿

SERVES 4
675 g/1½ lb ripe tomatoes
small bunch spring onions
1 garlic clove
2 tablespoons olive oil
1 tablespoon lemon juice
few basil leaves
salt and freshly ground black
   pepper
iced water
To garnish:
4 tablespoons yogurt
4 tablespoons finely diced
   green pepper
4 tablespoons diced cucumber
2 tablespoons chopped parsley
   or chives

Skin the tomatoes and chop into pieces. Chop the spring onions and put some on one side to add to the garnish. Peel and crush the garlic. Liquidize the tomatoes with the remaining spring onions, the garlic, oil, lemon juice, basil leaves and seasoning to form a smooth purée. Add sufficient water to give a fairly thick pouring consistency.

Spoon into freezing trays and leave until lightly frozen; the mixture must not be too solid. Spoon into chilled soup cups or sundae glasses. Put the spoonful of yogurt on each serving and add the pepper, cucumber, parsley or chives and the reserved spring onions.

CUCUMBER-TOMATO ICE:
Use 450 g/1 lb tomatoes with ½ peeled and diced small cucumber.

Follow directions for Tomato ice but omit the cucumber garnish; add a little finely chopped celery instead.

Grapefruit Sorbet

Tomato Ice

Avocado and Bacon Hors d'Oeuvre   ▲ ✪

Serves 4

4 to 6 bacon rashers

2 large ripe avocados

1 tablespoon lemon juice

25 g/1 oz butter or margarine

To garnish:

green salad

oil and lemon dressing, see
    page 156

1 tablespoon chopped parsley

1 tablespoon chopped chives

De-rind the bacon and cut the rashers into 5 cm/2 inch pieces.
Halve and skin the avocados, remove the stones and slice the
flesh. Sprinkle with the lemon juice as soon as you have done
this.

Heat the butter or margarine in a frying-pan, add the bacon
rinds, heat for a minute and then remove them. Add the
pieces of bacon and fry for 1 to 2 minutes, depending on how
well done you like bacon. Add the avocado slices and heat
gently for just a few minutes.

Place the salad on individual plates and sprinkle with a little
dressing. Top with the hot bacon and avocado mixture and
the herbs. Serve at once.

Hot avocados:
This fruit is extremely good
served hot, providing it is not
over-cooked.

If cooked for too long, it
tends to develop a bitter taste.

Avocado slices are excellent
cooked with fried liver.

Hot Stuffed Avocados   ▲ to ▲ ▲ ✪

Hot Stuffed Avocados with
cheese and nut filling

When heating avocados with a filling, choose ingredients that
are cooked within a short time, as over-cooking tends to give
the avocados a bitter taste. The timing given in the recipe on
this page is ideal.

If an avocado is nearly, but not 100 per cent ripe, a few
seconds in the microwave will help to soften it.

Cheese and nut filling: To fill 4 avocado halves, mix 100 g/
4 oz cream or curd cheese with 75 g/3 oz grated cheese and
75 g/3 oz chopped nuts (walnuts, hazelnuts or cashew nuts are
ideal). Flavour with a little seasoning and mustard and bind
with 2 tablespoons single cream. Spoon into the avocado
halves, top with a few breadcrumbs and grated cheese. Cook
as for Baked avocados with crab (below).

Curried meat filling: Cook 1 finely chopped onion in 1½
tablespoons olive oil. Blend in 1 teaspoon curry paste or
powder, 100 g/4 oz diced cooked ham or chicken, 25 g/1 oz
soft breadcrumbs, 1 tablespoon chutney, 1 tablespoon single
cream and seasoning. Top with breadcrumbs and a little
desiccated coconut. Cook as for Baked avocados with crab.

Note:
Always sprinkle the cut edges
of the avocado with lemon
juice before adding the filling.

To cook in the microwave,
allow 2½ to 3 minutes,
depending upon the size of
the avocados, on FULL
POWER.

Baked Avocados with Crab   ▲ ▲ ✪

Serves 4

2 ripe avocados

salt and freshly ground black
    pepper

1 tablespoon lemon juice

For the filling:

100 g/4 oz crabmeat

1 tablespoon chopped spring
    onions

2 tablespoons diced red pepper

2 tablespoons finely diced
    green pepper

2 tablespoons single cream

few drops Tabasco sauce

For the topping:

25 g/1 oz butter or margarine

2 tablespoons breadcrumbs

1 tablespoon chopped parsley

Preheat the oven to 200°C/400°F, Gas Mark 6. Halve the
avocados and remove the stones. Put into an ovenproof dish.
Season the lemon juice and sprinkle over the cut surfaces.

Mix all the ingredients for the filling together and spoon in
the centre of the avocados. Melt the butter or margarine and
add the breadcrumbs and parsley. Sprinkle over the topping.
Bake for 10 minutes only. Serve immediately.

Shellfish blends well with avocados. It can be varied in many
ways; you can use chopped prawns, mussels or smoked fish
with or in place of the crab. Add chopped olives, herbs or
other flavourings that blend well with fish.

To skin peppers:
Although it is not essential in
this dish, the peppers can be
skinned before dicing. Halve
and place in a preheated oven
or under the grill, with the
rounded side uppermost.
Leave for a few minutes until
skins blacken; pull this away
from the flesh.

VEGETABLE HORS D'OEUVRE ▲ ✪

Many vegetables make excellent hors d'oeuvre. Serve hot globe artichokes, sweetcorn and asparagus with melted butter (remember to provide finger bowls). Cold globe artichokes and cold asparagus are delicious with an oil and lemon dressing.

Artichoke crumble: You need 8 small or 4 large cooked or canned artichoke hearts. Marinate them for a short time in seasoned olive oil. Artichokes bottled in olive oil are ideal.

Drain the vegetables and put into 4 individual ramekin dishes. Mix together 4 tablespoons single cream, or fromage frais, 50 g/2 oz grated cheese and seasoning. Spoon over the artichokes.

For the savoury crumble, melt 50 g/2 oz butter and mix with 100 g/4 oz fairly coarse breadcrumbs, 50 g/2 oz grated cheese, a shake of cayenne pepper and salt. Sprinkle over the artichokes and bake for 10 to 15 minutes in a preheated oven set to 200°C/400°F, Gas Mark 6.

Asparagus Creams ▲▲ ✪✪✪

SERVES 4 TO 6
350 g/12 oz asparagus, edible weight when cooked
liquid from cooking asparagus (see method)
1 sachet (1 level tablespoon) gelatine
3 tablespoons white wine
3 tablespoons mayonnaise, see page 157
150 ml/¼ pint double cream
150 ml/¼ pint natural yogurt
salt and freshly ground black pepper
½ to 1 tablespoon lemon juice
To garnish:
cooked asparagus

Cut the tips from the cooked asparagus and put them on one side. Sieve or liquidize the rest of the stalks. Measure the purée. If there is less than 300 ml/½ pint, add a little of the liquid in which the asparagus was cooked.

Sprinkle the gelatine on top of the wine. Alternatively, omit the wine and use 3 tablespoons of the asparagus cooking liquid. Allow to stand for 2 or 3 minutes, then dissolve over hot water or in the microwave cooker. Blend with the asparagus purée. Add the asparagus tips, stirring them in carefully so they are not broken.

Allow the mixture to become quite cold and then add the mayonnaise. Whip the cream until it just stands in peaks and fold this with the yogurt, seasoning and lemon juice to taste into the asparagus jelly. Spoon into the prepared moulds, see right, and leave until firm. Turn out and serve with freshly cooked hot or cold asparagus and crisp toast.

TO PREPARE MOULDS:
When making a savoury jelly, as in the recipe left, brush the inside of the moulds with a few drops of olive oil.

When making a sweet jelly, rinse in cold water only; drain but do not wipe dry.

TO TURN OUT OF THE MOULDS:
Wrap a heated tea towel around the outside of the moulds and leave for about ½ minute; then invert the mould(s) on to the serving dish or dishes.

Asparagus Creams

Fish hors d'oeuvre   ▲ to ▲ ▲ ▲

The range of smoked fish available means you can select one type or even small portions of different kinds. These fish do not need cooking. Arrange them in an attractive manner on individual plates. It is usual to serve lemon wedges and horseradish sauce with smoked eel, mackerel and trout, although a gooseberry or apple sauce is excellent with mackerel.

Lightly scrambled egg – hot or cold – also makes a very good accompaniment to smoked fish. Use a little extra cream or milk in cooking the egg(s) if you intend to serve them cold, as they stiffen as they cool. Garnish with very finely chopped chives, dill or parsley.

You need only lemon wedges and cayenne pepper with smoked salmon. The slices of smoked salmon can be rolled around Prawn cream, or a Smoked fish pâté, see pages 84 and 57.

Smoked sprats are less familiar than the fish suggested above, but they have an extremely good flavour; serve as smoked mackerel.

It is usual to have thin brown bread and butter with smoked fish.

Smoked fish pâté, page 57, looks appetizing with a salad garnish. Serve with hot toast and butter.

> When buying these ready-to-serve smoked fish, check that they look pleasantly moist and bright in colour. If they are in a polythene package, press this gently to see if the fish is soft. If it is hard, it can mean that it is far from fresh.

Watercress and Fish Roulade   ▲ ▲   ✿ ✿

SERVES 8
50 g/2 oz watercress leaves
1 teaspoon grated lemon zest
65 g/2¹⁄₂ oz self-raising flour or plain flour sifted with ³⁄₄ teaspoon baking powder
salt and cayenne pepper
4 large eggs
For the filling:
smoked trout pâté or Taramasalata, right

Prepare the tin and preheat the oven, as given in the recipe for Walnut and cheese roulade on page 61. Wash the watercress leaves and dry them very well. Chop finely; do not use any of the tougher green stalks.

Mix the chopped watercress, lemon zest and the flour or flour and baking powder together with a pinch of salt and good shake of cayenne pepper. Whisk the eggs until thick and creamy, then fold the watercress mixture into these.

Bake, then turn out, roll and cool as described in Walnut and cheese roulade.

When it is cold, unroll, fill with the fish mixture and re-roll.

TARAMASALATA:
Skin and blend 450 g/1 lb smoked cod's roe with 50 g/2 oz melted butter, 1 crushed garlic clove, 1 to 2 tablespoons lemon juice, 3 to 4 tablespoons single cream or fromage frais and a little black or cayenne pepper.

Use about half in the roulade; serve the rest with lemon and hot toast.

Warm Fish Salad   ▲   ✿

SERVES 4
For the salad dressing:
4 tablespoons mayonnaise
150 ml/¹⁄₄ pint thick yogurt
1 tablespoon chopped chives
1 tablespoon chopped fennel leaves
¹⁄₂ tablespoon lemon juice
For the salad:
few Chinese leaves
225 ml/7¹⁄₂ fl oz white wine
225 g/8 oz smoked haddock
2 large or 4 small scallops
100 g/4 oz peeled prawns
freshly ground black pepper
To garnish:
lemon wedges
sprigs of fennel

Mix all the ingredients for the salad dressing together. Place the Chinese leaves or lettuce on individual plates or a dish.

Pour the white wine into a pan, add the haddock and poach for 3 to 4 minutes. Do not cover the pan. Cut large scallops in slices; small ones can be left whole. Add the scallops to the haddock and cook gently for a further 3 or 4 minutes or until the fish becomes opaque. Add the prawns towards the end of this time, so they are heated. Season with pepper. Remove the pan from the heat, lift the haddock from the liquid and fork into large flakes. Mix with the scallops and prawns and keep hot. Boil the wine until it is reduced to 1 to 2 tablespoons. Add it to the fish. Spoon the warm fish mixture in the centre of the Chinese leaves or lettuce and top with the dressing. Garnish with lemon and fennel and serve at once.

USING THE MICROWAVE:
The fish can be poached in a flattish container in the microwave cooker. Follow the manufacturer's instructions for timing. Turn the dish once or twice during the cooking period. As liquid does not evaporate in the same way in the microwave, use only 150 ml/¹⁄₄ pint wine.

Smoked Trout Pâté

Whitebait

Smoked Trout Pâté ▲ ▲ ✿ ✿

SERVES 4 TO 6
50 g/2 oz butter
1 garlic clove
2 large smoked trout
1 tablespoon horseradish
   cream
4 tablespoons single cream or
   yogurt
1 to 2 tablespoons lemon juice
salt and freshly ground black
   pepper
To garnish:
parsley leaves
spring onions
strips of cucumber

Melt the butter, peel and crush the garlic, split the trout, remove the bones and all the skin. Flake the fish and blend with the butter, garlic and the remainder of the ingredients. Add the lemon juice and seasoning gradually to check the flavour. The ingredients can be blended in a basin, or a food processor, or in small batches in a liquidizer. If using a food processor, allow only a very short time, as over-processing spoils the texture of the fish.

Spoon the pâté into one dish or individual ramekin dishes, cover with foil and chill until ready to serve. Turn the pâté on to a plate and garnish with parsley, spring onions and strips of cucumber. If serving in small dishes, arrange the garnish on individual plates and place the dishes in the centre. Serve with hot toast and butter.

WATERCRESS AND TROUT
PATÉ:
Add 4 tablespoons chopped watercress leaves after blending the pâté.

A little finely chopped fennel root makes another interesting addition.

USING OTHER SMOKED FISH:
If using smoked mackerel, use only 25 g/1 oz butter.

With smoked salmon, you can omit the horseradish cream.

Whitebait ▲ ✿

SERVES 2 TO 4
450 g/1 lb whitebait
15 g/¹/₂ oz flour
pinch salt
good shake cayenne pepper
For frying:
oil
To garnish:
lemon or lime slices
fennel or parsley sprigs

If the whitebait is frozen, it can be fried without thawing, but in that case, it is not possible to coat the small fish with flour. Frozen whitebait may also be defrosted.

Wash fresh or defrosted fish in cold water and dry well on absorbent paper. Mix the flour with the seasoning. Put the fish in this seasoned flour and turn until evenly coated.

Heat the oil to 185°C/365°F, or check the temperature as described in the right-hand column. If you are using a deep-fryer on the cooker or an electric fryer, lower the basket into the oil to become hot. This prevents the fish sticking to the wire mesh.

Add the fish and fry rapidly for 2 to 3 minutes. You may need to do this in more than one batch, so the fryer is not over-filled. Drain on absorbent paper, then tip on to a heated dish. Garnish and serve as soon as possible after cooking.

TESTING THE TEMPERATURE:
Drop a cube of day-old bread into the hot oil or fat and note the time it takes to become golden. This shows the temperature of the oil or fat.
1 minute – it is 170°C/340°F
³/₄ minute – it is 185°C/365°F
¹/₂ minute – it is 190°C/375°F

If it takes longer, continue heating the oil or fat and test again.

If it browns in a shorter time, allow the oil or fat to cool slightly and test again.

MEAT HORS D'OEUVRE   ▲ to ✿✿✿

There are many meats that make excellent hors d'oeuvre. Follow the French fashion of serving a selection of various kinds of salami, cooked ham, etc. Arrange these in a border of sliced hard-boiled eggs, tomatoes and lettuce. Serve some of the interesting versions of French mustard with the meats, such as those containing herbs and peppercorns.

Parma ham is one of the most popular meats for an hors d'oeuvre. It is excellent with melon, fresh figs or dessert pears. It is expensive but so thinly sliced that it weighs 'lightly'.

Italian bresaola – beef cured in salt and air-dried – is another meat that makes a luxury hors d'oeuvre. Just before serving, add a little dressing, made by blending virgin olive oil with a squeeze of lemon juice and freshly ground black pepper. Take great care when buying this meat that it is freshly sliced, for it dries out very quickly.

Two easily made pâtés are on this page.

Speedy Liver Pâté   ▲▲ ✿✿✿

SERVES 4
2 bacon rashers
I small onion
I garlic clove
225 g/8 oz lambs' liver
50 g/2 oz butter or margarine
I teaspoon Dijon mustard
2 tablespoons beef or chicken stock
2 to 3 tablespoons single cream or fromage frais
2 teaspoons chopped parsley
salt and freshly ground black pepper

Remove the rinds from the bacon and cut the rashers into small pieces. Peel and finely chop the onion and garlic. Dice the liver. Heat the butter or margarine with the bacon rinds in a good-sized frying-pan. Add the onion and garlic and cook for 3 to 4 minutes, put in the liver and bacon, continue cooking for 4 to 5 minutes, turning the liver once or twice; do not overcook it.

Remove all the ingredients from the frying-pan with a perforated spoon and discard the bacon rinds. Add the mustard, stock, cream or fromage frais to the pan. The amount of liquid depends on the stiffness required. Stir well to absorb all the meat juices. Add the parsley and seasoning.

Put the ingredients into a food processor or, in batches, into a liquidizer or through a mincer until the pâté is as smooth as desired. Spoon into a container, cover and chill. Serve with hot toast.

CHICKEN LIVER PÂTÉ:
Substitute the same weight of chicken livers for lambs' liver in the recipe left.

Halve them and cook for 5 to 6 minutes. Then continue as the recipe left.

WARM PÂTÉ:
Both the lamb and chicken liver pâtés are very pleasant when served warm.

Spoon on to a bed of cold crisp salad and serve at once.

Boudin with Apples   ▲ ✿

SERVES 4
4 to 8 bacon rashers
225 to 350 g/8 to 12 oz blood sausage (see right)
2 to 4 dessert or cooking apples (see right-hand column)

The French know this savoury as boudin or 'blood sausage', whereas in Britain, it is called 'black pudding'. There are white 'blood sausages', too, which have a more pleasing appearance than the black variety. Cooked apple is an excellent accompaniment. The choice of apple depends upon whether you prefer a sweet or sharp flavour. Choose a type of dessert apple that cooks well.

De-rind the bacon and put the rinds into a frying-pan, heat for a few minutes to extract the fat, then remove. Meanwhile, slice the boudin and core and slice the apples. Add the bacon rashers to the pan and cook for 2 or 3 minutes. Add the boudin and apples and cook steadily for about 5 to 6 minutes, turning the slices over once or twice.

Serve as an hors d'oeuvre with a garnish of salad and French mustard or a mustard-flavoured salad dressing. It can also be served as a breakfast dish or for a main meal with creamed potatoes and a green vegetable.

CHOOSING APPLES FOR COOKING:
If you want an apple that cooks to a soft purée, choose a good cooking apple, such as a Bramley Seedling.

If you need the apple to soften but retain its shape, a dessert apple, like a Cox's Orange Pippin or a Golden Delicious, is ideal.

NOTE:
Do not over-cook bacon and sausages; remove them from the pan to heated plates, if necessary, while you complete the cooking of the apples.

Chicken Liver Salad

SERVES 4

12 chicken livers
1 garlic clove
50 g/2 oz butter
2 teaspoons grated lemon zest
2 tablespoons chopped parsley
salt and freshly ground black
   pepper
various kinds of lettuce
Oil and lemon dressing, page
   156
about 100 g/4 oz white
   seedless grapes

Halve the livers and peel and halve the garlic clove. Heat the butter and add the garlic and lemon zest. Put in the livers with half the parsley and seasoning. Cook steadily for 5 to 6 minutes, or until just tender.

Meanwhile, arrange the lettuce in a dish and add a very little dressing. Remove the garlic from the pan and tip the warm cooked livers on to the lettuce. Top with the grapes and remaining parsley and serve at once.

To prepare ahead: Prepare the salad and get the ingredients ready for cooking the livers, but only cook them ahead if you can reheat them for a very short time in a microwave.

TO DESEED GRAPES:
Seedless grapes are not always in season.
   Insert the tip of a small knife into each grape, carefully pull out the pips.

LIVER AND HARD-BOILED EGGS:
Cook strips of calves' or lambs' liver. Serve topped with chopped hard-boiled eggs and chopped parsley.

Chicken Liver Salad

Eggs as an hors d'oeuvre　▲ ✿

An egg mayonnaise is a simple but pleasant hors d'oeuvre.

Make the hard-boiled eggs look attractive by placing them on a colourful salad and garnishing the whole or halved eggs and mayonnaise with a topping of chopped herbs, or paprika, or narrow strips of red and green pepper.

Stuffed eggs make the dish more interesting. Remove the hard-boiled egg yolks and mash with a little butter or mayonnaise then mix with anchovy essence, or chopped prawns, or mashed canned sardines, or chopped asparagus, or curry powder.

Some of the egg dishes in the section beginning on page 136 may be served as interesting hors d'oeuvres.

Egg and Watercress Mousse　▲▲ ✿✿✿

Serves 6

6 eggs

4 tablespoons white wine

1 sachet (1 level tablespoon) gelatine

salt and cayenne pepper

4 tablespoons mayonnaise

1 tablespoon lemon juice

150 ml/¼ pint whipping cream

4 tablespoons finely chopped watercress leaves

To garnish:

watercress sprigs

Danish mock caviare (optional)

Hard-boil 4 of the eggs, shell and chop finely. Pour the wine into a basin, add the gelatine and allow to stand for 2 to 3 minutes, then dissolve over a pan of hot water or in the microwave cooker.

Separate the last 2 eggs, put the yolks into a bowl with the salt and pepper and whisk over a pan of hot water until thick and creamy. Add the warm gelatine liquid to this mixture. Allow to become cold, then add the mayonnaise, lemon juice and the chopped eggs.

Whip the cream until it stands in peaks and blend into the cold ingredients, together with the watercress leaves. Finally whisk the 2 egg whites until stiff, gently fold into the watercress mixture.

Spoon into 6 individual dishes, leave until firm, then top with small watercress sprigs and a little mock caviare.

Amounts of gelatine: Powder gelatine is extremely satisfactory. If you buy small packets, the gelatine is packed in individual sachets, each containing 11 g/a scant ½ oz. This is the amount needed to set 600 ml/1 pint of a clear liquid.

In larger catering packs, the gelatine is loose. Use 1 level tablespoon instead of 1 sachet.

Egg and Watercress Mousse; Walnut and Cheese Roulade

Quails' Eggs Tartlets ▲▲ ✿

MAKES ABOUT 24
For the tartlets:
50 g/2 oz butter or margarine
6 sheets phyllo (filo) pastry
For the filling:
12 quails' eggs
75 g/3 oz cream cheese
2 tablespoons grated
   Parmesan cheese
little cayenne pepper

Phyllo pastry has many uses; it is very good for cocktail sized tartlet cases. You need very small baking tins. Melt the butter or margarine, use a little to brush the metal cases. Preheat the oven to 200°C/400°F, Gas Mark 6.

Place the first sheet of phyllo pastry on the board (keep the rest covered so they do not dry). Brush with a little melted butter or margarine, add the second sheet, brush again with melted fat, add the third sheet and brush with fat.

Cut 12 rounds from the triple thickness and press into the tins. Repeat with the other 3 sheets of pastry. Bake for approximately 8 minutes. Allow to cool.

Put the eggs into boiling water, cook for 2 minutes, cool and halve. Blend the cream and Parmesan cheeses together, add a shake of cayenne. Spoon or pipe into the pastry cases.

Top with the halved eggs, placing the cut side downwards. Sprinkle with more cayenne pepper.

OTHER FILLINGS:
Use Taramasalata, see page 56, or soft Liver pâté, page 58 under the eggs.

STUFFED QUAILS' EGGS:
These are ideal for canapés, as the eggs are so small.

Hard-boil and halve, scoop out the yolks, mash and blend with cream cheese, or mayonnaise or mashed sardines. Pipe or spoon into the egg white cases.

Garnish with mock caviare.

CHEESE AS AN HORS D'OEUVRE ▲ ✿

Serve diced or grated cheese with an interesting salad at the start of the meal. The subtle taste of smoked cheese is particularly suitable.

Fried Camembert or Brie is a quick and easy dish. Coat with seasoned flour, then beaten egg and a good layer of fine crisp breadcrumbs.

Heat oil to 190°C/375°F, or until a cube of day-old bread turns golden within 1/2 minute.

Fry the cheese until golden. Drain on absorbent paper. Serve hot with a purée of gooseberries or apples or other sharp fruit, or Cranberry sauce, see page 161.

Walnut and Cheese Roulade ▲▲ ✿✿

SERVES 8
65 g/2 1/2 oz walnuts
40 g/1 1/2 oz self-raising flour or
   plain flour sifted with a
   scant 1/2 teaspoon baking
   powder
pinch salt
4 large eggs
For the filling:
175 g/6 oz Stilton or Danish
   blue cheese
175 g/6 oz cream cheese
3 tablespoons mayonnaise
To garnish:
a few halved walnuts
parsley sprigs

Line a 20 × 30 cm/8 × 12 inch Swiss roll tin with greased greaseproof paper or lightly greased baking parchment. Preheat the oven to 190°C/375°F, Gas Mark 5.

Chop the walnuts very finely and mix with the flour or flour and baking powder and the salt. Leave this mixture on a flat plate in the warm for a short time; it lightens the flour.

Whisk the eggs until thick and creamy; until you see the trail of the whisk. Gently fold in the walnut and flour mixture, using a metal spoon. Spoon into the tin and bake for approximately 12 minutes, or until the sponge feels firm.

To roll the roulade: put a clean teacloth into hot water, wring out well and lay flat on the working surface. Cover with a sheet of baking parchment or greaseproof paper. Invert the cooked walnut sponge on to this and remove the cooking paper. Place a second sheet of greaseproof or parchment on the sponge and roll firmly. Lift on to a wire cooling tray.

To make the filling, blend the cheeses with the mayonnaise, beating until soft and smooth.

To complete the roulade, carefully unroll the walnut sponge, spread with most of the cheese mixture and roll up again. Pipe or spoon small amounts of the remaining cheese mixture on top and garnish with walnuts and parsley.

SWEET WALNUT ROULADE:
Use the same proportions of nuts and flour but only 3 large eggs. Whisk these with 100 g/ 4 oz caster sugar until thick and creamy, then fold in the nuts and flour and bake as in Walnut and cheese roulade.

There is no need to use a damp cloth; cover greaseproof paper with a generous amount of caster sugar and turn out the sponge.

Spread with warm, but not hot jam and roll firmly. Alternatively, roll without a filling as for Walnut and cheese roulade. When it is cold, unroll and fill with sweetened whipped cream or cream and fruit, such as raspberries. Roll again.

GOOD SOUPS

HOMEMADE STOCK:
The recipe on page 97 gives a
very simple way of making
stock. While this is very
satisfactory you can achieve a
rather better flavour if you add
diced vegetables and heat
these with the bones until
golden in colour, then add the
liquid and simmer gently.

For a white stock:
Use the carcass of chicken or
turkey or veal bones and do
not brown these first.

For a brown stock:
Use beef, or mutton or
venison bones or the carcass
of game birds or duck or
goose.

A first-class soup depends upon a subtle blending of flavours. Some soups need a
good-flavoured stock. If unavailable, substitute a stock cube or use water with a more
generous quantity of the strongly-flavoured ingredients in the mixture. Some recipes
may appear to have a relatively small proportion of stock cube; this is because the
fairly pronounced flavour can overshadow the taste of the other ingredients in the
soup. Information about making homemade stock is given on the left.

When making a vegetable soup do not over-cook, as it is important to retain the
fresh flavour of the ingredients.

Microwave cooking of soups: Because of the high liquid content of soups you will not
save a great deal of cooking time, but it is an advantage to be able to cook the mixture
in a large bowl, without fear of its boiling over. Consult your manufacturer's instruction
book for details. Generally speaking, soup should be brought to simmering point on
FULL POWER, then the setting lowered to continue the cooking process.

The microwave cooker is ideal for heating individual bowls of soup. Take care to let
these stand for a minute in the microwave before removing; this ensures that the very
hot soup will not boil over as you bring it out of the microwave. Also ensure that the
soup bowls do not have metal rims or decorations.

Freezing soups: Most soups freeze well. A puréed soup tends to separate in freezing,
but the original consistency is generally returned by heating and whisking briskly. If a
soup that is to be served cold has separated, whisk when it has defrosted and if that is
not successful, liquidize it.

Tomato Soup

SPEEDY SOUPS   ▲ ✪

Many homemade soups can be cooked within a very short time if you make use of some ready-prepared or left-over ingredients and cut raw foods into small pieces. This can be done by grating or shredding by hand, or by using the attachments on a mixer or food processor.

A liquidizer or food processor also means you can achieve a beautifully smooth texture with the minimum of time and trouble. Each soup serves 4.

Chicken soup: Finely dice 175 g/6 oz ready-cooked chicken breast, chop several spring onions and a little celery heart. Simmer in 450 ml/$^3/_4$ pint of really good chicken stock, with $^1/_2$ teaspoon chopped rosemary and/or thyme and seasoning for 10 minutes.

Add 150 to 300 ml/$^1/_4$ to $^1/_2$ pint single cream and heat gently. Liquidize to make a smooth texture. Top with chopped parsley.

Chicken and almond soup: Use the ingredients above, but add 25g/1 oz ground almonds to give a thicker texture. Top with chopped almonds.

Cream of vegetable soup: Shred, grate or finely dice about 225 g/8 oz vegetables; these can be a mixture, such as carrots, green beans, onions, leeks, mushrooms etc., or use just a single vegetable or a packet of frozen vegetables.

If using fresh vegetables, heat 50 g/2 oz butter or margarine. Cook the vegetables in this for 5 minutes, stirring well so they do not discolour. Blend 15 g/$^1/_2$ oz cornflour with 600 ml/1 pint vegetable stock, add to the pan, stir well as the soup comes to the boil, then add chopped herbs and seasoning to taste. Cook fairly briskly for 10 minutes, or until the vegetables are tender. Add 150 ml/$^1/_4$ pint single cream and heat for 2 minutes. Top with chopped parsley.

If using frozen vegetables, do not defrost them. Make a sauce with 50 g/2 oz butter or margarine, either 25 g/1 oz flour or 15 g/$^1/_2$ oz cornflour and only 450 ml/$^3/_4$ pint stock. Add the frozen vegetables, with seasoning and chopped mixed herbs to taste then proceed as above.

The soup can be liquidized for a smooth texture.

Tomato Borsch: Use the ingredients in the Tomato soup on this page, but substitute beef stock for the vegetable or chicken stock. When it is cooked, add 175 g/6 oz grated or shredded cooked beetroot and heat for 1 or 2 minutes. Top with soured cream.

Tomato Soup   ▲ ✪

SERVES 4
1 medium onion
1 garlic clove
1 tablespoon sunflower oil
1 × 425 g/15 oz can chopped plum tomatoes
salt and freshly ground black pepper
1 fresh bay leaf or $^1/_2$ dried bay leaf
450 ml/$^3/_4$ pint vegetable or chicken stock
1 to 2 teaspoons brown sugar
To garnish:
single cream or yogurt

Peel and chop the onion and garlic. Heat the oil and cook the onion and garlic for 5 minutes. Add the tomatoes and liquid from the can, the seasoning, bay leaf and stock. Bring to the boil, lower the heat and simmer for 10 to 15 minutes. Remove the bay leaf then liquidize the soup. Reheat with any extra seasoning required and the sugar.

Garnish with the cream or yogurt.

NOTE: When fresh tomatoes are plentiful, use 550 g/1$^1/_4$ lb of these. Do not skin before cooking; you obtain a better flavour and colour. Liquidize well or sieve to remove all skin and pips.

CHILLED TOMATO SOUP:
Liquidize 600 ml/1 pint tomato juice with 2 tablespoons chopped spring onions, 4 tablespoons peeled and chopped cucumber, pinch celery salt and sugar.

Top with yogurt and chopped chives.

FROSTED TOMATO SOUP:
Lightly freeze the recipe above or the one on the left. Fork briskly then spoon into chilled soup cups.

Soups make a meal   ▲▲ ✿

There are many soups that can be served in place of a meal, as they are sustaining and full of nutritious ingredients. These range from soups made from pulses, as on page 66, to one of the famous American chowders, as well as the fish, meat and cheese soups.

Corn chowder: Derind 4 bacon rashers and cut into small pieces. Save the rinds. Peel 2 medium onions and 2 medium potatoes. Chop the onions finely and cut the potatoes into dice. Finely chop 4 or 5 celery sticks. Deseed and dice 1 green pepper.

Heat the bacon rinds with 25g/1 oz butter add the onions and diced bacon and cook for 5 minutes. Discard the bacon rinds. Add 300 ml/$\frac{1}{2}$ pint chicken stock, 300 ml/$\frac{1}{2}$ pint milk, the potatoes, the celery, 1 teaspoon paprika, salt and pepper to taste. Simmer for 10 minutes. Add the green pepper and 225 to 300 g/8 to 10 oz cooked or well-drained canned sweetcorn. Heat for a few minutes. Garnish with chopped chives and parsley.

Bean Sprout Soup   ▲▲ ✿

SERVES 4

75 g/3 oz steak
1 small bunch spring onions
1 or 2 garlic cloves
350 g/12 oz fresh or canned
    bean sprouts
900 ml/1$\frac{1}{2}$ pints chicken stock
    or water and 1 chicken
    stock cube
2 tablespoons dark soy sauce
salt and freshly ground black
    pepper
2 tablespoons sake* or dry
    sherry (optional)

* rice wine

This soup has the flavour we associate with the Far East and it makes an excellent start to a Chinese meal. It can also be served by itself as a light supper dish. You do need really tender steak.

Vegetarians could make the soup, see right-hand column, substituting other ingredients for the meat.

The choice of chicken stock may seem strange, but this does not spoil the delicate taste of the bean sprouts.

Cut the meat into small dice. Chop the onions and garlic. If using canned bean sprouts, drain and rinse them in cold water. Heat the stock or water and stock cube, add the steak, onions and garlic, together with the soy sauce and a little seasoning. Simmer for 10 minutes, then put in the bean sprouts. Bring to the boil and boil briskly for 2 to 3 minutes. Add the wine, if using this, heat for a few seconds and serve.

FOR VEGETARIANS:
If you are a fish eater, add 75 g/3 oz prawns at the last minute.

Tofu or Quorn could be used instead of the meat, or you could use fresh or frozen peas.

BEAN SPROUT AND CHEESE SOUP:
Use vegetable stock omit the steak and soy sauce. Add 100 g/4 oz grated cheese just before serving.

Sopa de Pescadores (Fishermen's Soup)   ▲ to ▲▲▲ ✿✿

SERVES 4

1 onion
1 to 2 garlic cloves
3 tomatoes
2 tablespoons olive oil
1.2 litres/2 pints fish stock, see
    page 74
bouquet garni, see right
1 teaspoon grated lemon rind
1 tablespoon lemon juice
50 g/2 oz rice*
pinch saffron powder or few
    strands
salt and freshly ground black
    pepper
550 g/1$\frac{1}{4}$ lb white fish,
    without skin and bone
shellfish (optional)
$\frac{1}{4}$ of a cucumber to garnish

This Spanish soup is typical of the delicious and very sustaining soups that are made in countries around the Mediterranean. It can be as economical or luxurious as you like. The shellfish can include mussels, prawns, crabmeat, even lobster flesh. If these are pre-cooked, they should be added to the soup towards the end of the cooking period, so they do not become over-cooked and tough.

Peel and neatly chop the onion. Crush the garlic. Skin and chop the tomatoes. Heat the oil and cook the onions, garlic and tomatoes gently for 5 minutes, pour in the stock with the bouquet garni, lemon rind and juice. Bring to the boil and add the rice, saffron and seasoning. Cook steadily for 30 minutes if you are using short grain rice; only 15 minutes for long grain rice.

Cut the white fish into neat dice, add to the liquid and lower the heat, so this simmers gently for approximately 10 minutes, or until the fish is tender but unbroken. Dice the cucumber. Add to the soup a few minutes before serving.

TO MAKE A CHANGE:
Omit the rice in the soup and use slightly more fish; buy a mixture of various kinds of white fish if possible. When the mixture is cooked, sieve or liquidize it to make a smooth consistency. This produces a simplified version of the delicious Italian soup – Ciuppino.

*use short grain rice to give a thicker texture to the liquid; this takes about 40 minutes to cook. Long grain only about 25 minutes in this dish.

Sopa de Pescadores

Saffron Fish Soup

Saffron Fish Soup ▲ ✪

SERVES 4 TO 6

350 g/12 oz white fish, such as plaice or whiting
2 medium old potatoes
1/4 small cucumber
750 ml/1 1/4 pints fish or chicken stock
salt and freshly ground black pepper
pinch saffron powder or saffron strands
1/2 teaspoon paprika
150/1/4 pint single cream or fromage frais

To garnish:
paprika

Skin and dice the fish; remove any bones. Peel and finely dice or grate the potatoes and cucumber. Put the fish and vegetables into a saucepan with the stock, a little seasoning, the saffron and paprika. Cover the pan and cook steadily for 15 minutes.

Sieve or liquidize the mixture, return to the pan and heat with the cream or fromage frais. Do not allow to boil. Top with a sprinkling of paprika.

A Fish Chowder makes a very satisfying meal. Chop 4 bacon rashers as in the Corn Chowder page 64. Fry until crisp then add the diced, not grated potatoes and diced cucumber. Continue as above.

VARYING THE FLAVOUR:
Omit the cucumber and add a small portion of diced fennel root plus 1 tablespoon chopped fennel leaves.

Use a mixture of white fish and shellfish.

Omit the saffron and flavour the soup with chopped fennel leaves.

Partan Bree ▲▲ ✪✪

SERVES 4 TO 6

1 medium cooked crab
75 g/3 oz long grain rice
600 ml/1 pint fish stock, see page 74 or water and 1/2 fish stock cube
600 ml/1 pint milk
1/4 teaspoon anchovy essence
salt and freshly ground black pepper
150 ml/1/4 pint single cream

To garnish:
fried or baked croûtons see page 118
chopped parsley

This soup is famous in Scotland and it has all the good flavour of really fresh crabmeat. You could use canned crab if a fresh one is not available. Buy a 227 g/8 oz can.

Remove all the flesh from the body and claws of the crab. Put 2 tablespoons of the white meat and 1 to 2 tablespoons of the dark meat on one side to float on top of the soup.

Put the rice, stock or water and stock cube and milk into a saucepan. Cook steadily for about 20 minutes or until the rice is tender. Add the anchovy essence, a little seasoning and most of the crabmeat. Heat, but do not cook for any length of time, as this makes the crabmeat rather tough.

Add the cream just before serving and heat gently. Spoon into soup cups and top with the reserved crabmeat, croûtons and parsley.

HADDOCK SOUP:
Poach about 350 g/12 oz smoked haddock in 600 ml/ 1 pint milk. Lift the fish from the milk, discard the skin and bones and flake the haddock.

Cook the rice in the stock as in Partan bree; add the milk left from poaching the haddock.

When the rice is tender, add the flaked haddock and cream but omit the anchovy essence. Season lightly and top with chopped hard-boiled egg, parsley and croûtons.

Spiced Lentil Soup   ▲ ✪✪

SERVES 4 TO 6
3 medium onions
3 medium tomatoes
50 g/2 oz butter or margarine
175 g/6 oz split lentils
1.2 litres/2 pints stock, see
   right
1/2 teaspoon turmeric
1/4 teaspoon ground cinnamon
1/4 teaspoon ground ginger
salt and freshly ground black
   pepper
For the topping:
little cream or yogurt
cashew nuts

Peel and chop the onions. Skin and chop the tomatoes. This soup can be served without sieving or liquidizing, in which case, chop the onions and tomatoes finely and neatly.

Heat the butter or margarine and cook the onions and tomatoes for 5 minutes. Add the lentils, stock and spices, together with a little seasoning. Simmer for 45 minutes, or until the lentils are tender. Sieve or liquidize for a smooth texture, then return to the pan and reheat.

Adjust the seasoning and serve topped with cream or yogurt and the nuts.

STOCK TO CHOOSE:
If you are serving this as a vegetarian dish, choose a vegetable stock.

For non-vegetarians, it is best made with the stock from cooking a piece of boiled bacon or even lamb. Failing this, use chicken stock or water and 1 stock cube.

Tarragon Carrot-Orange Soup   ▲ ✪✪✪

SERVES 4
1 medium onion
sprig of fresh tarragon or 1/2
   teaspoon dried tarragon
600 ml/1 pint vegetable stock
   or water and 1 vegetable
   stock cube
2 teaspoons grated orange
   rind
225 g/8 oz young carrots
   (weight after grating)
salt and freshly ground black
   pepper
300 ml/1/2 pint orange juice
To garnish:
few tarragon leaves
orange slices

Peel the onion but leave whole. Place in a saucepan with the tarragon, stock or water and stock cube and orange rind.

Bring to the boil. Cover the pan and simmer for 20 minutes to extract the flavour from these ingredients, then strain and return the liquid to the pan.

Peel and grate the carrots. Add to the liquid in the pan, together with a little seasoning. Cook for only a few minutes, so the carrots retain both flavour and texture. Sieve or liquidize, then allow to become cold. Add chilled orange juice, together with any extra seasoning required. Top with the tarragon and orange slices.

TO SERVE AS A HOT SOUP:
The soup can be served with a smooth texture, as the recipe on the left, or without sieving or liquidizing. In this case the carrots should be fairly finely grated.

The orange juice needs to be heated, but do not add it too soon or heat for any length of time in order to retain the maximum vitamin content.

Green Milk Soup   ▲ ✪✪

SERVES 4 TO 6
4 medium leeks, see method
2 small onions
2 small potatoes
450 ml/3/4 pint lamb or chicken
   or bacon stock*
50 g/2 oz butter or margarine
50 g/2 oz plain flour
600 ml/1 pint milk
salt and freshly ground black
   pepper
4 tablespoons single cream
   (optional)
To garnish:
chopped parsley

The tougher parts of the leeks are very good for giving additional flavour to this soup, so you can use virtually every part of the vegetables. You could then reduce the number of whole leeks to 2 or 3.

Cut the leeks into very thin strips. Peel and finely dice the onions and potatoes. If using the tougher green parts of the leeks, chop fairly finely; simmer in the stock, in a covered pan, for about 15 minutes to extract the flavour, strain the stock and return to the saucepan. Bring to the boil and add the prepared vegetables. Cook for about 15 minutes, or until tender.

Heat the butter or margarine in a second saucepan, stir in the flour and then the milk. Stir or whisk as the sauce comes to the boil and thickens. Gradually stir in the vegetable mixture and the cream, if using this. Reheat the soup, but do not cook for any length of time, for the vegetables should retain their texture. Garnish with the parsley.

GOLDEN MILK SOUP:
Omit the leeks and the potatoes in the recipe left. Instead, use 3 to 4 finely diced carrots and about 100 g/4 oz grated swede. Add 2 or 3 tablespoons cooked sweetcorn towards the end of the cooking time.

* the stock from boiled lamb, chicken or bacon is ideal for this soup

Minestrone Soup

Minestrone Soup   ▲ ✪✪

SERVES 4
2 medium onions
2 garlic cloves
2 bacon rashers
2 large tomatoes
2 medium carrots
2 tablespoons olive oil
600 ml/1 pint chicken stock or
    water and 1 chicken stock
    cube
salt and freshly ground black
    pepper
small portion cabbage
50 g/2 oz penne or macaroni
75 g/3 oz frozen petit pois
1 × 227 g/8 oz can haricot
    beans in tomato sauce
For the topping:
Parmesan cheese
chopped basil

Peel and finely chop the onions and garlic. Derind and dice the bacon rashers. Skin and chop the tomatoes and peel and finely grate the carrots.

Heat the oil and bacon rinds in a large pan. Add the onions, garlic and diced bacon and cook gently for 5 minutes. Remove the bacon rinds. Add the chicken stock or water and stock cube and bring to the boil. Add the tomatoes and carrots. Cover the pan, cook steadily for 15 minutes and add a little seasoning if desired. At the end of this time, check there is adequate liquid left to cook the cabbage and pasta. If it is insufficient add a little more stock or water and bring to boiling point.

Shred the cabbage finely and add to the boiling liquid, together with the pasta and petit pois. Cook for 15 minutes or until the pasta is tender. Add the canned beans and heat for a few minutes.

To serve, grate enough Parmesan cheese for a generous helping. Serve the portions of soup and top with the basil and cheese.

NOTE: Vegetarians should omit the bacon and use vegetable stock.

MEATY MINESTRONE:
Cook 225 g/8 oz minced beef with the onions. Add 4 instead of 2 tomatoes. Use vermicelli instead of short pasta. Bacon and basil can be omitted from the recipe left, as well as the beans, although these are a very traditional ingredient in Minestrone.

USING DRIED BEANS:
Soak 50 g/2 oz dried beans in water for 12 hours. Drain, then simmer in 900 ml/1½ pints stock for 1 hour. Cook onions etc., as recipe left, then add stock and beans. Proceed as recipe.

COLD SOUPS

A cold soup is wonderfully refreshing. Although it may seem more appropriate for hot weather, it can be very welcome in winter-time too. Make sure that the serving cups or plates are very well chilled before adding the really cold soup.

To decorate the containers: Dip the rim of the cups or bowls in lightly whisked egg white and then into very finely chopped parsley before chilling.

Prawn Vichysoisse

▲ ▲   ✿ to ✿✿✿

SERVES 4 TO 6
225 g/8 oz old potatoes
    (weight when peeled)
3 medium leeks
1 small onion
750 ml/1 ¼ pints fish stock, see
    page 74 or water and ½ fish
    or chicken stock cube
salt and freshly ground black
    pepper
175 g/6 oz peeled prawns
150 ml/¼ pint single cream
4 tablespoons white wine
2 teaspoons lemon juice
To garnish:
chopped chives
chopped parsley
few prawns

This is a very delicious version of the classic Vichysoisse soup, see recipe right. Traditionally, this soup is served cold, but both versions make a very good hot soup, with certain changes in the way the ingredients are added.

Peel and dice the potatoes. Slice the white part of the leeks thinly, (the green part of the leeks can be used in the Green milk soup on page 66). Peel and finely chop the onion. Although the soup is liquidized or sieved, it is important that the vegetables are cut into small pieces, so they cook in the shortest possible time to retain the maximum flavour.

Bring the stock or water and stock cube to the boil, add the vegetables and cook steadily for about 15 minutes, or until just tender. Season lightly.

If serving cold, allow the vegetable mixture to become cold, then liquidize or sieve with the prawns, cream, wine and lemon juice. Add extra seasoning if desired.

Serve in chilled soup cups, topped with the garnish.

If serving hot, add the prawns to the hot cooked vegetable mixture, then sieve or liquidize. Return to the pan and heat. Whisk the cream, wine and lemon juice into the hot, but not boiling soup and heat gently. Season to taste and garnish as above.

TO MAKE A CHANGE:
Use crabmeat or cooked white or smoked fish instead of prawns.

VICHYSOISSE:
Increase the quantity of leeks to 6 to 8; the onion and the prawns can be omitted.

Use double instead of single cream and a little more wine.

CHILLED GREEN PEA SOUP:
Omit the potatoes and leeks in the Vichysoisse and use 350 g/12 oz shelled peas.

Cook as the recipe left. The prawns can be added or omitted.

Guacamole Soup

▲ ▲   ✿

SERVES 4
2 or 3 spring onions
½ red pepper
½ green pepper
1 or 2 garlic cloves
2 ripe avocados
2 tablespoons lemon juice
600 ml/1 pint tomato juice
salt and freshly ground black
    pepper
few drops Tabasco sauce
To garnish:
2 tablespoons thinly sliced
    spring onions
2 tablespoons finely diced
    green pepper

As this soup can be put into a liquidizer to blend, the ingredients can be roughly chopped. If you do not want a very smooth soup, then finely and neatly, chop the onions, peppers and peeled garlic. Halve the avocados, scoop out the pulp and dice this finely. Mix or liquidize all these ingredients with the lemon juice, tomato juice, seasoning and the Tabasco.

Garnish with the onions and green pepper and serve cold with toast or cheese biscuits.

GUACAMOLE DIP:
Peel and finely chop 1 garlic clove and enough onion to give 2 teaspoons. Skin and chop 2 large tomatoes, blend with the onion, garlic, 1 tablespoon lemon juice and the pulp from 2 large avocados. Add a few drops Tabasco sauce and a little seasoning.

Delicious with raw vegetables.

Apple and Orange Soup

▲ ✿✿✿

SERVES 4

450 g/1 lb cooking or dessert*
    apples
2 large oranges
600 ml/1 pint water
1 tablespoon lemon juice
sugar to taste

* use a type of apple that
    cooks well; dessert apples
    save adding too much sugar

Many Continental countries make delicious fruit soups; they
are refreshing and make a good start to the meal.

Peel and slice the apples. Grate just the top zest from the
oranges and squeeze out the juice or remove the pulp if you
prefer pieces of orange in the soup.

Put the apples, water and lemon juice into a saucepan and
simmer until the fruit is soft. This can be done in a covered
bowl in the microwave cooker – the fruit retains more of its
flavour and needs a little less sugar.

Liquidize or sieve until smooth. Add the sugar while the
soup is hot, so it dissolves. Add the orange juice or chopped
pulp and chill well.

TO GIVE A MORE SAVOURY
FLAVOUR:
Use half chicken stock.

BLOMME SUPPE (PLUM
SOUP):
This Danish soup can be
served hot or cold.

Stone 450 g/1 lb ripe plums
and cook in 1.2 litres/2 pints
water with a little ground
cinnamon and sugar to taste.

Sieve or liquidize and blend
with a little white wine. Heat
or chill. Top with cream.

Lemon Avocado Soup

▲ ▲ ✿

SERVES 4

2 medium avocados
1 to 2 teaspoons finely grated
    lemon zest
2 to 3 tablespoons lemon juice
450 ml/³/₄ pint vegetable or
    chicken stock
150 ¹/₄ pint single cream or
    yogurt or fromage frais
salt and ground black pepper

Halve the avocados, remove the stones and the peel. Either
mash them with the lemon zest and juice or liquidize with all
the ingredients. The amount of lemon juice is a matter of
personal taste.

If mashing the fruit, gradually add the stock and cream, or
yogurt or fromage frais, beating briskly to give a smooth
texture.

This soup looks most colourful if garnished with finely
chopped spring onions and/or finely diced raw tomatoes. Add
the garnish at the last minute.

TO ADD MORE FLAVOUR:
Put in a few drops of Tabasco
sauce and/or a shake of
cayenne pepper.

Use half stock and half
tomato juice.

Do not prepare the
avocados until you have the
rest of the ingredients
available.

Lemon Avocado Soup

Soups for slimmers

There is a belief that all soups are fattening and that you cannot enjoy them if you are on a diet or trying to lose a little weight. That is not true; it depends upon the ingredients used. There are many low-calorie foods that make good soups, and ordinary recipes can be adapted by using low-fat yogurt or fromage frais in place of cream. Omit the fat in the recipes where possible.

Cucumber Soup   ▲   ✪

Serves 4
½ large cucumber
1 tablespoon lemon juice
1 small bunch spring onions
sprig of mint
300 ml/½ pint vegetable or
   chicken stock
450 ml/¾ pint fromage frais
salt and freshly ground black
   pepper
To garnish:
chopped chives
chopped mint

Peel and dice most of the cucumber, but save one or two portions with the peel on to give both colour and more flavour to the soup. Too much peel creates a rather bitter taste.

Liquidize all the ingredients to give a smooth soup. Serve cold topped with chives and mint.

This mixture is very refreshing if it is lightly frosted as described under Frosted Consommé, below. Allow only a short time in the freezer.

To serve hot:
Liquidize the cucumber, onions, stock and mint. Then heat. Add the fromage frais, lemon juice and seasoning to the hot, but not boiling mixture. Heat again; do not boil.

Courgette soup:
225 g/8 oz uncooked or lightly cooked courgettes can be used in place of the cucumber. Make either the cold or hot version of cucumber soup.

Speedy Gazpacho   ▲   ✪

Serves 4
1 garlic clove
900 ml/1½ pints tomato juice
8 tablespoons finely diced
   green pepper
8 tablespoons finely diced
   cucumber
8 tablespoons finely chopped
   spring onions
salt and freshly ground black
   pepper
2 tablespoons white wine,
   optional
lemon juice to taste

Peel and crush the garlic and mix with the tomato juice. Put half the diced green pepper, cucumber and spring onions into small dishes so everyone can add these to the soup, as desired. Blend all the other ingredients with the tomato juice. Serve cold.

If you would like a more piquant flavour add either a little lemon juice or wine vinegar to the tomato juice or the fresh tomato purée, mentioned on the right.

To give a thicker soup:
Either make a fresh tomato purée and dilute this with a little water, or add 2 to 3 tablespoons soft breadcrumbs to the ingredients.

To give a rich flavour:
There is no olive oil in the recipe on the left. This makes it low in calories; add a little, if desired.

Frosted Consommé   ▲   ✪✪

Serves 4
2 × 427 g/15 oz cans of beef
   consommé
2 tablespoons dry sherry
To garnish:
curd or cream cheese or thick
   yogurt
chopped parsley
lemon slices

This makes a delicious start to the meal. Tip the consommé into a basin and add the sherry. If the consommé is very thick, you may need to warm it to incorporate the sherry.

Pour into freezing trays and leave until lightly frosted. Whisk with a fork until frothy looking and spoon into chilled soup cups. Top with the cheese or yogurt and the parsley. Place lemon slices on one side of the soup cups.

Home made beef or chicken stock can be used in place of the canned consommé.

Jellied consommé:
Allow 1 teaspoon gelatine to each 600 ml/1 pint canned consommé.

Soften the gelatine in a little cold consommé, then dissolve and add to the rest of the consommé. Add either a little lemon juice or sherry to flavour. Set lightly then whisk or cut into neat squares and spoon into chilled soup cups.

Garnish as the recipe left.

Mushroom Soup   ▲ ✿

SERVES 4
175 g/6 oz mushrooms
1 garlic clove, optional
2 medium onions
900 ml/1 1/2 pints beef or
    chicken or vegetable stock
1/4 to 1/2 teaspoon yeast
    extract
salt and freshly ground black
    pepper
To garnish:
yogurt or fromage frais
chopped parsley

If you do not want to sieve or liquidize the soup, then dice all the ingredients neatly.

Wipe and chop the mushrooms. Peel and finely chop the garlic and onions. Pour the stock into a pan, add the mushrooms, garlic, onions, yeast extract and seasoning. Cook for 15 minutes, then sieve or liquidize and reheat. Top each portion with yogurt or fromage frais and parsley.

It increases the calories in this soup but does add a good flavour if the mushrooms, garlic and onion are tossed in 25 g/1 oz beef dripping or butter.

CREAMY MUSHROOM SOUP:
Cook the vegetables for 5 minutes in 25 g/1 oz butter or margarine. Add the liquid, yeast extract and seasoning. Cook as before.

Blend 15g/1/2 oz cornflour with 300 ml/1/2 pint milk. Add to the ingredients in the pan. Stir until thickened. Liquidize or sieve for a smooth soup and reheat. Garnish as the recipe on the left.

Brown Fish Soup   ▲ ✿

SERVES 4 TO 6
1 bacon rasher
1 medium onion
1 medium leek
2 teaspoons sunflower oil
1 litre/1 3/4 pints fish stock, see
    page 74
1 to 2 tablespoons tomato
    purée
salt and freshly ground black
    pepper
pinch saffron powder or
    strands
2 teaspoons chopped fennel
225 to 350 g/8 to 12 oz raw
    or cooked white fish
1 to 2 tablespoons dry sherry,
    optional
1 tablespoon chopped parsley

Remove the rind from the bacon and dice the rasher. Peel and finely dice the onion and dice the leek. Heat the bacon rind and the oil and gently cook the onion and leek for 2 or 3 minutes. Add the bacon pieces and continue cooking for 3 minutes. Add the stock, tomato purée, a little seasoning, the saffron and the fennel and bring just to boiling point.

If using raw fish, skin and dice this neatly, add to the other ingredients and cook for 15 minutes.

If using cooked fish, skin and flake this, add to the other ingredients and cook for 5 to 10 minutes.

Add the sherry and parsley. Heat for 1 minute, then serve.

To reduce the calorific value of the soup omit the bacon and the sherry. Use 1 tablespoon lemon juice in place of the sherry.

FISH TO USE:
Inexpensive white fish or smoked fish are equally good in this soup.

Canned salmon or tuna give it a good flavour; drain the oil from the can and use this instead of the sunflower oil.

FENNEL FISH SOUP:
Omit the bacon and use 2 to 3 tablespoons finely diced fennel head, together with 2 teaspoons of the chopped leaves.

Brown Fish Soup

FISH DISHES

We are fortunate in having a very wide selection of fish in this country. On the whole, though, many people tend to be conservative about the varieties they buy. From time to time, do try a fish you may not have sampled before, as each kind has a different flavour and texture.

Fish is a very adaptable food and can be cooked in many different ways. The recipes in this section provide a range of ideas, from the very simple to the more elaborate. Fish is not only delicious, but highly nutritious, too. Medical opinion stresses that we should include as much fish as possible in our meals.

Information about buying and preparing fish is given on pages 22 to 23. It is important that fish is not over-cooked, even by conventional methods, for this makes it needlessly dry.

Microwave cooking of fish: The flavour of fish cooked by this method is excellent, but special care must be taken to time the cooking process correctly, for over-cooking in a microwave makes the fish tough and hard.

When cooking fillets of fish, where one end is appreciably thinner than the other, protect the thin end for part of the cooking time by covering it with a small piece of foil – make sure this does not touch the sides of the cooker. You may prefer to tuck the thin end under, instead, to give an even thickness to the fillets.

Food continues to cook during the standing time. This is an essential part of microwave cooking.

Freezing fish: Unless you are sure that the raw fish is 100 per cent fresh, it is better not to freeze it. Cooked dishes containing fish can be frozen, but great care should be taken when reheating to make sure the fish is not over-cooked.

TO BAKE FISH

The recipes that follow are based upon baking fish in the oven. This is an excellent method of cooking, for many ingredients can be added to make the fish more interesting. These should be of the kind that cook fairly quickly, so there is no possibility of the fish over-cooking. Baking times vary, according to the other ingredients added. The temperature and timing for a simple form of baked fish follows.

To prepare fish for baking: Wash, dry and season the fish lightly. Sprinkle with a little lemon juice or tomato juice, or top with melted butter or margarine or a few drops of oil. You can add chopped herbs to the melted fat; dill, fennel leaves, chives, parsley, a very little tarragon or rosemary all blend well with fish. The baking dish should be greased, so the fish does not stick to it. If you want the fish to brown slightly during cooking, do not cover; if you want to keep it more moist but with less browning, cover the dish with foil or a lid.

The microwave can be used for this method of cooking. Check the timing in your manufacturer's instruction book.

Timing: Preheat the oven to 190°C/375°F, Gas Mark 5; do not use lower temperatures except for specific dishes. When cooking very thin fillets of fish, you can use a slightly hotter temperature, i.e. 200°C/400°F, Gas Mark 6. Allow 10 to 15 minutes for thin fillets, 20 to 25 minutes for thicker fillets and up to 30 minutes for very thick cutlets. When baking whole fish, allow approximately 12 minutes per 450 g/1 lb. If the dish is covered, allow a few extra minutes. If the fish is completely wrapped in foil, as in the recipe right, it will need at least 5 minutes extra cooking time.

Barbecued Fish in Foil

Foil-Baked Fish

▲ to ▲   ✿ to ✿✿

SERVES 4

4 portions of fish,
    see method for flavouring
very little oil or butter or
    margarine
4 squares of foil
salt and freshly ground black
    pepper
To garnish:
see method

Prepare the fish for cooking, i.e. skin or bone it if desired. The flavourings used in the foil can be very diverse – sliced tomatoes, mushrooms, very finely chopped spring onions (these are not as strong as ordinary onions), sliced cucumber or courgettes, chopped herbs etc. Whatever you choose must be suitable for cooking in the same length of time as the fish, see Timing under Baked fish (left).

1 or 2 tablespoons liquid, such as milk, single cream, white wine, cider, apple juice or lemon juice, can be used. If using seasoning, add it sparingly.

Place the pieces of foil on a flat baking sheet or tin. Rub a few drops of oil or melted butter or margarine over all parts of the foil that will come in contact with the fish. This method of cooking is ideal if you want to cut down on fat. If the flavourings are juicy or you are adding liquid, even this small amount of fat can be omitted.

Put a little of the flavouring on the foil first, or save it to place beside or on top of the fish. Lay the fish in the centre of the foil, add the flavourings and any liquid required. Wrap the foil around the fish and other ingredients. Bake as the timings given on page 72.

Open the foil carefully, as the contents are very hot and steam rises as the parcels are unwrapped. Serve garnished with the flavourings or with lemon or lime slices.

BARBECUED FISH IN FOIL:
Flavour the fish with chopped garlic, olive oil, and a little soy sauce. Then wrap in foil and cook in the oven or over a barbecue.

Thinly sliced courgettes, flavoured with crushed garlic and chopped fennel can be wrapped with the fish; season lightly.

The attractive markings on top of each portion of fish were made after cooking by pressing them with a heavy heated skewer.

Choose a fish with plenty of flavour, such as cod or hake, to cook with these particular flavourings.

Sole Véronique

Sole Véronique   ▲ ▲ ✪ ✪

SERVES 4

4 medium sole

For the fish stock:

450 ml/³/₄ pint water

1 small shallot or onion,
   optional

salt and freshly ground white
   pepper

sprig parsley

To cook the fish:

150 ml/¹/₄ pint white wine

100 g/4 oz black or white
   grapes

To make the sauce:

25 g/1 oz butter

20 g/³/₄ oz flour

150 ml/¹/₄ pint double cream

To garnish:

few extra grapes, optional

fennel or dill leaves

If the fishmonger has skinned and filleted the fish, ask for the heads and skins to make the fish stock. If this has not been done, follow the directions on page 82 for removing skin etc.

To make the stock, put fish heads, skins and water into a saucepan. Peel the shallot or onion, but leave it whole, and add to the pan with a little seasoning and the parsley. Cover the pan and simmer steadily for 20 minutes. Strain the liquid; you need 225 ml/7¹/₂ fl oz. Add this to the white wine.

To cook the fish, skin and deseed the grapes. Put one or two on each fillet of sole before rolling these tightly. Secure the rolls with fine wooden cocktail sticks. Put them into an oblong casserole and cover with the liquid; add any remaining skinned grapes. Cover and cook in a preheated oven set to 200°C/400°F, Gas Mark 6 for 25 minutes, or until tender.

Lift the fish rolls and grapes from the liquid; remove the cocktail sticks from the rolls. Place the fish on a heated dish, cover with foil so it does not dry and keep hot. Keep the liquid from the casserole.

To make the sauce, heat the butter in a pan, stir in the flour, then blend in 225 ml/7¹/₂ fl oz of the strained liquid from cooking the fish. Stir as the sauce thickens, then gradually blend in the cream and any extra seasoning required. Heat gently, without boiling, then add the skinned grapes. Spoon the sauce, with the grapes, on to heated plates. Arrange the fish rolls on top. Garnish with a few extra grapes, if desired – these should be deseeded but not skinned – and the fennel or dill leaves.

Serve with crisp mangetout peas and new potatoes.

TO COOK MORE QUICKLY:
Poach the fish in the liquid in a covered pan on top of the cooker for 10 to 15 minutes, or do this in the microwave cooker.

SOLE BERCY:
Prepare the sole fillets, but do not roll them. Put into the dish with the fish stock and wine, as for Sole Véronique. Add 2 small, finely chopped shallots or onions, 2 teaspoons chopped parsley and the wine and seasoning.

Cook as recipe left or variation above. Make the sauce with the unstrained fish liquid but no cream. Add a little extra chopped parsley.

Savoury Haddock

▲ ✿✿

SERVES 4
4 portions of fresh haddock
    fillet
1 tablespoon lemon juice
salt and freshly ground black
    pepper
For the stuffing:
100 g/4 oz mushrooms
2 medium carrots
2 tablespoons chopped parsley
1 teaspoon grated lemon rind
1 tablespoon lemon juice
25 g/1 oz soft breadcrumbs
1 tablespoon sunflower oil

Place the haddock portions in a greased dish. Moisten with the lemon juice and season very lightly. Preheat the oven to 190°C/375°F, Gas Mark 5. Wipe and thinly slice the mushrooms. You can use the stalks; chop them very finely. Peel and finely grate the carrots. Mix the mushrooms and carrots with the rest of the stuffing mixture. Season to taste. Spoon on top of each of the pieces of haddock. Cover the dish with a lid or greased foil and bake for 35 to 40 minutes.

USE OTHER WHITE FISH:
This stuffing blends well with cod or fillets of plaice, which should be skinned and rolled around the stuffing.

For a more piquant flavour, finely chop an onion and cook in the oil, then mix with the other ingredients.

Mariniette Herrings

▲ ✿✿

SERVES 4 TO 8
4 herrings with soft roes
150 ml/¹/₄ pint white wine
    vinegar
2 tablespoons water
1 tablespoon brown sugar
1 lemon, sliced thinly
2 fresh bay leaves or 1 dried
    bay leaf
¹/₂ to 1 teaspoon ground
    mixed spice or cinnamon
salt and cayenne pepper
4 tablespoons soured cream
To garnish:
lettuce
lemon slices

Bone and fillet the herrings if the fishmonger has not done this, see page 23. Put the roes on one side. Pour the vinegar and water into a pan, add the sugar and bring to boiling point. Add the lemon, bay leaves or leaf, spice and seasoning to the vinegar and heat for 4 to 5 minutes.

Put the soft roes into a basin and mash with the soured cream and seasoning. Spread a little on each of the 8 herring fillets and roll firmly from the heads to the tails, secure with wooden cocktail sticks. Put into a container.

Pour the very hot vinegar mixture over the fish, cover and allow to become quite cold. Place in the refrigerator for 24 hours. Turn the fish rolls over once or twice during this time.

Garnish with lettuce and lemon slices.

If you would rather have the fish as a cooked dish, put the herrings into an ovenproof dish and pour the hot vinegar over the fish, as above. Cover and place into a preheated oven set to 180°C/350°F, Gas Mark 4 and cook for 30 minutes.

Serve hot or cold, as an hors d'oeuvre or main dish.

TO COOK HERRING ROES:
Soft roes make an excellent savoury dish. Wash and dry them and either cook in a saucepan with a small knob of butter or margarine and a little milk and seasoning for 5 to 10 minutes, or in a covered dish in the microwave cooker, or between 2 plates over a pan of boiling water. The roes are cooked when they become opaque. Serve on hot toast.

Hard roes should be coated very lightly with seasoned flour and fried in a little hot oil or fat for 5 minutes.

Mackerel in Green Sauce

▲ ✿✿

SERVES 4
4 mackerel
100 g/4 oz button mushrooms
3 teaspoons French mustard
300 ml/¹/₂ pint white wine or
    water with 1 tablespoon
    lemon juice
2 tablespoons finely chopped
    chives
3 tablespoons finely chopped
    parsley
1 teaspoon fennel leaves,
    unchopped
2 tablespoons thinly sliced
    spring onions, include a little
    of the tender green stems
salt and freshly ground black
    pepper

Ask the fishmonger to bone the fish or follow the instructions on page 23. Wipe and thinly slice the mushrooms. Spread the cut side of the fish with half the mustard and top with the mushrooms. Fold the fish to enclose the mushrooms and secure with wooden cocktail sticks. Place in a shallow casserole.

Blend the rest of the mustard with the wine or water and lemon juice, the herbs, onions and seasoning. Pour over the fish and cover the dish. Bake in a preheated oven, set to 190°C/375°F, Gas Mark 5 for 25 minutes.

When cooked, lift the fish from the liquid on to a heated dish; strain the liquid, top the mackerel with some of the herbs and a spoonful of the cooking liquid.

MARINATING THE FISH:
To emphasize the flavour of the herbs and wine, place the fish in the liquid for an hour before cooking.

TO SERVE COLD:
Allow the fish to cool in the liquid. Strain it. Blend the herbs into the mayonnaise, made as page 157, and serve with the fish.

FOR A HOTTER FLAVOUR:
Use made English mustard instead of the French kind.

TO FRY FISH

This is the most popular of all methods of cooking fish. While nutritionists decry the use of fat, it must be said that the fish retains all its flavour, which is kept in by the coating. There is a way of cooking fish in the oven that gives much the same appearance and taste to the fish as shallow-frying. This is described right.

To prepare fish for shallow-frying: Coat the fish in a very little seasoned flour, then with beaten egg and fine crisp breadcrumbs.

To shallow-fry: Use a polyunsaturated oil, such as corn, sunflower or safflower. Heat 2 or 3 tablespoons in a large pan, then add the fish.

Timing: Thin fillets take 2 to 3 minutes on either side; thicker portions 3 to 5 minutes on either side. Turn the heat down slightly when the outside is golden in colour. If frying ready-coated frozen fish, follow the directions for cooking on the packet.

To prepare fish for deep-frying: Although a large quantity of oil is used in deep-frying, less is absorbed by the food than in shallow-frying. Coat the fish as above, or in seasoned flour then a thin coating of the following batter. Blend 100 g/4 oz plain flour, a pinch of salt, 1 egg and 225 ml/7½ fl oz milk and water. This coats up to 6 portions.

To deep-fry: Heat the oil to 180°C/355°F or when a cube of day-old bread turns golden in ¾ to 1 minute. You can heat the oil to a slightly higher temperature – 185°C/365°F for thinner portions. It is important to have these high temperatures to crisp the outside. Heat the frying-basket in the hot oil before adding the fish; this makes sure it does not stick to the wire mesh.

Timing: Allow about 3 minutes for thin portions of fish, 4 to 5 minutes for thicker portions and 5 to 6 minutes for really thick steaks. Lower the heat if the fish is getting too brown towards the end of the cooking time or if the oil has become slightly too hot, simply lift out the frying basket containing the fish, allow the oil to cool down slightly, replace the basket and the fish and continue frying.

Always drain fish on absorbent paper after shallow or deep-frying.

To prepare ahead: If frying for a large number complete the cooking in the oven. Fry the fish until just brown; place on hot dishes in a preheated oven, set to 190°C/375°F, Gas Mark 5 and cook for 10 to 15 minutes. Drain and serve.

Oven 'frying': This may sound a strange method of frying, but it is one that is highly successful for cutting down fat. It is a wise solution if your family prefers fried fish to that cooked by any other method. See left for method.

Oven 'fried' potatoes: Although there are commercially prepared potatoes for oven-cooking, you will find this method of cooking fresh potatoes excellent. Peel potatoes and cut into slices – these are better than the more solid chips. Dry well. Prepare and heat flat baking tins, as described under the method of cooking fish. Carefully place the potatoes onto the hot tins and brush them with a few drops of oil. Cook in the preheated oven set to 200°C/400°F, Gas Mark 6 for 12 to 15 minutes.

COOKING FISH MEUNIÈRE

This is a method of frying in which the fish is NOT coated. It is fried in butter; you could use a mixture of ⅔ butter and ⅓ oil, but the buttery taste must predominate. The recipe on page 77 is typical of this method of cooking. It is used with fillets of sole, plaice and whiting and portions of skate, as well as shellfish like scallops. For an adaptation of this method, see below.

Skate in black butter: Use portions of skate instead of scallops. Cook until tender, remove from the pan, check there is enough butter. Allow this to become dark golden-brown but not black. Add a few capers and a generous amount of lemon juice, parsley and black pepper. Pour the hot butter over the fish.

TO OVEN 'FRY':
Coat the fish with beaten egg and breadcrumbs or omit the egg coating and brush the fish with a few drops of oil and then coat in crisp breadcrumbs. This helps to keep the flesh of the fish moist during cooking; the outside crisps and browns, just as it does when fried.

Brush a flat baking sheet or tin with a very little oil and place in the oven; this should be preheated to 220°C/425°F, Gas Mark 7 for cooking thin fillets or to 200°C/400°F, Gas Mark 6 for thicker pieces of fish.

Place the fish on the very hot oiled sheet or tin. Bake thin fillets for 12 to 15 minutes. Bake thicker portions for about 20 minutes at the slightly lower heat.

There is no need to turn the fish over during cooking. Serve as you would ordinary fried fish, garnished with lemon and parsley.

Herrings in Oatmeal;
Scallops Meunière

Scallops Meunière   ▲ ▲ ✪

SERVES 4
8 to 12 scallops
75 to 100 g/3 to 4 oz butter
1 to 2 teaspoons lemon juice
1 to 2 tablespoons chopped
   parsley
shake white pepper
To garnish:
creamed potatoes or croûtons
lemon slices
parsley

Remove the scallops from their shells; retain any liquid that
may be on the shells to add to the butter when you are cooking
the fish. If the fishmonger has cut the scallops from the shells,
wash in cold water and dry on absorbent paper before cooking.

Heat the butter in a pan, add the scallops and cook for 4 to
5 minutes, or until they turn opaque. Do not over-cook the
scallops, for, like all shellfish, they become tough. Lift from
the butter, then heat this with the lemon juice, parsley, and
pepper. Spoon over the fish.

If garnishing with creamed potatoes spoon or pipe them in
a neat ring on the serving dish. Heat and brown in the oven,
or under the grill, then spoon the fish into the centre.
Croûtons should be placed beside the fish just before serving.

Top with the lemon slices and parsley.

TO USE QUEENIES:
This is the name given to very
small scallops. You will need
to buy about 450 g/1 lb to take
the place of the larger
scallops.

SCALLOPS IN BROWN BUTTER:
Follow the recipe left, but
allow the butter to turn a dark
brown before adding the
lemon juice and parsley.

Herrings in Oatmeal   ▲ ✪

SERVES 4
4 herrings
1 tablespoon flour
salt and freshly ground black
   pepper
For coating:
1 egg
50 g/2 oz fine or medium
   oatmeal or rolled oats
For frying:
50 g/2 oz fat or 2 tablespoons
   oil
To garnish:
parsley sprigs
lime wedges

Split and bone the herrings and remove the heads. Each fish
can be divided into 2 fillets, see page 23. Mix the flour with a
little seasoning. Dust the fish with this, then coat in beaten egg
and the oatmeal or rolled oats.

Heat the fat or oil and fry the herrings until crisp and brown
on both sides. Drain on absorbent paper. Serve garnished
with parsley and lime.

A more interesting coating is made by adding 2 tablespoons
finely chopped mixed fresh herbs to the oatmeal coating.
Chopped parsley, dill and fennel leaves are a good choice with
a very little finely grated lemon rind.

RED HERRINGS:
Split and bone 4 herrings;
save the roes.

Place the flat herrings plus
the roes in a casserole.

Heat 300 ml/½ pint beer
with a little seasoning. Pour
over the fish, leave for 1 hour.
Remove the fish from the
liquid, drain, then brush with
melted butter and grill until
tender.

Chinese-Style Fried Fish

▲ to ▲▲ ✪

SERVES 4

675 g/1½ lb monkfish or cod or other white fish

For the coating:

3 teaspoons cornflour

3 teaspoons grated root ginger

good pinch salt

For the batter:

50 g/2 oz self-raising flour, or plain flour sifted with ½ teaspoon baking powder

150 ml/¼ pint milk and water

1 egg white

For frying:

oil

Cut the fish into neat 2·5 to 4 cm/1 to 1½ inch dice. If using defrosted fish, drain away all surplus liquid. Dry the fish well on absorbent paper.

Mix the cornflour, ginger and salt and toss the fish in this mixture. Blend the flour or flour and baking powder with the milk and water. Whisk the egg white until it stands up in soft peaks. Fold into the batter.

Heat the oil to 180°C/355°F, or when a cube of day-old bread takes slightly over ¾ minute but under 1 minute to turn golden brown.

Fry the fish until crisp and golden brown; drain on absorbent paper. Top with sesame seeds and garnish with spring onions, these can be made into flower shapes, see right, or thinly sliced.

TO MAKE SPRING ONION FLOWERS:

Trim part of the green tops from the onion but leave some of the green stems.

Carefully make cuts down the stems, right to the white part.

Put into ice cold water for some time so they open out.

Stir-Fried Squid (Calamares)

▲▲ ✪

SERVES 4

450 to 550 g/1 to 1¼ lb squid

1 red pepper

1 green pepper

small bunch spring onions

3 celery sticks, sliced

2 tablespoons sunflower oil

1 teaspoon sesame oil

salt and freshly ground black pepper

little lemon juice

To garnish:

parsley

lemon wedges

Squid is almost better known by the Italian name of calamares; it is now much more readily available in fishmongers. You may find that it is sold ready-prepared and cut into rings, but if this is not done, then prepare as follows.

First wash the squid. Pull back the top of the body pouch and remove the pen. This is shaped like a quill and it should be pulled carefully away from the flesh. Discard the pen, together with the head and ink sac, which is not needed in this recipe. Wash and skin the body and the tentacles. Discard the mouth of the squid at the base of the tentacles.

Finely chop the tentacles and cut the body of the fish into rings. Deseed the peppers and cut into narrow strips. Cut the spring onions into small lengths.

Heat the oils in a wok or frying-pan, add the peppers, spring onions and celery and stir-fry for 2 or 3 minutes. Add the squid and continue stir-frying for 3 to 4 minutes. Do not cook any longer, as this will toughen the fish. Add a little seasoning and lemon juice. Serve garnished with the parsley and lemon.

FRIED SQUID:

Coat the rings of fish with batter, as described above, then deep-fry for 2 to 3 minutes.

TYPES OF PARSLEY:

The parsley shown in the picture is the flat-leaved type. The more usual herb is curly parsley. Flat-leaved parsley has a very good flavour.

Stir-Fried Squid

Seafood Kebabs

TO GRILL FISH

Grilling is an ideal way of cooking fish because you have rapid and even heating. Always preheat the grill very well before the fish is placed under it. Before putting the fish on to the grid of the grill pan, brush it with a little oil or other fat or place a sheet of foil over it. This makes washing-up much easier and as all juices or basting mixtures are on the foil, it is easy to tip them on to the serving dish or plates, so no flavour is lost.

Keep fish well basted with butter, margarine or oil during cooking.

To cut down on fat: To avoid using too much fat in cooking, baste the fish with skimmed milk or with lemon or orange juice.

Timing: Thin fillets of fish take about 4 to 5 minutes and there is no need to turn them. Thicker fish fillets or steaks need 8 to 10 minutes and should be turned over halfway through the cooking period. Whole, larger fish will take about 15 minutes; it may be better to cook these in the oven, as they need turning over several times to make sure they are evenly cooked.

Grilled Shark Steaks   ▲▲ ✪✪✪

SERVES 4

4 shark steaks, each about 175 g/6 oz in weight

For the marinade:

6 tablespoons white wine

2 tablespoons olive oil

4 tablespoons chopped onion or spring onions

few drops Tabasco sauce, optional

1 teaspoon light soy sauce, optional

salt and freshly ground black pepper

To cook the fish:

1 tablespoon oil

To garnish:

lemon wedges

Although not obtainable in all shops, shark has become a much more readily-available fish. It has a firm texture, is very satisfying and has a good flavour. Marinating is not essential, but it adds more taste to the fish and gives a moister texture, for shark is inclined to be dry if not kept well basted during cooking or marinated in a mixture containing enough oil. It is an excellent choice of fish to cook over a barbecue fire, see page 166.

Place the fish in a dish, add the marinade ingredients, turn the fish around so it absorbs the mixture and leave for at least 30 minutes, preferably longer.

Lift the steaks from the marinade, drain and brush with a little oil. Keep the marinade, see below. Place on foil under a preheated grill and cook for 5 to 6 minutes. Turn over, brush again with oil and continue cooking for the same time on the second side, or until quite tender. Garnish with the lemon.

Any marinade left could be heated and spooned over the fish just before serving.

BAKED SHARK:

Skin and chop 450 g/1 lb tomatoes. Peel and chop 2 garlic cloves. Heat 2 tablespoons oil in a pan, add the tomatoes, garlic, 3 tablespoons water, 4 tablespoons white wine, a squeeze of lemon juice and 1 tablespoon chopped parsley and cook until a purée. Season well. Place half the mixture in a dish. Add 4 shark steaks, top with the tomato mixture. Cover the dish and bake for 40 minutes in a preheated oven, set to 190°C/375°F, Gas Mark 5.

Seafood Kebabs   ▲▲ ✪✪

SERVES 4

450 g/1 lb firm white fish, see method

12 large prawns in their shells

For the marinade:

2 tablespoons light or dark soy sauce

2 tablespoons sunflower oil

2 tablespoons orange juice

1 tablespoon lemon juice

salt and freshly ground black pepper

To garnish:

mango and melon slices

shredded endive or lettuce

Mix all the ingredients for the marinade together. Cut the fish into neat cubes. Monkfish is shown in the picture and this is ideal for kebabs, but hake, halibut, salmon or turbot or sliced scallops could be used. Place the diced fish and prawns into the marinade and leave for 30 minutes.

Lift the fish from the marinade, drain well and arrange on long barbecue skewers. Keep the marinade for basting the fish. Cook for 10 minutes over a barbecue or under a preheated grill. Turn the skewers several times and brush the fish with the marinating mixture. Garnish with the fruit slices and arrange on a bed of endive or lettuce.

COOKING KEBABS:

It is important that all the food placed on the skewers will cook within the same time. Always turn the skewers during cooking, to ensure even cooking.

Handle the skewers carefully, as they become very hot.

NOTE: Never eat the hot food directly from the skewers; you could burn your mouth badly. Pull the food off the skewers with a fork.

Orange-Flavoured Red Mullet

Grilled Sardines   ▲ ✪

SERVES 4
12 to 16 fresh sardines
1 to 2 garlic cloves
1 tablespoon sunflower oil
2 tablespoons chopped parsley
2 teaspoons lemon juice
salt and freshly ground black
   pepper
For garnish:
lemon wedges

The heads can be removed or left on the fish, but each
sardine should be split along the belly and the intestines
removed. Peel the garlic and crush this finely as explained on
the right. Blend the garlic with the oil, half the parsley, the
lemon juice and seasoning. Spoon over the fish.

   Preheat the grill and cook the sardines for 6 to 8 minutes,
turning over halfway during the cooking period and basting
with the garlic mixture. Top with the rest of the parsley and
garnish with lemon.

TO CRUSH GARLIC:
Put a little salt on a chopping
board. Dip the point of a firm
knife in it to give a better grip
and press the garlic clove until
reduced to pulp.

   Garlic presses are available
to do this job.

Devilled Sardines   ▲ ✪

SERVES 4
12 to 16 fresh sardines
1½ tablespoons sunflower oil
½ to 1 teaspoon curry powder
few drops Tabasco sauce
1 teaspoon Worcestershire
   sauce
salt and freshly ground black
   pepper

Remove the intestines from the sardines, as described in the
recipe above. Blend the oil with the rest of the ingredients and
spoon over the fish.

   Preheat the grill and cook the sardines for 6 to 8 minutes,
turn over halfway through the cooking period and brush with
the devilled mixture. Serve as a light main dish with a crisp
green salad.

COOKING SPRATS:
These small fish are much
cheaper than fresh sardines
and they can be cooked in the
same way.

   You may prefer to cook
them in the oven. Allow
15 minutes at 200°C/400°F,
Gas Mark 6.

Orange-Flavoured Red Mullet

▲ ▲ ▲ ✪ ✪

SERVES 4

4 medium or 8 small red
    mullet

For the marinade:

2 tablespoons olive oil

2 tablespoons orange juice

2 teaspoons finely grated
    orange zest

2 teaspoons lemon or lime
    juice

I tablespoon chopped fennel
    leaves

salt and freshly ground black
    pepper

To garnish:

orange slices

lime or lemon slices, halved

fennel sprigs

Scrape away any loose scales from the fish and cut away the
fins if this has not been done. Mix together the ingredients for
the marinade and marinate the fish for 30 minutes; turn once
or twice.

Preheat the grill, lift the fish from the marinade onto a sheet
of foil on the grill pan. Grill for 5 to 8 minutes on either side,
depending upon the size of the fish. Baste with any marinade
left when the fish is turned over.

Serve on a heated dish with the sliced oranges, lemon or
lime slices and fennel.

When red mullet is not available use fresh mackerel or trout
instead.

As mackerel is a very oily fish use only 1 tablespoon olive oil
in the marinade. Increase the amount of lemon or lime juice to
4 teaspoons.

USING GREY MULLET:
This is a far bigger fish and
considered to have a stronger,
less interesting flavour than
red mullet. If it is small, grill as
in this recipe, allowing 8 to 10
minutes on either side.

If it is large, marinate as left,
then bake, see page 72 for
timing.

Scallops and Bacon

▲ ▲ ✪

SERVES 4

8 scallops

2 tablespoons lemon juice

I tablespoon olive or
    sunflower oil

salt and freshly ground black
    pepper

8 rashers of long streaky
    bacon

To garnish:

lemon wedges

If the scallops are still in their shells, cut them away; pour any
liquid from the shells on to a plate. Halve the scallops, put on
the plate with the lemon juice, oil and seasoning. Leave for
10 minutes.

Remove the rinds from the bacon. Stretch the rashers, see
right, and cut them in half. Lift the halved scallops from the
plate, drain and wrap the bacon around them. Thread the rolls
on to 4 long skewers. Place under a preheated grill or over a
hot barbecue and cook for 8 to 10 minutes. Turn over once
during cooking so the bacon becomes evenly crisp.

Garnish with lemon and serve with crusty rolls.

TO STRETCH BACON:
Stroke the rashers with the
back of a knife. This not only
lengthens them but makes
them easier to roll.

Devilled Crabs

▲ ▲ ✪

SERVES 4

4 small or 2 medium cooked
    crabs, see page 82

75 g/3 oz soft fine white or
    wholemeal breadcrumbs

75 g/3 oz butter or margarine

shake cayenne pepper

$\frac{1}{2}$ to I teaspoon curry
    powder

$\frac{1}{2}$ teaspoon Worcestershire
    sauce

salt, optional

For garnish:

lemon wedges

watercress

small crab claws

Take all the crabmeat from the shells and blend the light and
dark flesh together. Add about 25 g/1 oz of the breadcrumbs
to the crabmeat. Heat all the butter in a pan or dish in the
microwave cooker and spoon 1 tablespoon of it into the
crabmeat. Add the pepper, curry powder and Worcestershire
sauce with a very little salt, if required. Mix thoroughly and
spoon into the well-cleaned shells or individual flameproof
dishes.

Mix the remaining breadcrumbs and butter together and
spoon over the crabmeat. Cook for 5 to 10 minutes under a
preheated grill set to a low heat, or for 10 to 15 minutes in the
oven preheated to 200°C/400°F, Gas Mark 6. Garnish with the
lemon, watercress and small claws. Serve with a crisp green
salad as a main dish or with hot toast as an hors d'oeuvre.

CRAB CUTLETS:
Peel and finely chop 1 small
onion. Heat 50 g/2 oz butter or
margarine and cook the onion
until soft.

Mix with 225 g/8 oz flaked
crabmeat, 50 g/2 oz soft
breadcrumbs, 1 beaten egg
and a little seasoning. Flavour
with a squeeze of lemon juice
or pinch of chilli powder.

Chill well. Form into small
cutlet shapes, coat in
seasoned flour, beaten egg
and crisp breadcrumbs.

Fry until golden brown on
both sides.

TO POACH FISH

This is the term used when fish is cooked in liquid. People often talk about 'boiled fish', but it is wrong to boil fish rapidly, as the outside flesh cooks too quickly and breaks before the centre of the fish is cooked. A lot of flavour may be lost by rapidly boiling.

The term court bouillon describes a liquid with more flavour, in which to cook the fish. It is made by adding a sliced onion and carrot, plus a bay leaf, sprig of parsley, sprig of fennel or dill and 1 or 2 tablespoons of lemon juice to 600 ml/1 pint of fish stock or water and white wine.

Timing: Let the liquid come to simmering point and add the fish. Start timing from the moment the liquid returns to a gentle simmer. Thin fillets take 6 to 7 minutes; thick fillets, steaks or cutlets 10 to 12 minutes. When cooking a whole fish, allow 10 minutes per 450 g/1 lb for really solid fish but only 6 to 7 minutes per 450 g/1 lb for a more delicate kind. The fish is cooked when white flesh turns opaque or when the flakes separate if tested gently with the tip of a knife. If you have a fish kettle with a rack, use it for cooking whole fish.

POACHING IN THE MICROWAVE:
You can poach fish in liquid in the microwave, so saving a little time. Follow the manufacturer's instructions and remember the fish continues to cook during the standing time.

Plaice Roulades   ▲ ▲ ✿

SERVES 4
8 small plaice* fillets
For the filling:
4 medium tomatoes
100 g/4 oz mushrooms
2 tablespoons chopped parsley
$^1/_2$ teaspoon chopped lemon thyme or pinch dried thyme
1 tablespoon lemon juice
few drops soy sauce
salt and freshly ground black pepper
For cooking the roulades:
300 ml/$^1/_2$ pint white wine or fish stock

* or use whiting or sole or part of small codling fillets

Skin the plaice fillets, as described below, if this has not been done by the fishmonger. Skin, halve and deseed the tomatoes and chop the pulp; this is known as 'concassing'. Wipe and finely chop the mushrooms. Mix them with the tomatoes and add the herbs, lemon juice, soy sauce and seasoning.

Spread the stuffing over the fillets, roll firmly from head to tail. Tie with fine string or cotton or secure with wooden cocktail sticks. Pour the wine or stock into a frying-pan and add a little seasoning. Put in the plaice rolls and poach for 10 minutes. Turn over once or twice during the cooking period.

Remove the rolls with a fish slice. Drain very well and remove the string, cotton or cocktail sticks. The cooking liquid can be discarded after cooking or boiled until 2 tablespoons only remain – to give an intensive flavour – which can be spooned over the fish. It can also be made into a thickened sauce, see right.

Serve with a lightly cooked green vegetable or salad and crisp croûtons.

TO MAKE A LOW-CALORIE SAUCE:
Blend 1 level teaspoon cornflour with 150 ml/$^1/_4$ pint of the liquid used to poach the fish. Pour into the pan, stir briskly until thickened then remove from the heat.

Whisk in 150 ml/$^1/_4$ pint low-fat yogurt or fromage frais. Heat gently, without boiling, then add a little chopped parsley or dill or fennel leaves, a squeeze of lemon juice and seasoning to taste.

TO PREPARE FISH:

Make a deep incision down the centre of one side of the fish. Loosen the flesh for the first fillet.

Cut around the edge of the one side of the fish. Cut away the first fillet. Repeat these steps to give 4 fillets.

Hold the tip of the fillet in your hand. Make a cut at this end then gently cut the flesh from the skin.

Lobster Americaine

Lobster Americaine

▲ ▲ ▲ ✪

SERVES 2 TO 4

2 freshly cooked lobsters, see right
1 small onion
450 g/1 lb tomatoes
75 g/3 oz butter
150 ml/¹/₄ pint white wine
squeeze lime or lemon juice
salt and freshly ground black pepper
1 to 2 tablespoons brandy, optional
To garnish:
lime or lemon wedges
mint sprig

This dish would serve 4 people as a starter or a light lunch and 2 as a sustaining main course.

Split the lobsters and remove the inedible parts, see right. Take all the meat from the body and crack the large claws and remove the flesh. Dice this neatly. Clean the lobster shells if using them for serving the fish.

Peel and finely chop the onion. Skin, halve and deseed the tomatoes and cut the pulp into small pieces. Heat the butter and cook the onion and tomatoes until a pulp. Add the wine and lime or lemon juice, together with the lobster.

Heat for a few minutes only, then season to taste. Add the brandy. The mixture can be ignited before spooning into the lobster shells or a heated dish. Garnish and serve.

To prepare ahead: Cook the tomato mixture and add the wine and lobster in advance. Do not heat the mixture until just before the meal. Keep in the refrigerator until heated.

TO BUY LOBSTERS:
A freshly cooked lobster has a softer texture and even better flavour than one cooked several hours ahead. Check when the fishmonger is boiling them.

TO COOK AT HOME:
Secure claws with elastic bands. Either plunge into boiling water and cook until bright red or put into cold water, bring up to boiling point then continue as before.

TO REMOVE INEDIBLE PARTS:
Discard the intestinal vein and small bag by the head.

Coconut-Ginger Fish

▲ ✪

SERVES 4

75 g/3 oz creamed coconut
225 ml/7¹/₂ fl oz water
1 tablespoon chopped ginger
2 small onions
2 garlic cloves
2 tablespoons sunflower oil
1 tablespoon tomato purée
4 cod cutlets
salt and freshly ground black pepper
150 ml/¹/₄ pint yogurt
To garnish:
preserved ginger
1 tablespoon blanched flaked almonds

Cut the coconut into small pieces and place it in a basin. Boil the water, pour over the coconut and add the ginger. Peel and finely chop the onions and garlic. Heat the oil in a frying-pan and cook the onions and garlic gently for 5 minutes. Add the coconut and ginger mixture, together with the tomato purée. Heat for 2 to 3 minutes, then place the fish in the liquid. Poach gently for 5 minutes, turn over and cook for the same time on the second side, or until just tender.

Lift the fish out of the liquid with a fish slice and place on a heated dish. Add a little seasoning and the yogurt to the liquid remaining in the pan, stir to blend and heat, without boiling, for 2 to 3 minutes. Pour around the fish. Slice the ginger and sprinkle this on top of the fish, together with the almonds.

Serve with a mixture of cooked white and wild rice.

TO MAKE COCONUT MILK:
Instead of creamed coconut, prepare coconut milk. To do this, put 75 g/3 oz grated fresh coconut or 40 g/1¹/₂ oz desiccated coconut into a basin. Add 225 ml/7¹/₂ fl oz boiling water. Leave for 10 minutes, strain and use the liquid. Coconut milk is frequently used in a curry.

Prawn Cream   ▲ ▲ ✿

SERVES 4

350 g/12 oz peeled prawns
1 tablespoon lemon juice, or
   to taste
1 teaspoon anchovy essence
2 tablespoons mayonnaise, see
   page 157
pinch celery salt
shake cayenne pepper
150 ml/¼ pint double or
   whipping cream

Defrost frozen prawns and dry well. Put all the ingredients, except the cream, into a liquidizer goblet or food processor. Switch on until smooth.

Lightly whip the cream and blend with the purée, taste and adjust the amount of lemon juice and seasoning as desired.

Serve with hot toast and butter or as a filling in smoked salmon rolls.

BUYING PRAWNS:
The best flavoured prawns are judged to come from cold water areas, so look at the label to check. They are often termed Atlantic prawns.

Seafood Platter   ▲ ▲ ▲   ✿✿✿

SERVES 6

12 large prawns in shells
675 g/1½ lb mussels, prepared
   as right
150 ml/¼ pint white wine
2 tablespoons chopped parsley
salt and freshly ground black
   pepper
2 medium tomatoes
1 medium cooked crab,
   prepared as below
100 g/4 oz smoked salmon
Prawn cream, see recipe
   above
For the avocado dressing:
2 tablespoons lemon juice
150 ml/¼ pint mayonnaise, see
   page 157
150 ml/¼ pint fromage frais
1 large avocado
To garnish:
lemon wedges
parsley sprigs
dill sprigs

This makes an impressive dish and the variety of fish provides interesting variations of colour and flavour.

To prepare the prawns, peel the tail ends but you can leave the heads on the fish to look more colourful.

To prepare the mussels, scrub the shells. Discard any that do not close when sharply tapped. Put into a saucepan with the wine, half the parsley and a little seasoning. Heat until the shells open. Concass – skin, deseed and finely chop – the tomatoes, mix with the remaining parsley and just a very little of the mussel liquid. Mix with the mussels.

To prepare the crab follow the 4 stages shown below. Mix the flesh from the claws with the white meat from the body. Clean out the shell. Season the flesh and arrange light and dark meat on separate sides of the shell.

To arrange the platter, place the crab in the centre of the dish. Arrange the prawns, mussels in their sauce and small strips of smoked salmon rolled around the Prawn cream on the dish.

To make the avocado dressing, blend the lemon juice, mayonnaise and fromage frais together. Halve the avocado, scoop out the flesh, mash it well and blend with the other ingredients. Season to taste. Keep well covered and chill so the mixture does not darken. Serve this separately.

Cover the fish platter and keep in the refrigerator. Garnish just before serving.

FISH CAKES:
Crabmeat or other kinds of cooked fish make excellent fish cakes. To 225 g/8 oz of flaked fish allow 225 g/8 oz mashed potatoes. These ingredients can be bound together with an egg or a little double cream or thick white sauce. Flavour with chopped herbs or anchovy essence or Tabasco sauce.

Season to taste.

Form into 8 medium sized cakes or 12 smaller cakes.

Coat these in seasoned flour, then beaten egg and fine crisp breadcrumbs. Fry in a little hot oil or fat until crisp and brown on both sides. Drain on absorbent paper and serve hot with slices of lemon.

TO PREPARE A CRAB:

Pull away the claws from the body of the crab. These can be very sharp, so take care not to cut your fingers.

Turn the crab so the shell is downwards, then take the body from the shell, remove the stomach bag in the body.

Pull the centre body of the crab out, discarding the 'dead men's fingers' – the poisonous spongy sacs and the stomach sac lying behind the head.

Crack the large crab claws and remove all the flesh from these. Take the white and dark flesh from the body of the crab.

Seafood Platter

Croustades of Salmon ▲ ▲ ✿

MAKES 8
½ large uncut sandwich loaf
For frying:
oil
For the filling:
100 g/4 oz cooked or canned
    salmon
100 g/4 oz smoked salmon*
3 eggs
25 g/1 oz butter or margarine
2 tablespoons mayonnaise or
    yogurt
2 teaspoons chopped dill or
    fennel leaves
salt and freshly ground black
    pepper

* buy salmon pieces if possible;
    they are less expensive

Croustades is the name given to square cases of food,
generally fried bread, which are used to hold a filling. They
are very like a vol-au-vent, but made much more quickly. The
fried bread cases freeze well and only need defrosting and
reheating in a microwave cooker or the oven.

Cut the crusts from the bread, then divide the loaf into
2 slices, each about 5 cm/2 inches thick. Divide each slice into
4 small squares. Carefully scoop out the centre to make neat
cases. The bread removed can be made into breadcrumbs.

Heat the oil to 180°C/350°F and cook the bread cases until
golden in colour. Drain on absorbent paper and keep warm if
serving as a hot dish.

Drain and flake the salmon and dice the smoked salmon.
Beat the eggs. Melt the butter or margarine in a pan. Add the
eggs and scramble lightly, remove from the heat, add the
mayonnaise or yogurt, the herbs and salmon. Season to taste.
Spoon into the cases.

Serve hot or cold with salad as an hors d'oeuvre or light
snack with grilled mushrooms or tomatoes.

TO COOK CROUSTADES
WITHOUT FRYING:
Brush the inside and outside
of the cases with a very little
corn or sunflower oil. Bake for
10 minutes in a preheated
oven, set to 200°C/400°F, Gas
Mark 6.

STEAMING FISH

This is often considered the best method of cooking fish as no fat or other ingredients are added. The fish is simply steamed between two plates or a piece of greaseproof paper or foil in a steamer. In fact, it is one of the best ways to retain both texture and flavour in fish.

If you top the fish with interesting sauces, such as Cucumber, Tomato, or Cheese, see pages 158 to 162, this will add colour and extra flavour.

You can add lemon juice, as well as very small amounts of seasoning, plus chopped herbs to the fish when steaming.

Seafood Cream   ▲ ▲   ✿ ✿ ✿

SERVES 4 TO 6
675 g/1 ½ lb white fish, see
    method (weight without
    skin and bones)
100 g/4 oz peeled prawns
1 small onion
25 g/1 oz butter
50 g/2 oz soft white
    breadcrumbs
2 eggs
150 ml/¼ pint single cream
salt and freshly ground black
    pepper

Choose turbot, halibut or sole for special occasions, and cod, fresh haddock or even prime huss or coley for family meals.

Chop the fish into small pieces; this can be done by hand or in a food processor, but do not over-process. The prawns may be left whole or chopped. Peel and finely chop the onion.

Heat the butter in a pan and cook the onion until soft, but do not allow it to discolour. Mix the onion with the fish and all the rest of the ingredients. Mix thoroughly.

Spoon into a 1·2 litre/2 pint mould, cover with greased greaseproof paper or foil. Steam over boiling water for just 50 minutes. Turn out and serve hot with Hollandaise sauce, see page 160. Garnish if desired.

FISH AND TOMATO MOULD
Follow directions for the Seafood cream, but use 150 ml/¼ pint freshly made tomato purée instead of the cream. You can also add 50 g/ 2 oz diced raw mushrooms to the other ingredients.

Steam as the recipe on the left. A Tomato sauce or Mushroom sauce goes well with this. Recipes pages 160 and 158.

Seafood Cream; Chinese Steamed Fish

Chinese Steamed Fish

▲ to ▲▲ ✿

SERVES 4
4 cutlets of white fish
2 teaspoons sesame oil
little light soy sauce
2 teaspoons sugar
2 teaspoons grated fresh
   ginger
2 teaspoons sesame seeds

Place the pieces of fish in a steamer. Blend the sesame oil, soy sauce, sugar and ginger and spread over the top of the fish. Sprinkle the sesame seeds over this mixture.

Cover the steamer and cook for 25 minutes over a pan of steadily boiling water. Serve with cooked noodles or rice.

FISH CAKES:
Steamed fish is ideal for making fish cakes, as it is firm and dry.

Follow the directions for Fish cakes on page 84 using steamed whole fish.

FISH DISHES FOR SLIMMERS

Fish is an excellent choice if you are anxious to lose weight. White fish is particularly low in fat and calories. While oily fish has more fat and calories, the particular oil in the various kinds of fish is especially valuable to health.

Often, it is the accompaniments or sauces that add the extra calories to the dish, but it is possible to serve fish dishes for slimmers if you choose the ingredients wisely.

Mushroom-Stuffed Fish

▲ ✿✿

SERVES 4
4 portions of white fish
2 tablespoons water or white
   wine or cider
squeeze of lemon juice
For the filling:
175 g/6 oz large mushrooms
3 large tomatoes
2 tablespoons finely chopped
   spring onions
1 tablespoon chopped parsley
1 teaspoon grated lemon rind
1 teaspoon sunflower oil
salt and freshly ground black
   pepper

Place the portions of fish with the water, wine or cider in a dish. Moisten the fish with the lemon juice.

Wipe and finely chop the mushrooms and skin and chop the tomatoes. Mix the mushrooms and tomatoes with the rest of the stuffing ingredients. Spread over the fish.

Cover the dish and bake for 20 to 30 minutes, depending upon the thickness of the fish, in a preheated oven set to 200°C/400°F, Gas Mark 6.

SORREL STUFFED FISH:
Cook 100 to 150 g/4 to 5 oz sorrel in slightly salted boiling water for a few minutes, or until just tender. Drain well and chop. Blend with 50 g/2 oz chopped mushrooms and the rest of the ingredients in the recipe left.

Harvest Herrings

▲ ✿✿✿

SERVES 4 TO 6
4 to 6 fresh herrings
2 large onions
2 dessert apples
2 firm dessert pears
600 ml/1 pint apple juice
5 cm/2 inch cinnamon stick or
   ¹/₂ teaspoon ground
   cinnamon
2 teaspoons honey
salt and freshly ground black
   pepper

Bone and fillet the fish if the fishmonger has not done this. Instructions are given on page 23. Roll each fillet from head to tail and secure the rolls with wooden cocktail sticks.

Peel and finely chop the onions. Core, but do not peel the apples. Cut them into thin rings. Peel, core and slice the pears. Put the fish rolls, with the onions and fruit into a casserole. Add the apple juice, cinnamon, honey and seasoning. Cover and cook in a preheated oven set to 160°C/325°F, Gas Mark 3 for 1 hour. Remove the cinnamon stick before serving. Serve hot or cold. This is delicious with new potatoes and a crisp green salad.

USING APPLE JUICE:
Apple juice has a natural sweetness, which is very useful when trying to lose weight. Add a little to fresh fruit salads; cook fruits in it, rather than in water – you will save an appreciable amount of sweetening.

FISH DISHES IN MINUTES ▲ ✿ to ✿✿

These are the fish dishes to choose when you have a hungry family waiting for a meal.

Do not defrost frozen fish before cooking, unless advised to do so.

Bacon-wrapped cod: Take individual portions of fresh or frozen cod. Spread with French mustard, or tomato purée, or sliced tomatoes. Wrap each portion of fish in a stretched bacon rasher (do not derind this as the extra fat helps to keep the fish moist).

Grill steadily until both bacon and fish are tender; turn over once or twice. For oven method see below, left.

Fish Duglère: Tip a 425 g/15 oz can chopped plum tomatoes into a deep frying-pan. Add 2 or 3 tablespoons finely chopped ordinary or spring onions, 2 tablespoons chopped parsley, a little seasoning and 150 ml/¼ pint white wine or water. Heat gently, then stir in 1 tablespoon tomato purée if you would like a stronger flavour.

Add 4 portions fresh or frozen white fish and spoon some of the tomato mixture over them. Cover the pan and cook steadily for 10 to 15 minutes; turn the fish over once or twice, so it becomes well flavoured. Top with chopped parsley and serve. This dish serves 4 people.

If it is more convenient, cook in a covered dish in a preheated oven. Allow 30 minutes at 200°C/400°F, Gas Mark 6.

If cooking in the microwave, heat the tomato mixture thoroughly and then add the fish; frozen fish need not be defrosted first.

Paprika fish: Prepare the tomato mixture, as above, but add 1 to 2 level teaspoons paprika and 2 tablespoons finely chopped red or green pepper to the mixture.

Salmon stir-fry: Cut some mushrooms, spring onions, mangetout peas, young carrots and red or green peppers into narrow strips. Stir-fry for a few minutes in a small amount of hot oil. Add a little soy sauce, seasoning and lemon juice.

Finally add flaked canned salmon. Heat for 2 or 3 minutes, being careful not to break the fish into too small pieces. Cooked white or smoked fish or tuna can be used instead of salmon.

For information about stir-frying in the microwave cooker see page 121.

Sweet and sour prawns: Chop enough celery to give 75 g/3 oz and finely chop enough spring onions to give 50 g/2 oz. Cut a deseeded red pepper into thin strips. Pour 1 tablespoon sunflower oil into a wok or frying-pan, add the celery and onions. Stir fry for 2 minutes. Add the red pepper, with 225 g/8 oz frozen or well-drained canned peas. Heat for 2 minutes.

Blend 1 teaspoon cornflour with 150 ml/¼ pint water or fish stock, 2 tablespoons white wine or dry sherry, 1 tablespoon white malt or wine vinegar, 1 tablespoon honey or brown sugar, 1 tablespoon light soy sauce. Pour into the wok or frying pan, stir until the sauce is slightly thickened.

Add 350 to 450 g/12 oz to 1 lb peeled prawns. Heat thoroughly, spoon the mixture onto cooked rice.

This dish serves 4 people.

Tuna Pancakes: Make pancakes, as described on page 139, or defrost and heat frozen pancakes. Tip canned tuna into a pan – do not drain it as the oil from the can keeps the ingredients moist. Add chopped tomatoes, chopped parsley and chopped mushrooms, if available. Heat thoroughly, spoon on to the pancakes, fold or roll and serve.

The pancakes can be topped with a little grated cheese and heated under the grill, in the oven or microwave cooker.

Yogurt fish au gratin: Cook portions of fish under the grill until nearly ready. Spread the top of each portion with thick yogurt. Flavour with a little lemon juice and/or chopped parsley, or other herbs. Cover with a thick layer of grated cheese and complete the cooking.

COOKING IN THE OVEN
The bacon-wrapped cod can be cooked in a preheated oven at 200°C/400°F, Gas Mark 6 for approximately 20 minutes. There is no need to turn the fish when baking it.

This dish can be cooked in a microwave. In order to prevent the bacon being over-cooked, defrost frozen fish before wrapping it in bacon. Follow timing instructions in the manufacturer's book.

ESPECIALLY FOR CHILDREN

FISHBURGERS:
Finely chop about 450 g/1 lb uncooked white or other kinds of fish. Peel and finely chop a large onion; cook in 2 teaspoons sunflower oil, add to the fish with a little chopped parsley. Blend in 25 g/1 oz soft breadcrumbs or cooked rice or uncooked rolled oats. Form into 8 small round cakes with floured hands. Fry in a very little hot oil for about 7 minutes, or until the fish is absolutely cooked. The burgers can be cooked for the same time under the grill.

Serve on toasted burger rolls with a tomato relish.

Many parents find that children are not over-fond of fish, except fried fish or fish fingers. There may be very good reasons for their choice. Both look appetizing, both have crisp outsides and both are easy to eat, for most fried fish is boned fish. Many children hate having to deal with skin and bones.

Do not be discouraged about their liking for fish fingers; these can be considered as an introduction to more varied kinds of fish and interesting fish dishes.

Fish fingers are based upon wholesome fish. If you feel they are not giving a sufficiently generous amount of protein to a growing child, you can top them with a little grated cheese or serve them with peas or beans.

Try the oven 'frying' method of cooking, given on page 76, if you are anxious that the children should have less fat in their diet.

Fish cakes: on page 84 make an easy-to-eat meal. They look particularly interesting in colour if they are made with canned pink salmon or tuna. Their round shape enables you to garnish them with green 'eyes' from peas and a red 'mouth' from a strip of skinned tomato – this may well encourage a small child to try them.

Older children may enjoy them more if they are coated in rolled oats rather than breadcrumbs; this gives them a pleasant nutty flavour. See recipe left.

Spaghetti alla marinara: Most children of today enjoy pasta. Cooked spaghetti can be blended with a mixture of cooked fish, such as diced white fish, prawns, whole sardines or tiny canned brisling. Heat with the pasta, adding skinned chopped tomatoes or a little milk, so the mixture does not dry as you reheat for just a few minutes. Adults can add chopped cooked onions and garlic and a little white wine.

Fishburgers; Spaghetti alla Marinara

MEAT DISHES

The quality and choice of meats available is excellent. Whatever method of cooking we choose, the result should be tender and succulent meat dishes. To achieve this, we must first buy meat carefully, see page 30, then choose the right cut and method of cooking. See under grilling, etc.

Both uncooked and cooked meats are highly perishable foods, so take care with storing the fresh or frozen products, see pages 16 and 32.

Modern medical opinion suggests we limit our intake of red meat to a reasonable amount. This can be done in two ways – either we have days when we base our meals on poultry, fish or vegetarian dishes, or we habitually cook a smaller amount of meat and augment it with other important foods, such as pasta, rice and pulses. Another important nutritional fact is that most of us eat too many fatty foods. Modern breeding of animals has produced leaner meat; all you have to do is cut any fat off the meat after cooking. This does not impair the texture and flavour.

All methods of cooking meat are simple, but the one that causes most problems is roasting. This is fully covered in the next few pages and the information ensures that you produce a joint with perfect flavour and tenderness.

TO ROAST MEAT

A roast joint is ideal for a family meal or when entertaining. It is an especially good choice if a friend who lives alone comes to a meal, for few single people buy joints.

If you have bought a joint of fresh meat, it is ready to roast immediately after purchase; but if you buy a frozen joint, you must allow it time to defrost, see page 32.

How to roast

Most joints contain sufficient natural fat to mean that the amount of additional fat you add can be kept to a minimum, or even dispensed with.

If you are roasting potatoes round the joint in the meat tin, you need a little fat. However, if the potatoes are well coated with this or brushed all over with oil when they are first put into the tin, they brown and crisp well.

Covering roasting meat: You can cover the meat in one of the following ways.

You can use a roasting bag. These are made to enclose the meat and keep it moist, but still enable it to become brown during cooking.

You can buy a covered roasting tin. Make sure it is deep enough to hold the meat without touching the top. A true roasting tin allows the meat to baste itself during cooking, for any fat in the tin splashes up inside the cover and falls back on to the meat.

You can use aluminium foil in one of two ways. Wrap the meat in it, but remove the foil for the last 15 to 20 minutes roasting time. Alternatively, you can simply place the foil over the roasting tin, rather like a tent. This does not alter the basic cooking times.

The advantage of covering meat is that it keeps beautifully moist and the oven keeps clean. The disadvantage is that the outside does not become crisp and it browns less. You also need to allow a slightly longer cooking time, see under Timing, page 91.

Do not cover the meat or the meat tin when you are cooking pork and want crisp crackling, or when roasting potatoes around the joint.

TIMING FOR ROAST JOINTS

The timing and temperature required for perfect roasting are given under each kind of meat, but there are certain general considerations below.

- Prime fresh joints can be roasted at the higher setting given under each kind of meat (**A**). This is particularly good for superb beef.
- Much of the meat sold today has been chilled and it is better roasted at a lower setting (**B**).
- Frozen joints should be roasted at the lower setting too (**B**).

If covering meat: Allow an extra 10 minutes' cooking time at the higher setting (**A**) or 15 minutes at the lower setting (**B**).

Allowing cooked joints to stand: It is advisable to allow the joint to stand for a short time after it has been cooked. This makes it a great deal easier to carve. Allow 5 minutes standing time for a small joint and 10 minutes for a larger one. Lift the joint out of the tin on to a heated dish.

Even if you have roasted the meat in an open tin, it is advisable to wrap it loosely in foil to retain the heat within it.

Carving the joint: Information is given under each kind of meat, but do make quite sure that one, or even two carving knives are really sharp.

Roasting in a microwave cooker: It is possible to roast in a microwave cooker. As the output of these varies, it is essential to consult the manufacturer's handbook.

Standing time when roasting in a microwave cooker: As you will see from the handbook, standing time is an essential part of the cooking process, never avoid doing it.

HORSERADISH SAUCE:
25 g/1 oz butter
25 g/1 oz plain flour
300 ml/¹/₂ pint milk
1 to 2 tablespoons finely grated horseradish
3 tablespoons single cream
salt and freshly ground black pepper
pinch of sugar
few drops of lemon juice or white wine vinegar

Heat the butter in a saucepan. Stir in the flour, then gradually add the milk. Stir over the heat until the sauce has thickened. Remove from the heat and add the horseradish, cream, a little seasoning, a pinch of sugar and lemon juice or white wine vinegar. Heat gently; do not allow to boil. Serve hot.

SERVES 4 TO 6

Roast Beef with Yorkshire Puddings and Horseradish Sauce

TO ROAST BEEF

YORKSHIRE PUDDING
115 g/4 oz plain flour
pinch of salt
280 ml/¹/₂ pint milk or milk and
    water
1 or 2 eggs
little fat

Blend the flour, salt, 1 egg
and the liquid, to make a
batter. Whisk before cooking.
For a richer batter; use the
same amount of flour but 2
eggs with 250 ml/8 fl oz liquid.

Preheat the oven to
230°C/450°F, Gas Mark 8.
Put 25 g/1 oz fat into a
Yorkshire pudding tin. Heat
well and add the batter.
Cook for 10 to 12 minutes
until well risen. Reduce the
oven setting to heat under **A**
or **B**. Return the meat.
Continue cooking the
pudding as indicated:
at 190°C/375°F Gas Mark 5
– for 15 to 20 minutes; at
200°C/400°F, Gas Mark 6 –
for 12 to 15 minutes.

INDIVIDUAL PUDDINGS:
Grease deep patty tins, heat
well and pour in the batter.
Cook at the higher temperature
for 5 to 8 minutes. Reduce
heat, as above. Continue
cooking for 8 to 15 minutes.

SERVES 4 TO 6

This is considered by many people to be the finest of all meats.

Prime joints for roasting: Fillet, rib, sirloin. Baron of beef is a ceremonial joint; it is a double sirloin, which is left uncut along the backbone.

Fillet can be grilled or fried, but a double fillet can be roasted as a Chateaubriand. It makes a joint for 2 or 3 people.

Both rib and sirloin joints can be bought on the bone or boned and rolled.

The prime joints can be roasted quickly at temperature **A** or more slowly at temperature **B**.

Less expensive joints for roasting: Good quality aitch-bone, fresh brisket, topside. Topside is a lean joint and, therefore, popular today. You may like to top this with 25 g/1 oz fat or brush the outside with oil before cooking.

Roast these joints at temperature **B**.

NOTE: Check the weight carefully, as over-cooked beef is spoiled for many people. If there is a bone, as with rib of beef, allow 1 or 2 minutes' less time per 450 g/1 lb.

Temperature A: Preheat the oven to 220°C/425°F, Gas Mark 7 if you have a fairly gentle heat, or to 200°C/400°F, Gas Mark 6 if your oven is inclined to be fierce.

Allow 15 minutes per 450 g/1 lb and 15 minutes over for under done beef; 20 minutes per 450 g/1 lb and 20 minutes over for medium-done beef; and 25 minutes per 450 g/1 lb and 25 minutes over for very well-cooked beef (normally not popular).

You can reduce the heat to 190°C/375°F, Gas Mark 5 after the first 1 hour's cooking.

Temperature B: Preheat the oven to 180°C/350°F, Gas Mark 4.

Allow 25 minutes per 450 g/1 lb and 25 minutes over for under done beef; 30 minutes per 450 g/1 lb and 30 minutes over for medium-cooked beef; and 35 minutes per 450 g/1 lb and 35 minutes over for very well-cooked beef.

You can reduce the heat to 160°C/325°F, Gas Mark 3 after 1¹/₂ hours' cooking time.

Usual accompaniments with beef: A thin gravy or the juice from under-done meat, with Yorkshire pudding and Horseradish sauce, recipes on pages 91 and 93.

As you will see from the recipe for Yorkshire pudding, the oven needs to be very hot when you start to cook this. To achieve this (an especial problem when using temperature **B**), time the cooking of the meat so that you can remove it from the oven for 15 to 20 minutes while the oven temperature is raised and the pudding starts to cook. When it has risen, lower the heat to the original setting. Return the meat to the oven and complete the cooking of the meat and pudding.

Beef with Red Wine Sauce

SERVES 6
joint of beef for roasting, or
    steaks for grilling, see pages
    92 and 100
For the red wine sauce:
6 shallots or 3 medium onions
75 g/3 oz butter
600 ml/1 pint red wine or
    300 m/¹/₂ pint red wine and
    300 ml/¹/₂ pint beef stock
2 tablespoons chopped parsley
1 tablespoon lemon juice
salt and freshly ground black
    pepper

Roast the joint or grill the steaks. If cooking steaks, start making the sauce in plenty of time, so the meat can be served as soon as it its cooked.

To make the red wine sauce, peel and finely chop the shallots or onions. Heat 25 g/1 oz of the butter in a pan, add the shallots or onions and cook gently until softened, but do not allow them to brown. Add the wine or wine and beef stock and simmer steadily for about 15 minutes. Do not cover the pan; the liquid should be reduced until about half the volume.

When you are ready to serve the meat, add the parsley, lemon juice and seasoning to the sauce, remove from the heat, then whisk in the remaining butter. Do this gradually, so the sauce is rich and creamy, not oily. Taste the sauce and add a little sugar if you feel it is slightly acidic.

UNTHICKENED SAUCES:
Although this is an old, traditional sauce to serve with grilled or fried steaks, it is equally good with a roast joint.

WHITE WINE SAUCE:
Use the recipe left and similar ingredients, but substitute 600 ml/1 pint white wine for the red wine or red wine and stock.

This is a good sauce to serve with roast lamb or veal.

Filet Vascongado; Stuffed Beef

Stuffed Beef   ▲ ▲   ✿ ✿ ✿

SERVES 4 TO 6
1.1 kg/2¹/₂ lb joint of beef,
    boned and rolled, see
    method
For the stuffing:
100 g/4 oz bacon rashers
2 medium onions
50 g/2 oz butter or margarine
75 g/3 oz soft breadcrumbs
2 tablespoons chopped parsley
1 teaspoon mustard powder
salt and freshly ground black
    pepper
1 egg

This is an ideal way of giving a moist texture to a topside of beef, although lean rib could be used instead.

Cut the joint downwards into two halves. This means that when the meat is carved, everyone will have some stuffing.

To make the stuffing, derind and chop the bacon rashers (the rind can be used in cooking to give more flavour; place it on top of the joint). Peel and finely chop the onions.

Heat the butter or margarine and cook the onions until nearly tender, add the chopped bacon and cook for 2 or 3 minutes then mix in all the other ingredients.

Press the stuffing between the two halves of meat and tie the joint with fine string. Wrap the sides with a double band of foil to keep the joint a good shape. Weigh the stuffed joint and cook as temperature **B** on the previous page.

CARVING BEEF:
A boned and rolled joint should be carved across the meat.

When carving rib or sirloin joints on the bone, carve from the outside of the meat towards the bone.

Give people who like fairly well-done beef outside slices, and those who like under-done beef slices from the middle of the joint.

Filet Vascongado (Basque-style Beef)   ▲ ▲ ▲   ✿ ✿ ✿

SERVES 4 TO 6
1.1 kg/2¹/₂ lb fillet of beef, but
    see right
40 g/1¹/₂ oz butter
For the topping:
2 Spanish onions
175 g/6 oz small button
    mushrooms
100 g/4 oz smoked sausage or
    cooked ham
25 g/1 oz butter
1 tablespoon olive oil
salt and freshly ground black
    pepper
2 tablespoons chopped parsley

Put the meat into the roasting tin, melt the butter and brush a little over the meat. As this is such a tender joint, it should be roasted as temperature **A** on the previous page. Baste the fillet with the rest of the butter during the cooking time, or cover the meat with buttered foil and add a further 10 minutes to the total cooking time. It is not necessary for this particular joint to brown, as it is topped with the savoury mixture.

While the meat is cooking, prepare the topping. Peel and thinly slice the onions and separate into rings. Wipe the mushrooms. Remove the stalks and chop them finely but leave the caps whole. Slice the sausage or chop the ham. Heat the butter and olive oil in a pan and cook the onion rings until nearly tender, but do not allow them to brown. Add the mushrooms, with the chopped stalks, the sausage or ham and cook for a few minutes. Add the seasoning and parsley.

To serve, cut the meat into thick slices and top with the onion mixture. Serve with the usual fairly thin gravy, see right.

CHOICE OF MEAT:
Fillet is an expensive joint; this dish is equally good made with boned rib of beef or topside.

THIN GRAVY FOR BEEF:
To make gravy for 4 to 6 people, pour away all the dripping from the pan except 1¹/₂ tablespoons (save the rest). Blend 1¹/₂ level tablespoons flour with the dripping in the pan. Heat until brown. You can use a little gravy browning. Gradually blend in 600 ml/1 pint beef stock. Stir as the gravy thickens slightly. Season and strain before serving.

TO ROAST LAMB

MINT SAUCE:
Wash and dry mint leaves.
Chop finely by hand, or in the
food processor or liquidizer. If
using these appliances, it is
better to add a little of the
vinegar to the mint.

Blend the chopped mint
with sugar and wine vinegar.

THICKENED GRAVY:
Follow the method of making
gravy given in the right hand
column of page 93 but
increase the amount of flour
to 2 to 3 level tablespoons.

Today's lamb is of excellent quality, whether home-reared or imported.
Prime joints for roasting: Best end of neck (also known as rack), leg (also known as
gigot), loin. Crown roast is made with two racks of lamb and saddle is a double loin.
These prime joints can be roasted at either temperature **A** or **B**.
Less expensive joints for roasting: Breast. Use the lower temperature, **B**.
Temperature A: See page 92

If you like lamb very pink, allow just over 15 minutes per 450 g/1 lb and a good 15
minutes over; for fairly pink lamb, allow 18 minutes per 450 g/1 lb and 18 minutes
over; for well-done lamb, allow 20 minutes per 450 g/1 lb and 20 minutes over.

You can reduce the heat to 190°C/375°F, Gas Mark 5 after 1 hour's cooking time.
Temperature B: See page 92.

Allow 30 to 35 minutes per 450 g/1 lb, depending upon how well you like the lamb
cooked, and 35 minutes over. It is harder to achieve really good pink lamb at this setting.
Usual accompaniments with lamb: Mint sauce and unthickened or thickened gravy,
depending upon personal taste.

Apricot and Orange Crown Roast   ▲ ▲   ✿ ✿ ✿

SERVES 6 TO 7
2 racks of lamb, containing
   12 to 14 chops
For the stuffing:
100 g/4 oz dried apricots,
   preferably tenderized type
50 g/2 oz walnuts
1/4 small celery heart
75 g/3 oz seedless raisins
1 teaspoon grated lemon rind
3 teaspoons grated orange
   rind
4 tablespoons orange juice
1 tablespoon lemon juice
100 g/4 oz soft breadcrumbs
1 egg
salt and ground black pepper
To garnish:
bay leaves
orange segments
walnut halves

Most butchers will prepare a crown roast if given notice, but
the illustrations below show how you can do it yourself. It
takes time, but it is not particularly difficult.

To make the stuffing, chop the apricots, walnuts and celery.
Add the rest of the stuffing ingredients and mix thoroughly.

Put the stuffing into the meat, weigh to calculate the
cooking time and place in the roasting tin.

Protect the ends of the bones with foil and cover the top of
the stuffing with foil. This prevents the tips of the bones from
burning and the stuffing from becoming too brown.

Roast according to the instructions above. Rack of lamb is a
tender joint, so you can choose temperature **A** or **B**. Remove
the foil from the top of the stuffing for the last 20 to 30
minutes cooking time.

Lift the crown out of the tin on to a heated serving dish.
Remove the foil from the bones and top them with cutlet frills.
Garnish with the bay leaves, orange and walnuts. Serve with a
thickened gravy, following the method above and flavour with
a little orange juice.

To carve a crown roast, spoon portions of stuffing on to
plates, then cut down between the bones.

OTHER FILLINGS FOR CROWN
ROASTS:
When the new season's young
vegetables are available, roast
the meat without a filling and
fill the centre with cooked
vegetables.

The Cranberry rice stuffing
on page 163 is another
excellent filling for the lamb.

TO PREPARE A CROWN ROAST:

Remove the skin from the two
joints of lamb. Trim away all
the fat from the ends of the
chops, so making these into
cutlets.

Cut (chine) between the
bones at the end of each joint
so the meat can be formed
into the round. Use a strong
knife or meat saw.

Arrange the two joints to
form a perfect round. You
can place an apple in the
centre to help to achieve a
good shape.

Use a trussing needle and fine
string to sew the joints
together. Remove the apple
from the centre if you have
used one.

Cinnamon Pot Roast; Apricot and Orange Crown Roast

Cinnamon Pot Roast

▲ ▲ ✿ ✿ ✿ ✿

SERVES 4 TO 6

1/2 leg of lamb – choose the fillet end

2 to 3 garlic cloves

1 tablespoon flour

salt and freshly ground black pepper

1 teaspoon ground cinnamon

350 g/12 oz carrots

225 g/8 oz small onions

1/2 celery heart

few mint or rosemary leaves

lamb stock or wine or water, see method

To garnish:

mint leaves

Heat the meat in a large pan until golden brown in colour. Remove on to a plate and cool sufficiently to handle.

Make small slits in the lamb. Peel the garlic and cut into thick slices. Blend the flour, seasoning and cinnamon. Roll the garlic in this mixture and insert into the slits in the meat. Peel the carrots and onions, but leave them whole. Chop the celery. Heat all the vegetables in the pan in which the lamb was browned for 5 to 10 minutes only. There should be sufficient fat from the meat to stop the vegetables sticking to the pan. Turn frequently.

Put the vegetables into the base of a deep casserole, season lightly, add the herbs with just sufficient stock or wine or water to cover them. Place the meat on top of the vegetables.

Cover the casserole tightly. If the lid is a poor fit, place a piece of foil under it. Cook for 2 to 2¼ hours in a preheated oven at 180°C/350°F, Gas Mark 4.

Lift the meat and some of the vegetables on to a serving dish. Liquidize the remaining vegetables and any liquid left in the casserole to make a sauce, adding more liquid if necessary. Season to taste. Garnish with mint.

TO CARVE LAMB:

LEG: Carve a fairly thick slice from the middle of the curved part of the joint towards the bone. Continue carving slices from either side of this.

If you hold the knife at an angle, you get longer slices. Turn the joint over and carve along the length of the leg.

SHOULDER: Cut the first slice in the middle of the rounded side between the shoulder blade and arm bone. Continue as for leg.

LOIN AND RACK: Cut between the bones.

BONED ROLLED JOINTS: Carve across the joint.

Rice-Stuffed Breast of Lamb   ▲ ✪ ✪ ✪

SERVES 4

For the stuffing:

2 large onions

2 garlic cloves

100 g/4 oz long grain rice

300 ml/¹/₂ pint water

salt and freshly ground black
    pepper

2 teaspoons grated lemon rind

I egg

I breast of lamb, weighing
    approximately I kg/2¹/₄ lbs

This could be said to be an 'old-fashioned dish'. The joint is a
very economical one and it is full of flavour, but it does have a
higher percentage of fat than other cuts so it is not chosen as
often as other parts of lamb. If you are anxious to reduce the
fat content of your meals, cut away excess fat before and after
cooking. The stuffing contains only the small amount of fat
from the egg yolk.

Peel and finely chop the onions and the garlic. Put the rice
into a pan with the cold water, onions, garlic and a little
seasoning. Bring the liquid to the boil, stir the rice with a fork,
cover the pan and simmer until the rice is just tender. If any
excess liquid remains, boil briskly in an uncovered pan until
drier. Add the lemon rind and the egg, with any extra
seasoning required.

Bone the breast of lamb if this has not been done by the
butcher. Spread the joint with the rice stuffing, roll firmly and
tie in several places with string. Put into the roasting tin, on a
rack if possible. Do not cover the meat. Cook for 30 minutes
in a hot oven, preheated to 200°C/400°F, Gas Mark 6; this
extracts much of the fat. Pour away any fat, then lower the
heat to 160°C/325°F, Gas Mark 3 and continue cooking for a
further 1 hour.

Remove the string and cut the joint into neat slices. Serve
with rosemary-flavoured gravy.

TO MAKE A CHANGE:
Use a generous amount of
chopped rosemary and a little
chopped marjoram in the rice
stuffing. Add to the cooked
rice.

HONEY GLAZED LAMB:
Cook the meat as the recipe
left. 15 minutes before the end
of the cooking time, brush the
outside of the meat with thin
honey, blended with a little
lemon juice. Continue cooking.

Rice-Stuffed Breast of Lamb

Lamb in Honey and Cider ▲▲ ✪✪✪

SERVES 6 TO 8
1 leg or shoulder of lamb
few sprigs of mint, optional
2 to 3 tablespoons thin honey
300 ml/¹/₂ pint dry or sweet
    cider, depending upon
    personal taste
For the sauce:
2 tablespoons dripping from
    the roasting tin
25 g/1 oz flour
300 ml/¹/₂ pint lamb stock
salt and freshly ground black
    pepper

Roast the lamb as the timing on page 94. Bring the meat out of the oven 30 minutes before the end of the cooking time, if using the higher temperature, **A**, or 40 minutes if using the lower temperature, **B**. Make slits in the lamb flesh.

Pour away any fat from the roasting tin, saving 2 tablespoons to make the sauce. Press mint into the cuts.

Carefully spread the honey over the hot meat; and pour the cider over the meat and into the tin. Return to the oven and complete the cooking. Lift the lamb on to a heated dish, cover with foil and strain the liquid from the tin.

To make the sauce, pour the dripping into a saucepan, stir in the flour, blend in the stock and liquid from the roasting tin. Stir as the sauce boils and thickens. Season to taste.

WAYS TO FLAVOUR LAMB:
Before cooking the meat, try these easy ways of flavouring it.

Insert thin slivers of garlic into slits in the skin, or use small sprigs of rosemary, or for a hot flavour, insert matchstick pieces of red chilli pepper. Roast as usual.

ORANGE AND HONEY LAMB:
Substitute orange juice for the cider.

TO ROAST PORK

Modern pork is much leaner than in the past. The only problem many people have is to produce crisp crackling. Try the following steps to succeed.

Dry the meat well. Chine the skin (cut at intervals).

Rub with oil or sprinkle with salt; some people do both, but this is not necessary.

Stand the meat on a rack in the roasting tin so surplus fat runs away. Never cover it.

If all of these steps are still unsuccessful, then try this method. Carefully cut away the skin and cut it into neat fingers. Put on to a separate tin and cook separately with the skin side uppermost.

Timing: Pork must be well cooked, so allow the same temperatures and timings as given for roasting veal, see page 99.

Prime joints for roasting: Leg, or part of the leg, loin, spare rib.

These joints can be roasted at either temperature **A** or **B**.

Less expensive joints for roasting: Blade, hand, spring.

Roast at the lower temperature, **B**.

Always weigh the joint after stuffing it to ascertain the correct weight.

Usual accompaniments with pork: Apple sauce, Sage and onion stuffing and thickened gravy.

TO MAKE STOCK:
Use the bones removed from meat to make stock.

To give a darker colour, heat the bones in a pan until brown. Add diced vegetables and water to cover. Simmer for 1 to 2 hours, or use a pressure cooker or microwave to shorten the cooking time.

Apple Sauce ▲ ✪

SERVES 4 TO 6

450 g/1 lb peeled, cored and
    sliced cooking apples
2 tablespoons water
1 to 3 tablespoons sugar
15 to 25 g/¹/₂ to 1 oz butter

Put the apples into a saucepan with the water. Cover and cook until they form a purée. Beat or liquidize until smooth.

The apples can be cooked in a covered basin in the microwave. They cook very quickly, so check progress after 2 minutes on FULL POWER.

Add sugar, depending upon personal taste and the sweetness of the fruit.

Stir in the butter. This is not essential, but it helps to give gloss and extra flavour to the sauce.

FOR THE FLAVOURING:
There are many ways of ringing the changes: add a little ground spice or nutmeg; add a few sultanas or raisins; use white wine instead of water; blend the grated rind of an orange with the apples and use orange juice instead of water.

Sage and Onion Stuffing

▲   ✿✿

SERVES 4 TO 6
2 large onions
150 ml/¼ pint water
50 g/2 oz soft breadcrumbs
25 to 50 g/1 to 2 oz shredded
    suet or margarine
2 teaspoons chopped sage or
    1 teaspoon dried sage
salt and freshly ground black
    pepper
1 egg

Peel and finely chop the onions; this can be done in a food
processor. Put the onions and water into a saucepan, cover
and simmer for 10 minutes, or until nearly tender. You can do
this in a covered basin in the microwave for about 3 minutes
on FULL POWER. Strain and keep the onion stock.

Add the breadcrumbs and suet or margarine, which will
melt with the heat of the onions. Blend in the sage and a little
seasoning. Bind with the egg or use onion stock instead; this
produces a less solid stuffing.

Either spread over a boned joint of pork and then roll it, or
cook in a covered dish for approximately 30 minutes at
temperature **A** or 40 minutes at **B**. The stuffing can be cooked
for 8 to 10 minutes in the microwave cooker on FULL POWER.

MORE STUFFINGS:

SAGE AND APPLE:
Add a diced, peeled cooking
apple to the other ingredients.

ONION AND PRUNE:
Add 100 g/4 oz diced,
tenderized prunes to the
stuffing and omit the sage.

TO CARVE PORK:
Carve boned and rolled joints
by cutting across the meat,
and carve loin by cutting
between the bones.

Loin of Pork

▲ ▲   ✿✿✿✿

SERVES 4 TO 6
1 kg/2¼ lb boned loin of pork
For the marinade:
1 garlic clove
1 medium onion
5 tablespoons white wine
1 tablespoon soy sauce
½ tablespoon hoisin sauce
1 tablespoon thin honey
1 tablespoon chopped fresh
    ginger

Put the meat into a deep dish. Peel and chop the garlic and
onion and mix with the rest of the ingredients for the
marinade. Spoon over the pork joint. Leave for 2 to 3 hours,
turning the meat over from time to time. Lift out of the
marinade and drain well. Keep the marinade.

Roast as temperature **B** on page 99. Brush with any
marinade left at least once during the cooking period.

Serve with Apple sauce, see page 97. The gravy served with
the joint can be flavoured with a little soy and hoisin sauces.

STUFFED LOIN OF PORK:
Spread the Onion and prune
stuffing, above, over the
boned pork. Roll and tie the
meat with fine string.

Weigh the joint. Roast as
timing under temperatures **A**
or **B** on page 99.

Loin of Pork with Onion and Prune Stuffing

Pork Chops with Orange Stuffing ▲▲ ✿✿

SERVES 4
4 pork loin chops
For the stuffing:
2 oranges
25 g/1 oz butter or margarine
75 g/3 oz soft white or
   wholemeal breadcrumbs
1/2 teaspoon finely chopped
   fresh sage or 1/4 teaspoon
   dried sage
1 tablespoon chopped chives
salt and freshly ground black
   pepper
To garnish:
watercress

Preheat the oven to 190°C/375°F, Gas Mark 5. Place the chops on a rack in the roasting tin, so the excess fat runs out. Cook for 20 minutes while you make the stuffing.

For the stuffing, grate sufficient zest from the oranges to give 1 tablespoon. Halve the fruit and scoop out the orange segments, leaving the pith and skin behind. Do this over a basin so no juice is wasted. Melt the butter or margarine and mix with the orange zest, segments, breadcrumbs and herbs. Moisten with the orange juice and season lightly.

Remove the chops from the oven, top the lean meat with the stuffing, then return to the oven for a further 15 to 20 minutes.

Serve garnished with watercress.

FRUIT ZEST:
The term 'zest' refers to the very outer rind of citrus fruits. Take care not to include any bitter white pith when grating the zest.

CRACKLING FROM CHOPS:
If you like to crisp the pork rind, cut it from the chops before cooking. Place on a tin and cook separately.

TO ROAST VEAL (AND PORK)

Veal is a very lean meat and needs extra fat to keep it moist during cooking. To lard veal insert strips of fat bacon through the meat.
Prime joints for roasting: Fillet, leg, loin with chump end of loin, shoulder.

These joints can be roasted quickly at either temperature **A** or more slowly at temperature **B**.
Less expensive joints for roasting: Breast, neck.

Roast at the lower temperature, **B**.
Temperature A: Preheat the oven to 220°C/425°F, Gas Mark 7 if you have a fairly gentle heat, or to 200°C/400°F, Gas Mark 6 if your oven is inclined to be fierce.

Veal should be well cooked, i.e. 25 minutes per 450 g/1 lb and 25 minutes over.

You can reduce the heat to 190°C/375°F, Gas Mark 5 after the first 1 hour's cooking.
Temperature B: Preheat the oven to 180°C/350°F, Gas Mark 4.

Allow 40 minutes per 450 g/1 lb and 40 minutes over.
Usual accompaniments with veal: Bacon rolls, sausages and thickened gravy.

TO MAKE BACON ROLLS:
Choose streaky bacon.

Cut off the rinds, stretch the rashers with the back of a knife and halve them.

Roll firmly and put several on to metal skewers; allow a little space between the rolls, so they become crisp.

Put on a metal tin and cook for 10 minutes at temperature **A** or 15 minutes at temperature **B**.

Veau en Papillote ▲▲ ✿✿

SERVES 4
4 veal chops
For the topping:
4 tomatoes
1 tablespoon olive oil
1 teaspoon lemon juice
1 tablespoon white wine
1 tablespoon chopped parsley
1 teaspoon chopped fresh
   rosemary
1 tablespoon chopped chives
   or spring onions
salt and freshly ground black
   pepper

Make 4 large squares of double thickness greaseproof paper, or use bags or foil, see right. The paper, bags or foil must be large enough to enclose the meat and topping. Preheat the oven to 190°C/375°F, Gas Mark 5. Place the veal chops on one side of the paper. Skin and slice the tomatoes and place over the chops. Blend all the ingredients for the topping.

Lift the sides of the paper to make shallow basin shapes and carefully spoon the topping liquid over the meat. Fold the greaseproof paper very securely to enclose the meat and topping. Place in a roasting tin.

Cook for 40 to 45 minutes, depending upon the thickness of the chops. Pierce the paper, then carefully open each parcel, see right. Tip the meat and juices on to a heated dish. Serve with mixed vegetables.

COOKING EN PAPILLOTE:
This means cooking in a parcel or bag. The food retains its flavour and a moist texture.

Instead of the parcels described left, large greaseproof paper bags can be used. Fold the tops very securely after filling. Foil is excellent, but allow 15 to 20 minutes extra time in cooking.

Always open the parcels or bags very carefully as the contents are full of steam.

TO GRILL MEAT

Grilling should be a speedy method of cooking meat, so it is essential that the grill is thoroughly preheated before the meat is placed underneath. It is a method of cooking that needs the minimum of additional fat. It is suitable for the following.

Beef: Various steaks, i.e. entrecôte (the cut between the ribs), fillet – the tenderest of all steaks, tournedos (rounds made from the fillet), minute steaks (cut from the rump and so thin that the meat is cooked within 1 to 2 minutes), porterhouse – a thick steak, rather like sirloin but including some fillet, rump – considered by many people to be the steak with the best flavour, point rump being the prime part, sirloin – slices from the sirloin, T-bone – the end of the sirloin near the bone giving a T-shape.

Lamb: Best end of neck chops or cutlets, chump and loin chops, fillets – from the top of the leg (often called escalopes), noisettes – boned chops rolled to give neat rounds.

Pork: Chump and loin chops, spare ribs, fillets – from the top of the leg (often called escalopes and, when small, medallions).

Veal: Loin chops or cutlets. The slices of meat known as escalopes are so lean that frying is a better method of cooking them.

To prepare for grilling: Lean meats, such as steaks, should be brushed with melted butter or oil. It is important to brush the food again when it is turned over. Chopped herbs can be incorporated into the butter or oil to give additional flavour.

Timing: This varies according to the individual meats.

Beef: To cook steaks approximately 2·5 cm/1 inch thick allow a total cooking time of 6 minutes for rare (red in middle); 8 minutes for medium rare and 10 minutes for well-done meat.

Lamb: For chops about 2·5 cm/1 inch thick, allow a total cooking time of 10 to 12 minutes. For cutlets and fillets, allow about 8 minutes.

Pork: For chops about 2·5 cm/1 inch thick, allow a total cooking time of 18 to 20 minutes. For cutlets and fillet, allow about 15 minutes. Snip the rind at intervals to encourage this to become crisp.

Veal: The timing is similar to pork; keep well brushed with butter or oil.

Bacon: Thin streaky or back rashers are better if placed under a grill that has not been preheated for any length of time beforehand. A very hot grill encourages the bacon to curl and parts could burn. Snip the rind at intervals unless it has been removed. Thicker gammon steaks need approximately the same time as pork and should be kept well brushed with a little melted butter or oil.

Satay Sauce   ▲ ▲ ✪

SERVES 4
100 g/4 oz peanuts
1 onion
2 garlic cloves
1 tablespoon lime or lemon
   juice
1 tablespoon soy sauce
2 tablespoons peanut butter
pinch chilli powder
salt and freshly ground black
   pepper
50 g/2 oz creamed coconut
150 ml/¹/₄ pint water

Preheat the oven to 190°C/375°F, Gas Mark 5. Put the peanuts on a flat baking sheet and roast for 5 minutes.

Peel and finely chop the onion and garlic. Add the lime or lemon juice, soy sauce, peanut butter, chilli powder and seasoning.

Add the roasted peanuts and pound until smooth or liquidize until the mixture forms a purée. Meanwhile, heat the creamed coconut with water. Add to the other ingredients.

Spoon into a bowl to serve with the Satay Lembu, page 101.

The flavour of this sauce can be changed by using either a smooth or crunchy peanut butter with the peanuts.

SPEEDY SATAY SAUCE:
Omit the whole peanuts; use 100 g/4 oz crunchy peanut butter and slightly less water with the creamed coconut.

If you have no creamed coconut, prepare as coconut milk, but use only half the amount of water.

Satay Lembu

▲ ▲   ✪ ✪ ✪ ✪

SERVES 4

450 to 550 g/1 to 1¼ lb rump
steak

For the coconut milk:

100 g/4 oz fresh coconut or
50 g/2 oz desiccated
coconut

300 ml/½ pint water

For the marinade:

2 garlic cloves

pinch ground cardamom

pinch ground cinnamon

pinch ground cumin

pinch curry powder

2 teaspoons chopped ginger

freshly ground black pepper

lime wedges and parsley to
garnish

To make the coconut milk, grate fresh coconut and put it into a bowl. Alternatively, put the desiccated coconut in a bowl. Boil the water, pour over the coconut and leave for several hours. Strain through a fine sieve. A speedier method is to put the fresh coconut and water into a liquidizer and switch on until smoothly blended. This gives a thick mixture that can be diluted with more water, or you can use only half the quantity of coconut.

Pour the coconut milk into a container. Peel and crush the garlic, add to the coconut milk with the other marinade ingredients.

Cut the steak into neat 2·5 cm/1 inch pieces. Put into the marinade and leave for several hours.

Thread onto bamboo sticks or long metal skewers. Drain well and cook under the preheated grill or over a barbecue fire. Make sure the barbecue is well heated.

Garnish with wedges of lime, parsley and serve with cooked rice and Satay sauce, page 100, and a crisp salad.

MOROCCAN KEBABS:

The diced meat (known as kababs) is marinated in a buttery spice mixture for several hours before it is placed on metal skewers.

For 550 g/1¼ lb diced lamb or beef, blend 75 g/3 oz melted butter with pinches of the spices used left, plus saffron and cayenne pepper.

Remove from the marinade mixture and press crushed garlic and crushed onion into the meat.

Thread on skewers. Cook under the grill or over a barbecue.

Satay Lembu

Minute Steaks with Mushrooms   ▲ ▲ ✿

SERVES 4

2 teaspoons sunflower oil

40 g/1½ oz butter

4 minute steaks

175 g/6 oz button mushrooms, thinly sliced

2 tablespoons soured cream

1 tablespoon lemon juice

2 teaspoons snipped chives

2 teaspoons chopped fresh parsley

Heat the oil and half the butter in a large frying pan. When the foam subsides, add the steaks and cook over a moderately high heat for 2 minutes on each side for medium steak, or a little longer for well done steak. Transfer the steaks to a heated serving dish and keep hot while preparing the sauce.

Heat the remaining butter in the pan and add the mushrooms. Reduce the heat and cook, stirring, for a few minutes until the mushrooms begin to soften. Stir in the soured cream and lemon juice, then spoon the mushrooms and their juices over the steaks. Sprinkle with the herbs and serve immediately.

SERVING IDEA:

Serve with French fries and a green salad or sauté potatoes and ratatouille. Also good with this dish are glazed carrots and tiny onions.

Minute Steaks with Mushrooms

TO FRY MEAT

Meat is generally fried in a little heated fat or oil. It can be cooked in the fat that flows naturally from the meat. The method of cooking Hamburgers on page 107 shows that, even with lean meat, it is possible to cook with little or no extra fat. Just make certain that the pan is well heated. The one exception to heating the pan first is cooking bacon rashers. These are better placed in a cold pan for cooking.

Stir-frying in a wok requires only a little oil, so it is a popular method of cooking which is not only healthy, but also a very interesting way of preparing food.

The following recipe shows the method of frying coated foods. Once only butter would have been used, but nowadays, most people prefer a mixture of butter and oil.

Cuts of meat for frying are similar to those for grilling, and require similar cooking times, see page 100.

Pork Stroganoff ▲ ▲ ✿ ✿

SERVES 4
450 to 550 g/1 to 1¼ lb lean pork fillet
½ teaspoon mustard powder
½ teaspoon curry powder
salt and freshly ground black pepper
1 tablespoon flour
2 medium onions
100 g/4 oz button mushrooms
50 g/2 oz butter
2 tablespoons olive or sunflower oil
150 ml/¼ pint chicken stock
1 tablespoon tomato purée
150 ml/¼ pint soured cream
2 tablespoons brandy or dry sherry

If time permits, this dish is better if prepared to the stage before the soured cream and brandy or sherry are added and then allowed to cool and stand in the refrigerator for several hours. It is then reheated and the cream and alcohol put in. This gives a better blending of flavours.

Cut the pork into strips about 5 cm/2 inches long and 2·5 cm/1 inch in width and thickness. Blend the mustard powder, curry powder and seasoning with the flour. Toss the meat in the flavoured flour; there should not be a thick coating.

Peel the onions and cut into wafer thin slices. Wipe the mushrooms. Heat the butter and oil in a large frying-pan and cook the meat and onions steadily for 10 minutes. Stir continually, so the food does not become brown. Add the stock and tomato purée. Blend thoroughly, add the mushrooms and cook for a further 5 minutes. Remove from the heat for a minute, so the mixture is not too hot when you add the cream.

Pour in the soured cream and the brandy or sherry, heat gently and serve.

Cooked noodles or boiled potatoes and a crisp green salad are ideal accompaniments to this dish.

BEEF STROGANOFF:
This classic recipe is usually made with beef. Use fillet steak or very good quality rump steak, instead of the pork.

Follow the same method for making the dish, as given on the left. Shorten the cooking time by 5 minutes.

CHICKEN OR TURKEY STROGANOFF:
Both chicken and turkey breasts are delicious prepared and cooked as the Pork Stroganoff, left.

Shorten the cooking time by 3 or 4 minutes.

Escalopes of Veal ▲ ▲ ✿

SERVES 4
4 thin slices of veal, cut from the fillet (leg)
For coating:
salt and freshly ground black pepper
1 level tablespoon flour
1 egg
approximately 50 g/2 oz fine crisp breadcrumbs
For frying:
50 g/2 oz butter
1 tablespoon sunflower oil
To garnish:
lemon slices

The veal slices should be thin. If you would like them to be thinner, place each slice of meat between two sheets of greaseproof or waxed paper and roll gently with a rolling pin; this saves damaging the meat fibres. Blend a little seasoning with the flour and dust the meat with this.

Beat the egg, brush over the meat and then coat in the breadcrumbs. Pat the breadcrumbs into the sides of the meat.

Heat the butter and oil and fry the meat quickly on each side for 2 to 3 minutes until crisp and golden. Lower the heat and cook gently for a further 8 to 10 minutes.

Drain on absorbent paper and garnish with the lemon slices.
NOTE: If time permits, allow the coated food to stand in the refrigerator for a time; the coating adheres better.

TURKEY ESCALOPES:
Use thin slices of turkey breast. Add finely grated lemon zest to the flour in the coating.

LAMB OR PORK ESCALOPES:
These are prepared and cooked in exactly the same way as veal escalopes.

NOISETTES OF LAMB:
These are made by boning and rolling cutlets of lamb into neat rounds. They can be fried without coating or coated as the escalopes.

Lamb in Ginger Cream Sauce, Spiced Lamb Cutlets

Lamb in Ginger Cream Sauce   ▲ ▲   ✿ ✿ ✿

SERVES 4
550 to 675 g/1 to 1 1/2 lb lean
   lamb fillet, cut from the leg
1 tablespoon grated fresh
   ginger or 1/2 to 1 teaspoon
   ground ginger
225 ml/7 1/2 fl oz white wine
100 g/4 oz small button
   mushrooms
25 g/1 oz butter
1 tablespoon sunflower oil
300 ml/1/2 pint lamb or
   chicken stock
salt and ground black pepper
25 g/1 oz ground almonds
150 ml/1/4 pint single cream
To garnish:
25 g/1 oz blanched almonds
few preserved ginger slices
parsley

Cut the meat into 2·5 cm/1 inch slices and then into neat
fingers. Put them into a bowl with the ginger and wine. Leave
for about 30 minutes, turning over once or twice. Lift the lamb
from the marinade, but keep this to add to the sauce later.
Wipe the mushrooms.

Heat the butter and oil in a large frying-pan. Add the lamb
and cook steadily for 10 to 15 minutes, or until the meat is
nearly tender. Pour in the stock and the marinating liquid (this
can be strained if you do not want the small pieces of ginger),
together with the whole mushrooms and a little seasoning.
Cover the pan and allow the liquid to simmer for another 10
minutes, or until the lamb is quite tender.

Blend the ground almonds with the cream. Remove the pan
from the heat and stir the cream mixture into the liquid in the
pan. Return to the heat and cook very gently for a few
minutes, stirring all the time, until you have a very smooth
sauce.

Spoon into a heated dish and top with the browned
almonds and slices of preserved ginger.

Cooked rice or pasta are ideal accompaniments to this dish,
with a mixture of vegetables or a green salad.

USING OTHER MEATS:
Use lamb cutlets, very lean
pork or slices of turkey or
chicken. The poultry requires
a slightly shorter cooking time;
pork a few minutes longer.
When cooking pork, use only
half the butter.

IN A HURRY:
Use ready-cooked meat or
poultry. Prepare and marinate,
as recipe, left, then drain and
heat in the butter for 2 or
3 minutes. Add the marinade,
a little stock and the cream
and almond mixture. Heat for
5 minutes.

Spiced Lamb Cutlets   ▲ ✪

SERVES 4
8 lamb cutlets
For the marinade:
2 garlic cloves
1 teaspoon chopped mint
1 teaspoon allspice
$1/2$ teaspoon ground cinnamon
2 tablespoons oil
2 tablespoons white wine
    vinegar
2 teaspoons brown sugar
salt and freshly ground black
    pepper
To garnish:
cherry tomato halves
watercress and mint

Defrost the cutlets if they have been frozen and dry well with absorbent paper. Peel and crush the garlic. Mix all the ingredients together for the marinade and pour into a long shallow dish. Add the cutlets and allow to stand in the mixture for 1 hour; turn them over at the end of 30 minutes.

Lift the meat from the marinade and hold over the container for a minute so any excess liquid drips off the meat. Grill the cutlets as described on page 100. Add the tomatoes to the grill for the last 2 to 3 minutes of the cooking time. Place on a heated dish, garnish with the tomatoes, watercress and mint.

SAGE AND LEMON CUTLETS:
Grate the rind from 1 lemon and put into a dish with
1 tablespoon lemon juice,
1 teaspoon chopped sage,
2 tablespoons white wine,
1 tablespoon olive oil and a little seasoning.

Marinate the cutlets in this mixture; drain and grill as for Spiced lamb cutlets.

Sesame Lamb   ▲ ▲ ✪

SERVES 4
8 lean lamb cutlets
For the coating:
salt and freshly ground black
    pepper
1 tablespoon flour
1 egg
25 g/1 oz crisp breadcrumbs
1 tablespoon sesame seeds
For cooking:
$1 1/2$ tablespoons sunflower oil
1 teaspoon sesame oil
For the sauce:
1 teaspoon cornflour
pinch chilli powder
1 teaspoon paprika
$1/2$ teaspoon mustard powder
225 ml/$7 1/2$ fl oz chicken stock
    or water and $1/2$ chicken
    stock cube
2 tablespoons sweet sherry

Dry the cutlets well. Mix a little seasoning with the flour and sprinkle over both sides of the meat. Beat the egg and brush over the cutlets. Mix the breadcrumbs and sesame seeds and coat the meat. Chill for 5 to 10 minutes before cooking, if possible; this helps the coating adhere to the meat.

Heat the two oils in a frying-pan. Add the cutlets and fry quickly on either side for 3 to 4 minutes, or until golden brown, then lower the heat and cook for another 2 to 5 minutes, depending upon whether you like lamb well-done or slightly under-cooked. Lift on to a heated dish and keep hot, while you prepare the sauce.

To make the sauce, blend the cornflour, chilli powder, paprika and mustard with the chicken stock. Pour into the pan and stir until slightly thickened. Add the sherry and any seasoning required. Heat for 2 or 3 minutes.

Serve the sauce around the lamb. New potatoes and mangetout peas blend well with this dish.

CHANGING THE FLAVOURS:
A good alternative to the very hot chilli powder is to use a little grated or ground nutmeg.

A few drops of Tabasco sauce give much the same flavour as chilli powder.

Instead of sherry add a little light soy sauce.

NOTE: Never be too generous with sesame oil; it has a very strong flavour.

Lamb in Peanut Butter Sauce   ▲ ✪

SERVES 4
4 lamb chops
3 level tablespoons peanut
    butter
1 tablespoon lemon juice
salt and freshly ground black
    pepper
2 tablespoons soya or corn or
    sunflower oil
1 teaspoon finely chopped mint
150 ml/$1/4$ pint sweet cider or
    white wine
2 tablespoons chopped parsley

Place the chops on to a flat board and make several shallow cuts in the meat on both sides to enable the coating to penetrate better. Blend the peanut butter with the lemon juice and a very little seasoning. Spread over both sides of the meat, giving an even coating.

Heat the oil in a pan, add the chops and cook steadily for 3 minutes on either side. Add the mint and cider or white wine. Cover the pan and cook for 10 minutes, or until the meat is tender. Top with the parsley and serve with pasta or rice and a green vegetable or salad.

USING PEANUT BUTTER:
This is an excellent source of protein and ideal in sandwiches, etc for children, who generally like the flavour.

You can choose between a crunchy or smooth butter.

Peanut butter does not provide the fat in cooking; that is why you find other fats or oils used with it.

MINCED MEAT

The recipes that follow are based upon minced meat. Beef is the most popular, but you will find recipes for other meats and poultry too. The recipes include interesting meat loaves, which are ideal for picnics as well as hot meals at home, and meatballs from various countries; that specialize in them.

Butchers and supermarkets sell different kinds of minced meat, but you may prefer to buy a joint of meat and mince it or chop it in a food processor. Remember, minced meat, whether raw or cooked, deteriorates quickly because of the many cut surfaces.

Bolognese Loaf ▲ ✿✿✿

SERVES 4 TO 6
2 medium onions
2 garlic cloves
1 tablespoon sunflower or
    corn oil
1 × 227 g/8 oz can chopped
    plum tomatoes
1 tablespoon tomato purée
450 g/1 lb minced beef
2 tablespoons beef stock or
    red wine
25 g/1 oz soft breadcrumbs or
    rolled oats
2 tablespoons chopped parsley
2 eggs
salt and freshly ground black
    pepper

Grease a 900 g/2 lb loaf tin very well. Preheat the oven to 160°C/325°F, Gas Mark 3. Peel and finely chop the onions and garlic. Heat the oil in a good-sized saucepan, add the onions and garlic and cook gently for 3 or 4 minutes, taking care they do not brown. Add the tomatoes with the liquid from the can and the tomato purée. Mix together, then add the beef and stock or wine. Remove from the heat.

Stir briskly, so the beef is blended smoothly with the tomato mixture, then mix in the rest of the ingredients. Do not return to the heat.

Spoon into the prepared tin. Cover the top with greased foil and bake for 1$\frac{1}{4}$ hours. Turn out carefully and serve with hot vegetables and a sauce, such as the Onion sauce, page 161 or a Tomato sauce, page 160. If serving cold, place a light weight on top of the loaf; leave in the tin until quite cold.

CURRIED LOAF:
Add 2 teaspoons curry powder to the onions and blend 2 tablespoons smooth chutney into the mixture. Omit the stock or red wine. Serve with a curry sauce.

PORK LOAF:
Use minced lean pork or a mixture of pork and beef. Add 1 teaspoon finely chopped fresh sage or $\frac{1}{2}$ teaspoon dried sage and a peeled, grated dessert apple. Omit the stock or red wine.

Chilli Meatballs ▲ ✿✿

SERVES 4
For the meatballs:
25 g/1 oz soft breadcrumbs
2 tablespoons yogurt or milk
1 medium onion
1 tablespoon oil
450 g/1 lb minced beef or lamb
$\frac{1}{2}$ teaspoon chilli powder
salt and pepper
little flour
For the tomato sauce:
450 g/1 lb tomatoes
1 medium onion
1 small dessert apple
2 tablespoons oil
300 ml/$\frac{1}{2}$ pint water
1 tablespoon tomato purée
1 tablespoon brown sugar
pinch chilli powder (optional)
salt and cayenne or freshly
    ground black pepper

To make the meatballs, put the breadcrumbs into a basin, add the yogurt or milk, stir well and leave to stand while you prepare the other ingredients. Peel and finely chop the onion. Heat the oil in a pan, add the onion and cook for 5 minutes. Blend in the beef or lamb, the softened breadcrumbs and any liquid that might be left, together with the chilli powder and seasoning.

Flour your fingers and form the mixture into small balls, about the size of a walnut. Dust these with flour and leave in the refrigerator while you prepare the sauce.

To make the sauce, skin and chop the tomatoes. Peel and finely chop or grate the onion and apple. Heat the oil in a large frying-pan and cook the onion and apple for 5 minutes, then add the tomatoes and the remainder of the ingredients for the sauce. Stir well to blend, then allow the sauce to simmer gently for 2 or 3 minutes.

Add the meatballs and cook for 15 minutes, turning them over from time to time. The balls become coated with the sauce, which thickens during cooking.

Serve with noodles or other pasta or cooked rice or boiled potatoes and a green salad or firm vegetable, such as carrots.

TO PREPARE AHEAD:
Refrigerate the uncooked or cooked meatballs for a very short time only or freeze them. Prepare the sauce, cook for a few minutes before freezing.

ADAPTING THE RECIPE:
Instead of fresh tomatoes, use 3 × 227 g/8 oz cans of chopped plum tomatoes. Pierce the cans, drain off the liquid and measure this to give 300 ml/$\frac{1}{2}$ pint. Omit the water.

Bolognese Loaf with Tomato Sauce; Classic Hamburgers

Classic Hamburgers   ▲ ✿

MAKES 6
450 g/1 lb best quality chuck
   steak
salt and freshly ground black
   pepper
little fat or oil, for frying

The classic hamburger is incredibly simple to make; it consists of meat only. There are, however, a number of ways in which the meat may be flavoured and extended; these are given on the right and below.

Mince the steak just before cooking if that is possible. It can be chopped in the food processor, but care must be taken that it is not processed for too long, which makes the meat rather sticky in texture. A little salt and pepper can be added at this stage or later. Form into 6 round flat cakes.

If the meat is very lean, you will need to grease the frying-pan with a very little fat or oil. If there is a reasonable amount of fat in the meat, this is not necessary. The pan should be preheated, so the meat starts to cook the moment it touches the surface.

Fry the meat for 2 to 3 minutes – this is when some people like to add a small amount of seasoning. Turn over and cook for the same time on the second side.

Serve on toasted hamburger buns or with salad.

To extend the meat: Add up to 50 g/2 oz of soft fine breadcrumbs, 50 g/2 oz rolled oats, 1 medium sized freshly grated raw potato, 50 g/2 oz smooth mashed potato, 50 g/2 oz finely grated cheese or 50 g/2 oz grated carrots.

TO FLAVOUR HAMBURGERS:
Add a little grated or minced onion, chopped garlic, Worcestershire sauce and mixed chopped herbs.

Top the Hamburgers with rings of pineapple and slices of cheese, then melt under the grill. Add mixed salad and chutney, rings of raw or fried onions.

USE OTHER MEATS:
For an interesting change try using minced lean lamb or minced chicken leg.

Lamb Curry   ▲▲ ✿✿✿

SERVES 4 TO 6

flavourings as given on the
    right or use
1 tablespoon curry powder or
    to taste
1 teaspoon garam masala or to
    taste
To cook the curry:
2 onions
2 to 3 garlic cloves
550 g/1¼ lb lean lamb
50 g/2 oz ghee (clarified butter)
1 tablespoon sunflower oil
1 bay leaf
450 ml/¾ pint water
salt to taste

Heat the seeds in a pan for a few minutes to bring out the
flavours, then add to the other ingredients and grind in a food
processor. Use as desired and store the remainder. You could
use ground spices instead.

Curry powders vary a great deal, so experiment to find the
one you like best. Mix this or the other spices with the garam
masala.

To cook the curry, peel and chop the onions and garlic and
cut the meat into neat dice. Heat the ghee and oil and fry the
onions and garlic with the lamb for a few minutes. Add all the
spices and blend well. Put into a dish, top with the bay leaf.
Cover and leave to stand for an hour or so.

Put the meat mixture into the pan, add the water and a little
salt to taste. Cover and cook gently for 1¼ to 1½ hours.
Remove the bay leaf.

Serve with cooked rice, poppadums and yogurt.

FLAVOURINGS FOR CURRIES:
If you like to make this, you
have a good balance of
flavours with the following
proportions:
1 teaspoon cardamom seeds
2 teaspoons cumin seeds
2 teaspoons coriander seeds
1 teaspoon mustard seeds
1 teaspoon black peppercorns
2 hot dried chillies
1 teaspoon turmeric
pinch ground cloves and
½ teaspoon ground ginger

Gammon in Cider   ▲▲ ✿✿

SERVES 4 TO 6

1.1 to 1.3 kg/2½ to 3 lb boned
    unsmoked gammon
1 litre/1¾ pints sweet cider
225 g/8 oz small carrots
225 g/8 oz shallots or very
    small onions
1 teaspoon black peppercorns
    or good shake black pepper
1 small bunch parsley

Unsmoked or green bacon, as used in this recipe, does not
need soaking before cooking, although it can be rinsed in
plenty of running cold water before cooking.

A smoked bacon joint should be soaked in cold water to
cover overnight or for several hours. Discard the water.

Put the gammon in a pan with the cider. Bring the liquid to
the boil and simmer for 20 minutes. Peel the vegetables and
add to the pan with the pepper and parsley. Cover and
simmer for an hour, or until the bacon is tender.

Lift the gammon from the liquid, carve and serve with the
vegetables. Unthickened liquid can be spooned over the
gammon or used in the Cider parsley sauce, see right.

CIDER PARSLEY SAUCE:
Heat 25 g/1 oz butter or
margarine and stir in 25 g/1 oz
flour. Add 300 ml/½ pint cider.
Stir as the sauce comes to the
boil and thickens. Remove
from the heat and add 2 to 3
tablespoons chopped parsley
and 4 tablespoons single
cream. Heat without boiling.
Season to taste and add a
little French mustard.

Marinated Gammon   ▲▲▲ ✿✿✿✿

SERVES UP TO 8

1.5 kg/3½ lb joint lean smoked
    gammon
For the marinade:
6 juniper berries
150 ml/¼ pint white wine
150 ml/¼ pint pineapple syrup
2 tablespoons vinegar
1 teaspoon black peppercorns
1 tablespoon olive oil
2 fresh bay leaves
For the glaze:
3 tablespoons Demerara sugar
1½ teaspoons mustard powder
For the sauce:
2 level teaspoons arrowroot
150 ml/¼ pint water
2 teaspoons tomato purée
sugar to taste
To garnish:
pineapple rings
watercress

Smoked gammon, with its stronger flavour, is a good choice
for this dish, but unsmoked or green bacon can be used, in
which case omit the stage of soaking in water.

Place the smoked bacon into a bowl of cold water and leave
for 2 to 3 hours then drain.

Mix the ingredients for the marinade in a casserole, add the
gammon and leave for 24 hours, turning over once or twice.

Preheat the oven to 190°C/375°F, Gas Mark 5. Lift the
gammon from the marinade; keep this to add to the sauce.
Wrap the gammon loosely in foil and cook for 1¼ hours.

Unwrap the gammon, cut away the rind and score (cut) the
fat in a neat design. Blend the Demerara sugar and mustard
powder and press into the gammon fat.

Return the joint to the oven with the glazed side uppermost;
do not cover. Cook for a further 25 minutes.

To make the sauce, strain the marinade into a saucepan.
Blend the arrowroot with the water and add to the pan with
the tomato purée. Stir over a moderate heat until the sauce
thickens, then add a little sugar to taste, or see below.

Serve the gammon hot garnished with pineapple and
watercress. If serving the sauce cold, omit the sugar and add
2 tablespoons redcurrant jelly to the hot sauce.

CHEAPER JOINTS OF BACON:
Both the dishes on this page
are made from gammon – a
prime cut of bacon. It is very
lean and tender. You can use
forehock or collar joints
instead

If buying the same weight of
the cheaper bacon for this
recipe, soak and then simmer
the joint in water for 1¼
hours. Drain and dry well.
Marinate as before and roast
at 180°C/350°F, Gas Mark 4
for 1 hour.

In the recipe for Gammon
in cider, increase the cooking
time by 50 per cent.

Stifado

Stifado (Greek Beef Stew)   ▲ ✪ ✪ ✪

SERVES 4 TO 6
675 g/1¹/₂ lb stewing beef
450 g/1 lb very small pearl
    onions
2 medium onions
1 or 2 garlic cloves
3 tomatoes
3 tablespoons olive oil
300 ml/¹/₂ pint water
2 fresh bay leaves or 1 dried
    bay leaf
1 tablespoons red wine
    vinegar
salt and freshly ground black
    pepper
150 ml/¹/₄ pint red wine
50 g/2 oz feta cheese, crumbled
To garnish:
chopped parsley

There are many recipes for this famous Greek dish, but all
have a very high percentage of onions.

Cut the beef into small dice, peel the pearl onions and peel
and finely chop the larger onions and garlic. Skin and chop the
tomatoes. Heat half the oil in a large pan, add the chopped
onions, garlic and beef and cook steadily until golden in
colour. Add the water, bring just to simmering point then add
the tomatoes, bay leaves or leaf, the vinegar, seasoning and
the red wine. Cover the pan and simmer steadily for about
1¹/₂ hours or until the meat is tender.

Heat the remaining oil in a pan and cook the small onions
steadily until golden and tender. Stir the onions into the stew
and season to taste. Add the cheese to the stew and return
uncovered to the oven for a few minutes, until the cheese
begins to melt.

Remove the bay leaves or leaf and top with chopped
parsley.

TO REHEAT:
Like all stews, Stifado has an
excellent flavour if it is cooked
one day, allowed to cool,
stored in the refrigerator and
then reheated.

Make sure the food is
thoroughly reheated. This can
be done in the pan, or in a
dish in the oven for
approximately 40 minutes at
160°C/325°F, Gas Mark 3. Add
the cooked onions after 15
minutes.

If you are freezing this dish,
it is better to do so without
the small onions. Cook and
add when reheating.

Steak and Kidney Pudding   ▲▲ ✿✿✿✿

SERVES 4 TO 6

For the pastry:
300 g/10oz flour, see method
pinch salt
150 g/5 oz shredded suet or
    margarine or low-fat spread
water to bind

For the filling:
550 g/1¼ lb stewing beef
100 to 175 g/4 to 6 oz ox
    kidney
1½ tablespoons flour
salt and freshly ground black
    pepper
3 to 4 tablespoons beef stock
    or water

Most people like to use self-raising flour or add 2 level teaspoons baking powder to this quantity of flour to make the pastry but if you like a very delicate crust, use plain flour.

Wholemeal flour may be used, or half wholemeal and half white flour. Sift the flour, or flour and baking powder, and salt into a bowl. If using wholemeal flour, tip the bran – that does not go through the sieve – back into the flour.

Add the suet to the flour or rub in the margarine or low-fat spread. This is one of the recipes where low-fat spread can be used very successfully.

Add sufficient water to give a soft rolling consistency.

Roll out the dough and use just under three-quarters to line a greased 1·2 litre/2 pint basin.

For the filling, cut the beef into 2·5 cm/1 inch pieces. Skin the kidney and remove the core. Cut into similar sized pieces. The traditional method was to cut the beef into strips, cut the ox kidney into small pieces and then roll the beef around the kidney, so it was evenly distributed. Blend the flour and seasoning and roll the meat in it. Put into the pastry-lined basin and add just enough liquid to come three-quarters of the way up the basin.

Roll out the remaining pastry into a circle to cover the filling. Damp the edges of the pastry, put on the lid and seal the edges firmly. Cover with greased greaseproof paper and foil, see right hand column. Cook in a steamer over boiling water for 4 hours. Do not forget to fill up the saucepan under the steamer from time to time.

Serve with a slightly thickened gravy and mixed vegetables.

STEAK AND KIDNEY PIE:
Prepare the meat as in the recipe, left.

Coat in 25 g/1 oz seasoned flour. Heat 50 g/2 oz fat or 2 tablespoons oil in a pan, add the meat and cook gently until golden brown; stir to prevent the meat sticking. Add 600 ml/1 pint beef stock.

Bring to the boil and cook until thickened. Cover the pan and simmer gently for 1¾ hours, or until the meat is almost tender. Cool, put into a 1·2 litre/2 pint pie dish, with some of the gravy; the rest is served with the pie.

Cover with flaky pastry or several layers of phyllo pastry.

Brush with egg and bake for 20 minutes at 220°C/350°F, Gas Mark 7, then a further 15 to 20 minutes at 180°C/350°F, Gas Mark 4.

Kidneys in Tarragon

Salt Beef and Vegetables

▲ ▲   ✿ ✿ ✿ ✿

SERVES 4 TO 6
a joint of salted brisket or
    silverside, weighing about
    1 kg/2¼ lb
mixed root vegetables
freshly ground black pepper
For the dumplings:
ingredients as pastry, page
    110, plus chopped herbs or
    mustard to flavour

Soak the beef in water to cover overnight. Put into a pan with enough fresh water to cover and add the vegetables. Add the pepper and cover the pan. Bring just to boiling point, lower the heat and simmer for 1½ hours, or until the meat is almost tender.

Make the pastry, see page 110 but be slightly more generous with the water, so you have a softer mixture. Divide into 8 to 12 portions. Roll in balls with floured hands.

Make sure the liquid in the pan is boiling briskly and drop in the dumplings. Continue to cook in boiling liquid for 10 minutes, then lower the heat to simmering for a further 5 to 10 minutes. Serve the vegetables with the meat and dumplings.

If serving cold allow to cool in the liquid.

BOILED BACON:
Allow the same cooking time as in the recipe left for collar or forehock, but only 1¼ hours total cooking time for gammon.

These joints are ideal to serve cold with salad.

Kidneys Périgord

▲ ▲   ✿

SERVES 4
8 to 12 lambs' kidneys
100 g/4 oz small button
    mushrooms
25 g/1 oz butter
1 tablespoon sunflower oil
150 ml/¼ pint beef stock or
    canned beef consommé
4 tablespoons double cream
    or fromage frais
2 tablespoons brandy
    (optional)
salt and freshly ground black
    pepper
4 slices of bread
little butter or liver pâté

Skin and halve the kidneys and remove the core. Wipe the mushrooms. Heat the butter and oil and cook the kidneys with the mushrooms for 5 minutes. Add the stock or consommé and continue cooking for a further 5 minutes. Stir in the cream or fromage frais, heat very gently then add the brandy and seasoning.

Toast the bread, spread with the butter or pâté and spoon the kidneys on top. Serve at once.

Kidneys can be fried with bacon. Prepare them as above. Cook the bacon for 2 or 3 minutes, remove from the pan and then cook the kidneys in the bacon fat. Return the bacon to the pan just before serving.

USING THE MICROWAVE:
Cut the kidneys into quarters. Use just the butter or the oil, or half the quantities given left. You do not need as much fat in the microwave.

Cook the kidneys with the fat for 5 minutes in a covered dish. Add the mushrooms and cook for 2 minutes. Pour in the liquid and cook for 1 minute – all on FULL POWER.

Set to DEFROST, add the cream and seasoning and heat. Add the brandy while standing.

Kidneys in Tarragon

▲ ▲   ✿ ✿

SERVES 4 TO 6
450 g/1 lb lambs' kidneys
2 to 3 small onions
100 g/4 oz button mushrooms
3 streaky bacon rashers
50 g/2 oz butter or margarine
1 tablespoon sunflower oil
150 ml/¼ pint chicken stock
2 tablespoons dry sherry
2 teaspoons chopped tarragon
salt and freshly ground black
    pepper
150 ml/¼ pint soured cream
To garnish:
tarragon sprigs
fried or baked croûtons, see
    page 118

Remove the outer membrane (skin) from the kidneys. Halve each kidney and take out the white core and fat.

Peel and slice the onions and separate into rings. Wipe the mushrooms. Remove the stalks and chop them, but leave the mushroom caps whole. Derind the bacon and chop the rashers.

Heat half the butter or margarine with the oil and bacon rinds in a frying-pan. Fry the kidneys and onions until tender. Lift out of the pan and discard the bacon rinds. Add the remaining butter or margarine to the pan and fry the chopped mushroom stalks, whole mushrooms and chopped bacon for 5 minutes.

Replace the kidneys and onion rings. Add the stock, sherry, chopped tarragon and seasoning. Simmer for about 5 minutes to heat all the ingredients and allow the liquid to reduce by about half. Stir the soured cream into the mixture just before serving and heat gently for 2 to 3 minutes.

Spoon the kidney mixture into a heated serving dish. Garnish with tarragon and serve with croûtons and a green salad.

USING TARRAGON:
This is a strongly flavoured herb and should be used sparingly. It goes well with chicken, see below.

CHICKEN IN TARRAGON:
Follow the recipe on the left, but use 450 g/1 lb diced raw chicken. This is a good dish in which to use chicken legs. The cooking time for chicken is similar to that for kidneys.

Stir-Fry Liver

Stir-Fry Liver   ▲ ✪✪

SERVES 4

350 to 450 g/12 oz to 1 lb
   lambs' liver

For the marinade:

2 teaspoons thin honey
1 teaspoon sesame oil
150 ml/¼ pint orange juice
1 teaspoon finely grated
   orange rind

175 g/6 oz young green beans
100 g/4 oz young carrots
1 large red pepper
1 bunch spring onions or 8
   very small young leeks
1 × 227 g/8 oz can butter
   beans
2 tablespoons sunflower oil
1½ level teaspoons cornflour
150 ml/¼ pint lamb or chicken
   stock
1 tablespoon light soy sauce
seasoning

Cut the liver into slices and then into narrow fingers. Mix the ingredients for the marinade together, add the liver and allow to stand for 30 minutes, turning it over once or twice.

Cut the ends off the green beans; if large, cut into smaller pieces. Peel the carrots and cut into narrow strips. Halve and deseed the pepper, then cut the pulp into strips of about the same width and length as the carrots. Chop half the onions or leeks. Trim the remainder, but leave them whole. Drain the canned beans.

Lift the liver from the marinade. Keep the marinade for the sauce. Heat the oil in a wok or frying-pan, put in the green beans, carrots and chopped and whole onions or leeks. Stir-fry for 5 minutes, add the strips of red pepper and continue cooking for a further 2 minutes. Stir well throughout. Finally, add the liver and canned beans. Stir-fry for 2 to 3 minutes, depending upon how well you like liver cooked.

Blend the cornflour with the marinade, stock and the soy sauce. Pour into the wok or frying-pan and continue stirring as the sauce thickens. Season to taste.

Serve with a mixture of long grain and wild rice.

COOKING LIVER:

Calves' liver has the tenderest texture and most delicate flavour, but that would be less apparent in this recipe, so it is better to use lambs' liver, which is less expensive.

Liver can be pan-fried, grilled or baked. In order to keep the meat moist use a reasonable amount of oil or fat in cooking. Never cook for too long as the liver becomes hard and unappetising.

Liver with Apple Slices   ▲ ✿

SERVES 4
450 g/1 lb lambs' liver
2 teaspoons sunflower oil
2 to 3 dessert apples
300 ml/¹/₂ pint apple juice

Cut the liver into thin strips. Heat the oil in a wok or frying-pan and toss the liver in it for 1 or 2 minutes, just to colour it slightly. Transfer to a plate using a slotted spoon. Core the apples but do not peel them. Cut into thin slices or rings.

Pour the apple juice into the wok or frying-pan, bring to the boil, add the apple slices and cook for 5 minutes. Return the liver to the pan and cook for 2 to 5 minutes, according to how well you like it cooked.

ADDING SAGE:
Sage is an excellent herb to use with liver. It is strongly flavoured, so use only 2 small sprigs.

Sweet and Sour Lambs' Hearts   ▲ ▲ ✿✿✿✿

SERVES 4
6 to 8 lambs' hearts
2 medium onions
300 ml/¹/₂ pint dry white wine
salt and freshly ground black
    pepper
150 ml/¹/₄ pint lamb or chicken
    stock
1 × 227 g/8 oz can pineapple
    rings in syrup
2 tablespoons sunflower or
    corn oil
1 tablespoon brown sugar
2 teaspoons light soy sauce
2 teaspoons cornflour

Skin the hearts and cut away any gristle and fat. Cut the meat into thin fingers. Peel and finely chop the onions. Put the meat and onions into a casserole with the wine and a very little seasoning. Cover and cook in a preheated oven, set to 160°C/325°F, Gas Mark 3 for 1¹/₂ hours.

Pour the stock into a measure and add enough pineapple syrup to make a total of 225 ml/7¹/₂ fl oz. Cut the pineapple rings into neat pieces.

Lift the meat from the wine with a perforated spoon. Save the wine and onions to add to the sauce. Heat the oil in a wok or frying-pan, turn the hearts in it, then add the wine and onions from the casserole, half the stock and pineapple syrup, the brown sugar and soy sauce. Heat for 5 or 6 minutes.

Blend the cornflour with the remaining stock and pineapple syrup mixture. Pour over the other ingredients and stir until a slightly thickened and clear sauce is formed. Add most of the pineapple pieces and any extra seasoning required. Heat for 1 or 2 minutes. Garnish with the last of the pineapple pieces.

Cooked rice and a crisp green vegetable or salad go well with this dish. Pasta is another good accompaniment.

SWEET AND SOUR DISHES:
This clever blending of flavours is very popular. You can use exactly the same ingredients to add to other foods.

SWEET AND SOUR BEEF:
Cut good quality stewing beef into fingers and use instead of the hearts. Allow 1¹/₂ hours for the first stage of the recipe.

SWEET AND SOUR CHICKEN:
Follow the directions for lamb, using diced chicken from either the leg or the breast.

Golden Sweetbreads   ▲ to ▲ ▲
                                          ✿✿✿ to ✿✿✿✿

SERVES 4
450 g/1 lb lambs' or calves'*
    sweetbreads
1 tablespoon white vinegar
3 medium onions
4 medium carrots
40 g/1¹/₂ oz butter or
    margarine
1 pint/ 600 ml chicken stock
1 teaspoon grated lemon rind
salt and freshly ground black
    pepper
1 tablespoon chopped parsley
1 tablespoon chopped chives
¹/₂ teaspoon chopped thyme
To garnish:
lemon slices

* expensive and rather scarce;
    lambs' sweetbreads are
    much cheaper

It is advisable, if time permits, to soak the sweetbreads in several lots of cold water for 1 to 2 hours; add the vinegar to the last lot of water. Even if this stage is omitted, the next stage is important, for it whitens the sweetbreads.

Blanch the sweetbreads by putting them into fresh cold water, bringing this water just to boiling point and then discarding it.

Skin the sweetbreads and remove any gristle. A classic method of dealing with them is to put them on a board and put a second board and weight on top. Leave for a time to flatten, then slice. This is not essential; simply skin and remove the gristle.

Chop the onions and carrots fairly finely. Heat the butter or margarine and toss the vegetables in it. Add the chicken stock, lemon rind and a little seasoning. Cover and simmer for 20 minutes. Sieve or liquidize, return to the pan, add the sweetbreads and cook for 20 minutes with the herbs. Season to taste. Garnish with the lemon slices.

NEWER SAUCES:
The recipe for Golden sweetbreads illustrates how you can make a sauce with the vegetables in which the food was cooked.

In this case, the meat is cooked in the sauce, but in other cases, you can dish up the meat and make the sauce from any vegetables used to flavour it.

Do this when simmering bacon, salted beef, etc. You have a lighter and more interesting sauce than when using flour-based recipes.

POULTRY & GAME

Nowadays, the price of poultry makes it a most economical source of food. Both chickens and turkeys, whether as individual portions or whole birds, enable us to make a range of interesting dishes. Chicken, guinea fowl, turkey and game birds are low in fat and calories, so they fit within the modern recommendations for healthy eating. While duck and goose are higher in natural fat, they can be cooked in such a way that much of this is removed, see page 116.

There is advice on wise buying of these foods on pages 30 and 31. Always store poultry and game carefully, as they are highly perishable foods.

TO ROAST CHICKEN AND TURKEY

The weight is for a stuffed bird.
Fresh birds: Use temperature **A** (see page 92). Allow 15 minutes per 450 g/1 lb and 15 minutes over for birds up to 5·4 kg/12 lb in weight. When the weight exceeds this, add an extra 12 minutes per 450 g/1 lb up to 9 kg/20 lb. For every 450 g/1 lb over 9 kg/20 lb add an extra 10 minutes. You can reduce the heat to 190°C/375°F, Gas Mark 5 after the first 1 hour's cooking.
Defrosted frozen birds: Use temperature **B** (see page 92). Allow 25 minutes per 450 g/1 lb and 22 to 25 minutes over for a bird up to 5·4 kg/12 lb in weight. When the weight exceeds this, add an extra 20 minutes per 450 g/1 lb up to 9 kg/20 lb. For every 450 g/1 lb over 9kg/20 lb allow an extra 15 minutes.

Both chicken and turkeys to be roasted should be young and tender birds. General advice on buying poultry is given on page 32.

There are two kinds of chicken sold for roasting, the ordinary white-fleshed variety and golden-coloured, corn-fed birds.

When buying a frozen turkey, you can choose between ordinary birds and those labelled 'self-basting'. These have fat inserted under the skin to help cooking.

The advice on defrosting before roasting whole birds should be taken very seriously. It can be a health hazard if the bird is not entirely thawed. The flesh might well appear cooked perfectly, but the inside of the body could still be inadequately heated.

Stuffing chicken and turkey: Do not put stuffing inside the body cavity of the birds. This can prevent heat penetrating through all the flesh. Put the stuffing at the neck end or under the skin of the breast. The illustrations below show how to loosen the breast skin and insert the stuffing.

To keep the flesh moist: Brush the breast of the bird with softened butter or oil.

When roasting large birds, where the cooking time is long, place the bird breast-side downwards for the first half of the cooking time. This enables the fat to run down to the breast – the driest part. At the end of this period, turn the bird over so the breast is uppermost, and continue cooking.

One of the best ways of covering roasting poultry is simply to place foil over the roasting tin, rather like a tent, page 90.

Usual accompaniments with chicken and turkey: Bacon rolls, sausages, and a

TO STUFF A CHICKEN BREAST:

Insert two fingers under the skin at the neck end of the bird. Gently lift it to allow enough space to fill with stuffing.

Use a small spoon to spread the stuffing evenly over the breast. Press the skin down to make the bird a good shape again.

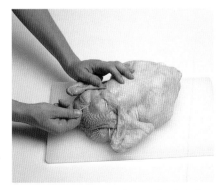

Insert one or two wooden cocktail sticks at the neck end of the bird to keep the stuffing and skin in position.

Roast Turkey with all the trimmings

TO TELL WHEN POULTRY IS COOKED:
Insert the tip of a knife into the bird where the leg joins the body. If any pink juice flows then the bird needs cooking for a little longer.

The timings given under both **A** and **B** are correct for the average bird, but today's methods of rearing poultry do produce some large turkeys that are exceptionally tender. This means they may be cooked in a slightly shorter time so it is wise to test the flesh, as described above, about three-quarters of the way through cooking.

If you find the bird almost cooked and the meal is not to be served for some time, either reduce the heat more, or take the bird out of the oven for a short period, then return it a little later.

thickened gravy with Bread and Cranberry sauces, pages 117 and 161. Try some of the newer sauces too.

Stuffings vary a great deal – Parsley and thyme is traditional and Chestnut stuffing is a modern favourite. These are on pages 116, 162 and 163.

To carve chicken and turkey: Allow a bird up to 5·4 kg/12 lb to stand for at least 10 minutes before carving and a larger bird to stand for 15 minutes. Cover with foil, so the bird keeps hot. This makes carving much easier. Smaller chickens can be cut into joints but larger ones are better carved like a turkey.

Have two heated meat dishes available; put the whole bird on one and have a second dish on which to put the carved portions.

First cut away one leg from the body of the bird. This is not difficult; simply feel the place where the leg bone joins the body and insert the knife there and make a firm, downwards cut.

Carve slices from the breast and slices from the leg. Give each person some of the breast (light) and the leg (dark) meat, unless they express a preference for just one, if necessary slicing meat from the thigh to serve to everyone.

Repeat with the second side of the bird if more meat is required.

Spoon portions of stuffing beside the meat.

TO ADD A NEW FLAVOUR WHEN ROASTING CHICKEN OR TURKEY
The following suggestions make a pleasant change. Where quantities are given, these are sufficient for a large chicken or small turkey or the size of bird(s) mentioned.

Cranberry glaze: Melt 3 tablespoons cranberry jelly. Brush over the breast about 20 minutes before the end of the cooking time. Redcurrant jelly may be used instead.

Garlic: Peel 2 garlic cloves, cut into thin slivers and insert under the skin of the bird before roasting. Alternatively, crush the garlic, blend with melted butter or oil and brush over the bird before roasting, as page 114.

Herbed chestnut stuffing: First loosen the skin under the breast, as described on page 114.

Blend 225 g/8 oz canned chestnut purée with 2 tablespoons melted butter or margarine, 2 tablespoons chopped parsley, 1 crushed garlic clove, 1 teaspoon chopped thyme, 2 tablespoons single cream and plenty of seasoning. Carefully insert the mixture under the skin. Roast as usual.

Lemon: Grate a little zest from 1 or 2 lemons. Blend with 50 g/2 oz melted butter, 3 tablespoons lemon juice and a little seasoning. Brush over the breast of the bird before roasting.

Lemon and herb coating: Blend 2 tablespoons melted butter with 1 tablespoon lemon juice and 2 tablespoons chopped mixed herbs (parsley, chives and a very little thyme). This is enough to coat 2 poussins or a medium-sized chicken.

Lemon and honey coating: Blend 2 tablespoons thin honey and 3 tablespoons lemon juice. Brush over the bird about 30 minutes before the end of the cooking time.

Rosemary: Make slits in the skin of the bird and insert single rosemary leaves in these. This is a strongly flavoured herb, so do not be over-generous with it.

Spiced coating: Blend 1 teaspoon curry paste (use curry powder if this is not available) with 75 g/3 oz softened butter or margarine, add ½ teaspoon ground cinnamon, several drops of Tabasco sauce or a pinch of chilli powder. Spread over the breast before roasting.

Stilton chicken: Blend 100 g/4 oz Stilton cheese with 50 g/2 oz soft cream cheese and 25 g/1 oz butter or margarine. Add 2 teaspoons chopped parsley and a shake of freshly ground black pepper. Loosen the skin away from the breast of the bird and insert the filling under it. It keeps the chicken so moist that very little oil needs to be brushed over the bird before roasting. This filling is enough for a medium-sized bird. It could be used for a small turkey or 2 to 3 poussins.

TO ROAST DUCK AND GOOSE

Although geese have become rather scarce and very expensive, ducks are plentiful, either as fresh or frozen birds, or cut into portions. They are reasonable in price.

Page 32 gives advice on buying poultry. It is important that whole birds are completely defrosted before cooking; see the information about this and method of roasting on page 114 under chicken and turkey. It is better to cook stuffing separately with these birds, so the skin becomes crisp.

For some people, the problem of cooking either duck or goose is to prevent them being greasy. Modern breeding of ducks, in particular, has produced lean birds, but it is the method of cooking which is of great importance.

If the skin does not become really crisp, raise the heat of the oven to temperature **A** for the last 15 minutes if cooking a duck, 25 to 30 minutes for a goose.

Usual accompaniments with duck or goose: Thickened gravy, apple sauce and Sage and onion stuffing. You will find recipes for both the sauce and stuffing under roasting pork, on pages 97 and 98.

Carving duck or goose: A duck is cut into neat joints; a goose is carved as a turkey, see page 115.

TO ADD A NEW FLAVOUR TO DUCK AND GOOSE
Both these birds blend well with fruits. Serve the roasted birds with Cranberry sauce, page 161. If you are making this specially, add a little orange juice to the cranberries.

The following suggestions give a new look to these birds. Where quantities are given, they serve 4 people.

HOW TO ROAST DUCK OR GOOSE:
Weigh the birds to ascertain the total cooking times. This is similar to that for chicken and turkey, see page 114 temperatures **A** and **B** page 92. To encourage the duck or goose to have a crisp skin place the bird on a rack in the tin. Do not cover.

Prick the birds lightly at regular intervals to encourage the fat to spurt out.

Use temperature **A** for prime birds and temperature **B** for defrosted frozen birds.

Roast Duck garnished with glazed clementines

BREAD SAUCE:
SERVES 4
A microwave is invaluable for making bread sauce. As the evaporation of liquid is less than in an ordinary pan, use just over half the amount of liquid given in the recipe below. Use a basin instead of the saucepan.

Pour 300 ml/$^1/_2$ pint milk into a saucepan, add a small peeled onion. 2 or 3 cloves may be inserted into the onion, if liked. Heat the milk and onion with a little seasoning. Remove from the heat and cover the pan. Infuse for at least 30 minutes. Remove the onion. Add 50 g/2 oz soft breadcrumbs, plus 25 g/1 oz butter or margarine. Heat gently, stirring all the time, until thickened. A tablespoon of cream can be added.

The sauce can be made in a basin over hot water to prevent it sticking to a pan.

Apricot sauce: Cook 450 g/1 lb apricots with 50 g/2 oz sugar, 1 tablespoon lemon juice and 150 ml/$^1/_4$ pint water. Sieve or liquidize and add 2 tablespoons apricot brandy just before serving. Garnish each portion of duck or goose with a halved apricot and a few flaked almonds.

Another version of this sauce can be made by adding sliced cooked or canned apricots to a gravy made with the duck giblets, then flavouring this with apricot brandy.

Black cherry sauce: Stone 450 g/1 lb black cherries by inserting the bent end of a hairpin into the fruit. Hook this around the stone and pull firmly. The cherries can be cooked with water or with very well-strained giblet stock to give a subtle savoury flavour.

Put the fruit into a pan with 300 ml/$^1/_2$ pint water or stock and 50 g/2 oz sugar. Poach gently for 15 minutes, then strain the fruit. Blend 2 level teaspoons arrowroot with the liquid and stir over the heat until thickened. Add the cherries. Heat and add 2 to 3 tablespoons cherry brandy just before serving, if desired.

This sauce can be made with Morello cherries, but as these are very sour, you will need more sugar. It is difficult to stone Morello cherries, so the fruit and liquid can be sieved to make a purée. In this case, there is no need to thicken with arrowroot.

Blackcurrant coulis: Cook 350 g/12 oz blackcurrants with 50 g/2 oz sugar and 150 ml/$^1/_4$ pint water. Sieve to give a clear thin sauce. Reheat with 2 to 3 tablespoons cassis. Top portions of duck or goose with a few cooked blackcurrants and serve with the coulis.

Orange sauce: Cut the peel from 2 large oranges. Discard the bitter white pith and cut the orange zest into matchstick pieces. Squeeze out the juice; add extra juice to make 225 ml/7$^1/_2$ fl oz. Simmer the zest in 225 ml/7$^1/_2$ fl oz well-strained duck stock or water for 15 minutes. Blend 2 level teaspoons arrowroot with the orange juice, add to the zest and liquid with 50 g/2 oz sugar, or to taste. Stir over the heat until thickened. You can add 2 tablespoons Curaçao just before serving.

Instead of the apple or redcurrant jelly you could use extra sugar to sweeten.

TO ROAST GAME BIRDS

GAME CHIPS:
Cut potatoes into wafer thin slices and dry very well before cooking. Heat the oil to 190°C/375°F. Put the potatoes into the heated frying-basket and lower into the hot oil. Cook for 2 to 3 minutes until softened. You can do several batches like this. Remove from the oil, check the temperature then add the potatoes for a second frying of 1 minute, or until very crisp and golden in colour. Drain on absorbent paper and serve.

Commercial potato crisps can be heated for a few minutes and served instead.

FRIED CRUMBS:
So often one is served very fine fried crumbs, but they are much nicer if slightly coarser.

To 100 g/4 oz breadcrumbs, allow 50 g/2 oz butter or 2 1/2 tablespoons sunflower oil. Heat the butter or oil in a frying-pan, add the crumbs and stir over the heat until golden in colour.

To save fat, crisp and brown the crumbs on a flat tin in the oven.

There is an excellent selection of game available, the most usual being pheasants, when in season, and the small quail, which are very good value.

All game birds tend to have dry flesh, so they need careful cooking. The hints on covering food when roasting, which are on page 90, are useful.

The breasts of birds can be covered with fatty bacon, a little oil or softened butter and you can put a small piece of butter – or soft cream cheese – inside the bird.

Roast young pheasants and grouse as chicken, on page 114. Allow the same cooking times given for chicken on temperature **A**. If you have bought frozen birds, defrost them completely and cook at temperature **B**, also on page 114.

Smaller birds, such as partridge and very young pigeon (known as squab), need about 45 minutes at temperature **A** or 1 1/4 hours at temperature **B**. Check very carefully that you really have bought young pigeons, for they can be tough when older and are better cooked as the Norfolk casserole on page 120.

The quail on sale is very young and tender and so, too, is most woodcock. These need about 30 minutes' cooking at temperature **A** or 45 minutes at the lower setting, given in temperature **B**. These small birds are often placed on toast before cooking, so any drippings flavour this and are not lost in the roasting tin.

The skin of wild ducks, like teal, mallard and widgeon, does not have crisp-up skins like that of cultivated birds, so they can be covered during roasting. Allow the same cooking times as given on page 92 under temperatures **A** and **B**. These birds are frequently fairly tough, so slower roasting is advisable.

Usual accompaniments with roast game birds: Bacon rolls, thickened gravy, game chips and fried crumbs, with redcurrant, apple, rowan or cranberry jelly. Bread sauce, see page 117, is frequently served with roast game, as it is with chicken and turkey.

Small sausages not only add flavour to the dish, but they help to 'eke out' the more costly game.

Wild ducks can be served with the same accompaniments as cultivated ducks, see pages 116 and 117. They are particularly good with cooked beetroot, on page 148 and red cabbage, page 148.

Guinea Fowl in Cherry Sauce   ▲▲ ✿✿✿

SERVES 4 TO 6
2 guinea fowl, with giblets if
    possible
450 ml/3/4 pint water
1 bay leaf
salt and freshly ground black
    pepper
225 ml/7 1/2 fl oz giblet or
    chicken stock, see method
75 g/3 oz butter
1 × 227 g/8 oz can black
    cherries in syrup
2 level teaspoons cornflour
150 ml/1/4 pint red wine
To garnish:
fried croûtons, see right

If you have giblets with the birds, put these into the water with the bay leaf and seasoning. Cover the pan and simmer for 1 hour. Strain off 225 ml/7 1/2 fl oz stock. If giblets are unavailable, substitute chicken stock. Use this in the sauce.

Preheat the oven at 190°C/375°F, Gas Mark 5. Take 40 g/1 1/2 oz of the butter, divide it into two and put one portion inside each bird. Spread the rest of the butter over the birds. Place in a roasting tin. Cover the tin tightly with foil, but do not wrap the birds. Roast for 55 minutes to 1 hour.

Strain the cherries and stone if necessary, as described on page 117. Blend the cornflour with 150 ml/1/4 pint of the cherry syrup.

Lift the guinea fowl on to a heated dish and keep hot. Pour 1 tablespoon of the fat from the roasting tin into a pan and add the cornflour stock and cherry syrup. Stir as the liquid comes to the boil and thickens slightly, then add the stoned cherries, red wine and seasoning. Heat, but do not allow to boil.

Carve the guinea fowl and arrange on a dish with the sauce. Add the croûtons immediately before serving.

TO MAKE FRIED CROÛTONS:
Cut slices of bread about 5 mm/1/4 inch thick. Cut into triangles or small rounds. Either deep-fry or cook in a little shallow fat until crisp and golden in colour. Drain on absorbent paper.

Croûtons can be made ahead and reheated for a few minutes on a flat dish in the oven. They can also be frozen then reheated.

Burgundy Pheasants   ▲▲▲ ✿✿✿

SERVES 4 TO 6

2 plump young pheasants with
   giblets

salt and freshly ground black
   pepper

small sprig of thyme or pinch
   dried thyme

50 g/2 oz butter

300 ml/¹/₂ pint red Burgundy
   wine

I level tablespoon arrowroot
   or cornflour*

2 tablespoons redcurrant jelly

2 tablespoons cocktail onions

2 tablespoons stuffed green
   olives (optional)

To garnish:

redcurrants

parsley sprigs

* Arrowroot gives greater
   clarity to sauces than flour
   or cornflour. It has the
   same thickening quality as
   cornflour. Use 15 g/¹/₂ oz
   arrowroot or cornflour in
   place of 25 g/I oz flour.

Put the pheasant giblets into a pan with water to cover, a little seasoning and the thyme. Cover the pan and simmer for 45 minutes. Strain the liquid and boil briskly, if necessary, until reduced to 300 ml/¹/₂ pint stock.

If you have no giblets from which to make stock, use chicken stock or water plus rather less than ¹/₂ stock cube.

Meanwhile, preheat the oven to 190 to 200°C/375 to 400°F, Gas Mark 5 to 6, as instructions on page 118 for roasting game birds. Put 25 g/I oz of the butter inside the birds and spread the remainder over the outer skin. Roast as the recipe on page 92, but bring the roasting tin out of the oven about 10 minutes before the birds are cooked. Lift them on to a dish and pour out all the fat from the tin. Replace the birds and pour 3 tablespoons of the wine over them. Return to the oven to complete the cooking while you make the sauce.

To make the sauce, strain 1 tablespoon of the fat removed from the roasting tin into a pan. Blend the arrowroot or cornflour with the remaining wine, add to the pan, together with the redcurrant jelly and the giblet stock. Stir as the sauce comes to the boil and thickens slightly and the jelly dissolves. Lift the pheasants onto a heated dish. Strain the juices from the roasting tin into the sauce. Boil briskly for a few minutes, then add the well-drained onions and olives and any extra seasoning required. Heat for 2 or 3 minutes.

Pour the sauce over the pheasants, garnish and serve with the traditional accompaniments, as suggested on page 118. NOTE: Any left-over fat poured from the roasting tin can be kept.

GOOD STOCK:

You will find a number of hints about preparing stock or using alternatives on page 62. In a recipe, such as the one on the left, where only a limited amount is used, do boil the stock well to ensure it has a sufficiently strong flavour to give a good balance with the other ingredients.

PHEASANTS IN CHERRY AND
RED WINE SAUCE:

Follow the directions in the recipe, left, but omit the olives.

Use only 150 ml/¹/₄ pint giblet or chicken stock, but still use the 300 ml/¹/₂ pint red wine. When making the sauce, use 150 ml/¹/₄ pint syrup from canned or cooked black cherries, as well as the stock, wine and juices from the roasting tin.

Add the onions and 4 to 5 tablespoons stoned cherries and heat for a few minutes.

Burgundy Pheasants; Guinea Fowl in Cherry Sauce

Norfolk Casserole

▲ ▲ ✿ ✿ ✿ ✿

SERVES 4

1 large pheasant or equivalent
    in grouse, pigeons or other
    game birds
300 ml/½ pint game or
    chicken stock, see method
25 g/1 oz flour
salt and freshly ground black
    pepper
¼ teaspoon mixed dried herbs
4 bacon rashers
2 medium onions
1 tablespoon sunflower oil
150 ml/¼ pint sweet cider or
    extra stock
2 dessert apples
2 tablespoons sweet sherry

This is an ideal way of cooking older birds.

Cut the pheasant into 8 pieces, i.e. halve each of the leg and breast joints so that each person will have part of a leg and part of the breast. Smaller birds can be halved. Put the bones, plus giblets if available, into a pan. Cover with water and simmer to make stock.

Blend the flour with the seasoning and dried herbs and use to coat the joints. Derind the bacon, saving the rinds, and cut the rashers into small pieces. Peel and finely chop the onions.

Heat the bacon rinds and oil in a pan. Add the coated game birds and cook steadily for 10 minutes, turning several times. Transfer to a casserole. Put the onions and bacon in the pan, cook for 5 minutes, then place on top of the game. Pour the stock and cider into the pan, stir well to absorb all the juices, add a little extra seasoning and boil briskly for 5 minutes. Discard the bacon rinds and pour the sauce into the casserole. Cover and cook for 1 hour in the oven, preheated to 180°C/350°F, Gas Mark 4.

Core, but do not peel the apples. Cut them into rings. Add to the other ingredients in the casserole, with the sherry. Continue cooking for a further 30 minutes to 1 hour.

HUNTSMAN'S CASSEROLE:
Use 550 g/1¼ lb diced venison in place of game birds, and red wine instead of cider. The venison can be marinated in the wine for several hours before cooking.

The cooking time depends upon the cut of venison used. Tender venison needs only a total of 1 to 1¼ hours in the casserole; stewing meat up to 2¼ to 2½ hours at the setting given, or about 3½ hours at the lower setting.

MAKING A SWEETER SAUCE:
In the recipes left and above you could blend 2 tablespoons apple jelly with the stock in the pan.

INDIVIDUAL CUTS OF POULTRY

The following recipes are based upon individual joints of chicken, turkey and duck. These are readily available in chilled or frozen form. The recipes indicate whether frozen portions should be defrosted before cooking.

When you buy chilled poultry, place it in the refrigerator as soon as possible after purchase. Frozen joints should be stored in the freezer until required.

Although the quantities in most recipes are given for 4 servings, you will find it very easy to reduce or increase them to serve fewer or more people. Portions of the various foods are invaluable for people living alone; they also make dishes very easy to serve when you are entertaining.

Chicken in Pine Nut Sauce

▲ ▲ ✿ ✿

SERVES 4

4 chicken portions, preferably
    leg joints
2 garlic cloves
4 medium tomatoes
4 tablespoons sunflower or
    corn oil
300 ml/½ pint chicken stock
few drops Tabasco sauce or
    pinch chilli powder
2 ginger nut biscuits
50 g/2 oz seedless raisins
2 tablespoons tequila or
    sherry
3 tablespoons pine nuts
salt and freshly ground black
    pepper

The ginger nuts in this recipe thicken the sauce as well as adding extra flavour. Fiery tequila gives a Mexican touch, but if this is not available, use sherry instead.

Skin the chicken joints. Peel and finely chop the garlic. Skin and chop the tomatoes. Heat 2 tablespoons of the oil in a frying-pan and add the chicken. Cook steadily for 10 minutes, turning over once or twice. Remove from the pan with a perforated spoon. Heat the rest of the oil and add the garlic and tomatoes. Cook for a few minutes. Meanwhile, blend the chicken stock with the Tabasco sauce or chilli powder and pour over the ginger nut biscuits. When these are slightly softened, mash them with the liquid, or sieve, or liquidize.

Pour this into the pan and stir to blend with the garlic and tomatoes. Add the chicken joints and raisins. Cover the pan and cook until the chicken is tender. Finally add the tequila or sherry, the pine nuts and any seasoning required. Heat for 2 minutes, then serve.

PINE NUT AND PRUNE
STUFFING:
This goes well with lamb, chicken and turkey.

Cut up 100 g/4 oz stoned prunes, cover with water and cook until just tender.

Strain and mix with 175 g/6 oz cooked brown rice, 75 g/3 oz pine nuts, 2 teaspoons lemon juice and 50 g/2 oz melted butter or margarine. Season and add 1 teaspoon chopped rosemary.

If baking separately, cook for 40 minutes at 190°C/375°F, Gas Mark 5.

Chicken in Pine Nut Sauce; Turkey and Orange Stir-Fry

Turkey and Orange Stir-Fry ▲ ▲ ✪ ✪

SERVES 4
350 g/12 oz turkey breast
   portions
For the marinade:
1 tablespoon soy sauce
2 tablespoons orange juice
For the stir-fry:
$^1/_2$ red pepper
$^1/_2$ green pepper
3 celery sticks
100 g/4 oz carrots
2 oranges
water, see method
1 teaspoon cornflour
salt and freshly ground black
   pepper
For frying:
1 tablespoon sunflower oil
1 teaspoon sesame seed oil

If using frozen turkey, defrost and dry well before using. The skin can be removed, if desired. Cut the turkey into strips about 4 cm/1$^1/_2$ inches in length and 1 cm/$^1/_2$ inch in width and thickness. Mix together the soy sauce and orange juice. Place the turkey in this marinade and leave for 30 minutes.

Cut the peppers into neat strips and dice the celery. Peel the carrots and cut into matchsticks. Grate the rind from the oranges and squeeze out the juice. Measure the juice and add sufficient water to give 150 ml/$^1/_4$ pint. Blend the cornflour with this liquid and add a little salt and pepper. Lift the turkey from the marinade and drain well. Save the marinade.

Heat the two oils in a wok or strong frying-pan. Add the turkey and stir-fry for 4 to 5 minutes, then add the orange rind, peppers, celery and carrots. Continue stir-frying for a further 3 minutes. Pour in the cornflour and orange juice mixture, together with any marinade that may be left. Stir as the liquid comes to the boil and thickens slightly.

Serve with cooked rice.

USING THE MICROWAVE:
Although ordinary frying cannot be carried out in a microwave, a modified form of stir-frying is possible. Follow the directions in the manufacturer's handbook.

DUCK AND ORANGE STIR-FRY:
Use breast of duck instead of turkey. In order to reduce the fat content, remove all skin and fat before cutting the duck into strips. Add 4 tablespoons chopped spring onions to the other ingredients.

Cumberland Chicken

▲ ✪✪

SERVES 4

4 chicken breasts
350 g/12 oz Cumberland
    sausage*
4 long streaky bacon rashers
4 tablespoons red or white
    wine or dry cider
salt and freshly ground black
    pepper
For cooking:
4 squares of foil

If using frozen chicken, make sure it is defrosted and well dried. Make a deep slit in each breast to form a pocket. Slice the sausage and insert into the breasts. Remove the bacon rinds and wrap the rashers around the chicken portions. Meanwhile, preheat the oven to 190°C/375°F, Gas Mark 5.

Place the chicken portions on the foil squares and bring up the sides to make individual casserole shapes. Pour in the wine or cider, add a little seasoning, then wrap the foil around the chicken. Place on a baking tray and cook for 35 minutes.

Open the foil parcels carefully. Place the chicken and any liquid on heated serving plates. Serve with cooked rice and salad.

CUMBERLAND SAUSAGE*:
A thick spiced sausage that is sliced before or after cooking.

USING THE MICROWAVE:
Place the chicken portions in a large dish, cover with a lid. Allow approximately 12 minutes on FULL POWER.

Herbed Chicken

▲ ✪✪✪

SERVES 4

4 chicken leg portions
For the marinade:
1 garlic clove
2 tablespoons sunflower oil
2 tablespoons lemon juice or
    white wine vinegar
2 teaspoons chopped
    rosemary or $^1/_2$ teaspoon
    dried rosemary
1 tablespoon chopped parsley
For coating:
salt and freshly ground black
    pepper
1 tablespoon flour
1 egg
50 g/2 oz dried breadcrumbs
For frying:
2 tablespoons sunflower oil

Frozen chicken joints must be defrosted and well dried for this dish so the flavour of the marinade impregnates the flesh. Slit the skin of the legs and carefully remove it. Make about 4 shallow cuts in each leg.

Peel and crush the garlic clove, then put all the ingredients for the marinade into a casserole and add the chicken. Leave for 1 hour. Any marinade left can be served with the chicken, see below.

Drain well, then coat the chicken lightly in seasoned flour. Beat the egg. Brush over the chicken legs, then roll them in the crisp breadcrumbs. Chill or freeze for a short time before cooking.

Heat the oil in a large frying-pan and fry the chicken legs steadily for 15 minutes, turning over once or twice. Drain on absorbent paper.

Top each portion with a trickle of the marinade and serve with salad or hot vegetables.

MARINATING FOODS:
A marinade generally contains acid ingredients, such as fruit juice, wine or vinegar. These tenderize the flesh as well as giving flavour. Do not leave normally tender foods, such as chicken, in the marinade for too long, as this makes the flesh over-soft. The purpose of making slits in the flesh, as in this recipe, is to allow the marinade to penetrate better.

Duckling with Orange and Honey Glaze

▲▲▲ ✪✪

SERVES 4

4 portions of duckling, either
    all breast or all legs
For the glaze:
2 tablespoons orange
    marmalade
2 teaspoons finely grated
    orange zest
$1^1/_2$ tablespoons thin honey
$1^1/_2$ tablespoons orange juice
For the sauce:
150 ml/$^1/_4$ pint orange juice
1 tablespoon Curaçao or
    brandy
To garnish:
rings of orange

There is no need to defrost the duckling portions before the initial cooking in the oven, although the skin tends to crisp better if the poultry is thawed out, then dried well before cooking.

Preheat the oven to 200°C/400°F, Gas Mark 6. Place the duckling portions in a roasting tin, with the skin side uppermost. Do not cover the tin. Cook breast portions for about 30 minutes and legs for 35 to 40 minutes. Allow a little longer if cooking from the frozen state. The duckling should be nearly, but not entirely cooked.

Blend together the ingredients for the glaze. Lift the tin from the oven and pour away any surplus fat. Cover the skin with the glaze and cook for 10 to 15 minutes. Heat the orange juice for the sauce in a saucepan. Add the Curaçao or brandy just before serving.

Arrange the duckling portions on a dish, pour the hot sauce around them and garnish with the orange rings. Serve with an Orange and Watercress Salad, see page 155, peas and new potatoes.

TO PLAN AHEAD:
This is an ideal dish when entertaining. To save too much cooking immediately before your guests arrive, partially roast the duck portions earlier in the day. Remove from the oven and drain away any surplus fat. Put on an ovenproof serving dish and top with the glaze. Reheat for 15 to 20 minutes at the oven setting given in the recipe. Serve with the sauce.

Duckling Goujons

▲ ▲   ✿ ✿

SERVES 6 TO 8

1 duckling, weighing
    approximately 2 kg/4½ lb or
    4 duck portions, see
    method
25 g/1 oz flour
salt and freshly ground black
    pepper
2 eggs
50 g/2 oz crisp breadcrumbs
For frying:
oil
To garnish:
watercress

Frozen duck should be defrosted and well dried before you attempt to cut the flesh. As it is easier to cut neat pieces from the breast of the duck, it is recommended that you buy 4 portions rather than a whole bird.

Cut away the skin from the flesh, then divide the meat into strips approximately 5 to 7·5 cm/2 to 3 inches in length and 2 cm/¾ inch in width and thickness. Mix the flour with a generous amount of seasoning and then use to coat the duck pieces.

Beat the eggs and brush over the duckling strips. Then coat in the crisp breadcrumbs. Spread on a flat dish and chill or even freeze the coated goujons before frying.

Either put enough oil in a large frying-pan to give a depth of 2 cm/¾ inch or use a deep-fryer. Cook the strips quickly for 3 to 4 minutes, or until crisp and brown. Lower the heat and continue cooking for 10 minutes or until tender. Drain on absorbent paper.

Garnish with watercress and serve hot or cold with a green salad. Spiced apple sauce or Cranberry and red wine sauce can be served as dips, see pages 97, 161 and 92.

TO MAKE A CHANGE:
Serve these goujons as an hors d'oeuvre. Make individual salads on small plates, add a little dressing, then top each portion with a few hot goujons just before the meal.

TO PREPARE AHEAD:
Fry the goujons for 3 to 4 minutes, drain and place in one flat layer on a baking sheet. Preheat oven to 190°C/375°F, Gas Mark 5. Cook goujons for 25 minutes, drain and serve.

Duckling Goujons with Spiced Apple Sauce

TO COOK VENISON

Much of the venison now available is of the farmed variety, but there is also wild venison meat, too.

The flesh varies, as much as cuts of beef vary. Tender joints of venison are roasted, just as beef. The timing given on page 92 is correct for venison. As this is a naturally lean meat, you must make sure it does not dry in cooking, so covering when roasting is a good idea; see page 90 for various suggestions about ways meat can be covered to keep it moist.

It was once traditional to marinade venison. This gives it a good flavour, as well as helping to tenderize the flesh, but it is not essential with today's more tender meat.

If you decide you would like to marinade the flesh – and that is wise if you are unsure of the tenderness – use the marinade recipe on page 125. This can be varied by the choice of wine you use and by adding juniper berries or herbs, such as tarragon.

Steaks of venison can be grilled or fried and the older stewing meat cooked more slowly, see Huntsman's casserole, on page 120.

Accompaniments with venison: These can be varied. The game chips, fried crumbs and redcurrant or other jelly served with game birds are just as appropriate for venison, but the fruit sauces suggested on page 117 give a more interesting flavour.

Venison in Apricot-Wine Sauce

Venison in Apricot-Wine Sauce ▲▲▲ ✿✿✿✿

SERVES 4

4 venison fillets, approximately
150 to 175 g/5 to 6 oz each

For the marinade:

2 onions

2 garlic cloves

300 ml/½ pint red wine

I tablespoon olive oil

**For cooking venison and
the sauce:**

50g/2 oz butter

I tablespoon olive oil

25 g/I oz flour

150 ml/¼ pint syrup from
canned or cooked apricots

2 tablespoons redcurrant jelly

8 to 12 canned or cooked
apricot halves

salt and freshly ground black
pepper

Tie the venison fillets into tournedos, see right.

To make the marinade, peel and chop the onions and garlic and put into a casserole with the wine and oil. Add the venison and leave for 1 to 2 hours, turning over once or twice.

Lift the meat from the marinade and drain well. Heat the butter and oil in a frying-pan, add the venison and cook on both sides until browned on the outside but still pink inside. Lift the meat onto a heated dish and keep hot. Blend the flour into the fat remaining in the pan, stirring well to absorb the meat juices. Strain the marinade into the pan, together with the syrup from the apricots and the redcurrant jelly.

Stir over the heat until the jelly has melted and the sauce thickens slightly. Add the apricot halves and seasoning and heat for a minute.

Spoon the sauce around the venison and garnish the meat with the apricot halves and parsley leaves.

TO MAKE TOURNEDOS:
Form fillets or thick cuts of meat into neat rounds. Tie with fine string. Remove the string before serving.

TO GIVE EXTRA FLAVOUR TO THE APRICOT SAUCE:
Add 1 or 2 tablespoons apricot brandy when heating the apricot halves. Reduce the amount of red wine by this amount.

TO COOK RABBIT AND HARE

The young rabbit sold today can be cooked in exactly the same way as chicken. Many people prefer rabbit to chicken, as they feel it has more flavour. Tender leg joints can be fried or grilled and the meat from the back used in a stir-fry dish, such as that on page 121.
Boiling or steaming rabbit, chicken and guinea fowl: This may sound a very dull way of cooking these, but it retains all the natural flavour. It has the added advantage that lean game and poultry do not become dry. The flesh is ideal for serving with an interesting sauce; see page 158 for suitable recipes.

Boiling is a misnomer, for the liquid in which the food is cooked should never boil; it should simmer very gently. It can be water or water with a little wine plus herbs and vegetables to flavour.

Allow 15 minutes per 450 g/1 lb and 15 minutes over.

Herb dumplings go well with these boiled foods. Follow the recipe on pages 110 and 111, but add 1 to 2 tablespoons of finely chopped herbs to the flour.

Steaming is ideal if you plan to have the meat in a salad, as it will be firmer than after boiling. Allow the same cooking time.

If you dislike the rather pallid colour of the flesh, then brush with a little oil or melted butter after steaming and put into a very hot oven for a few minutes only.

Guinea fowl, which can also be roasted like chicken or game birds, is extremely good cooked this way.

The back of hare, known as the saddle, is an excellent joint for roasting. It is very lean, so is better covered during this process. See the advice on page 90 about covering foods to keep them moist in cooking.

The joint, which provides smallish portions for 4 people, can be wrapped in bacon rashers.

It can be served with the same accompaniments as game birds. Several of the stuffings and sauces on page 158 to 163 are extremely good with hare.

The legs of hare could be used in the Norfolk casserole on page 120. Allow the same cooking time for rabbit and slightly longer for hare.

PASTA DISHES

Over the last few years, pasta has become a very much more popular food. The reasons are obvious. It is an economical food that can be cooked quickly, so it is ideal for busy people. It blends with a variety of different ingredients. Nutritionists recommend pasta highly for a number of reasons; it is made from wheat, it is an excellent source of fibre and it contains relatively little fat. There are many pasta shapes, but if you cannot obtain the type given in the recipe, use a different form.

There are three ways of obtaining pasta. You can buy the dried variety, which is an excellent standby in the store cupboard, or the fresh type. If you are buying fresh pasta, check the 'sell by' date and keep the packet in the refrigerator until it is used. The third way of obtaining pasta is to make it at home; this is not as difficult as it may seem. Commercially produced pasta is made from durum wheat – a very hard type – that keeps its shape in cooking. If you make your own pasta, buy strong flour, as used for bread.

The amount needed and the cooking times vary, depending on whether you use dried or fresh pasta. If the recipe instructs you to use 225 g/8 oz dried pasta, you will need 350 g/12 oz chilled, ready-made fresh pasta or homemade pasta to obtain the same amount when cooked.

Cook dried pasta according to the time recommended on the packet. Fresh pasta needs only about 3 minutes' cooking. The pasta should always be fairly firm, so you enjoy its texture, as well as the good flavour. The Italian term for correctly cooked pasta is 'al dente', i.e. firm to the bite.

PERFECTLY COOKED PASTA

PASTA WITHOUT EGGS:
Follow the recipe on page 127. Use the flour, salt and oil and bind with water or milk, and water, or even a little cream and milk.

SPINACH PASTA:
Use a very smooth purée of cooked and sieved spinach plus 1 egg to bind the flour etc. You will need approximately 4 tablespoons of spinach purée to the amount of flour in the recipe on page 127.

Pasta needs plenty of space in the water when it is being cooked. Too little water means it will stick together. Use a bowl when cooking pasta in a microwave.

Amount of water: Allow at least 1·2 litres/2 pints water to each 100 g/4 oz pasta whether you are cooking on the oven top or in a microwave.

Choose a good-sized pan or bowl, as the water must boil steadily, without any risk of boiling over, during the time the pasta is cooking. Add salt to taste before putting in the pasta. Make sure the water is boiling briskly when the pasta is added and that it returns to boiling point almost immediately. Do not cover the saucepan.

Adding oil to the water: A few drops of olive or other oil added to the water helps to prevent the pasta sticking together during cooking. Do not stir the pasta during cooking, as that could break it. Lift it in the water, with the help of two long spoons, once or twice.

Adding long pasta, like spaghetti, to the water: Hold the pasta in one hand, lower the ends into the boiling water, while holding the dry ends of pasta firmly.

When you feel the ends in the water soften, twist the pasta and lower more into the water. Continue like this until all the strands are completely immersed.

Testing pasta: Cook for the recommended time for the particular variety. Lift one or two pieces from the water; press against the side of the pan and try to cut them with a fork. They should feel slightly firm. Alternatively, taste the pasta; it should be firm to the bite, 'al dente', but not uncooked.

Rinsing cooked pasta: Some people like to rinse pasta, after straining, in boiling water to remove any stickiness; this is not essential — simply a matter of personal taste.

Home-made Pasta with Eggs

300 g/10 oz strong flour,
either all white flour or half
white and half wholemeal
flour
1 teaspoon salt
1 tablespoon olive oil
3 eggs, size 3

See page 126 for variations.

You can use a food processor to mix the ingredients together, but take care they are not over-handled. If using an electric mixer, choose the dough hook.

If mixing by hand, sift the flour and salt into a mixing bowl and add the oil. Beat the eggs, then add them gradually to the mixture and knead until the dough forms a ball and comes away from the sides of the bowl.

Turn the dough out of the bowl, cover with a cloth and leave for 15 minutes. Roll out on a floured board until the dough is the desired thickness. Allow to dry for a limited time, so it is not too sticky and it is easy to cut into the required shapes. Do not leave to dry for too long, as the pasta will crack as you cut it. You will find it less difficult to roll the dough thinly if you divide the total amount into 2 or 3 portions.

If you have a pasta-making machine, follow the manufacturer's instructions for using it.

PASTA DISHES IN MINUTES

Do not imagine that you need special sauces to turn pasta into an appetizing dish. You can heat one of the variety of ready-made sauces that are available and top the pasta with this.

The following suggestions are based on foods you may have in the storecupboard or refrigerator.

Pasta au naturel: The simplest way to serve pasta is just to strain it, return it to the pan and toss it in a little hot melted butter or margarine or olive oil, add a few chopped herbs and serve it with grated Parmesan or other cheese.

Pasta with meat: Heat left-over diced or minced ham, chicken or other meat in a little stock or oil and add to the hot pasta.

Pasta with fish: Heat cooked peeled prawns, mussels, tuna or white fish in a little wine, or cream or oil, add to the hot pasta with chopped fennel or dill.

Pasta with vegetables: Cook diced mixed vegetables while the pasta is boiling, strain and mix with the pasta.

Cannelloni Ripieni (see page 128)

Penne with Ham and Peas (see page 128)

EASY PASTA DISHES

The recipes on this and the following pages are based upon using dried pasta. The quantity of dried pasta is enough for 4 servings. When using the fresh type allow 50 per cent more, see page 126. Always allow at least 1.2 litres/2 pints boiling salted water to each 100 g/4 oz pasta.

Microwave cooking: Put the pasta into a bowl. Add boiling water, amount as above, plus a little salt. Cover and cook for three-quarters of usual time on FULL POWER. Stand for 4 minutes, strain and serve.

Cannelloni ripieni: Peel and finely chop 1 small onion. Wipe and chop 175 g/6 oz button mushrooms and chop 175 g/6 oz lean ham or minced beef. Heat 25 g/1 oz butter and 1 tablespoon olive oil and cook the onion and mushrooms until tender. Add the mince or ham, 1 beaten egg and 25 g/1 oz grated Parmesan cheese. Season to taste.

Cook 225 g/8 oz cannelloni until 'al dente', drain and fill with the mince or ham mixture. Put into an oblong casserole. Top with Tomato or Cheese sauce, see pages 160 and 158, and a layer of grated Parmesan cheese. Bake in a preheated oven, set to 180°C/350°F, Gas Mark 4 for 30 minutes.

Penne with ham and beans: Peel and chop 2 medium onions. Heat 2 tablespoons olive oil and cook the onions until tender, then add 150 ml/^{1}/$_4$ pint tomato juice and 350 g/12 oz shelled broad beans, with a little seasoning. Cook until the beans are tender. Stir 225 g/8 oz minced or finely chopped cooked ham into the mixture. Meanwhile, cook 225 g/8 oz penne or lasagne, cut into squares before cooking, until 'al dente'. Blend with the beans and ham. Serve with grated cheese.

Penne with ricotta: Penne are rather like thick short macaroni, which could be used as a substitute. Cook the pasta until 'al dente', drain and blend with a generous amount of ricotta cheese, chopped parsley, a little single cream to moisten and grated nutmeg or ground cinnamon to flavour.

Spaghetti Bolognese: It is worthwhile making a larger batch of sauce, as described below. This would serve 6 to 8; if the meal is for a smaller number of people, freeze any sauce left.

Peel and finely chop 2 medium onions, 2 garlic cloves and 2 small carrots. Wipe and chop 100 g/4 oz mushrooms. Heat 25 g/1 oz butter and 2 tablespoons olive oil and fry the vegetables for 10 minutes. Add 350 g/12 oz minced beef, 100 g/4 oz finely diced ham (optional), a 227 g/8 oz can chopped plum tomatoes and 300 ml/^{1}/$_2$ pint beef stock. Stir well to mix and continue stirring over the heat for 5 minutes, then add a little seasoning, pinch sugar, 1 tablespoon chopped parsley, 1 teaspoon chopped oregano, 150 ml/^{1}/$_4$ pint red wine or Marsala and a grating of nutmeg. Simmer in the open pan, stirring from time to time, for about 45 minutes to 1 hour. Serve with about 450 g/1 lb cooked spaghetti, or other pasta, and bowls of grated cheese.

Tortiglioni with beans: This pasta is medium-length twists, as shown opposite. Peel and chop a small bunch of spring onions, several sticks of celery and 2 tablespoons chopped parsley. Heat 2 tablespoons olive oil in a pan, fry the onions for a few minutes, add the celery, about 100 g/4 oz cooked or well-drained chopped canned green beans. Add the same quantity of canned chopped asparagus and a 227 g/8 oz can beans in tomato sauce. Heat well.

Meanwhile cook 225 g/8 oz tortiglioni, mix with the bean mixture and serve topped with the parsley.

Spaghetti alla carbonara: Cook 100 g/4 oz chopped bacon until crisp. Cook 225 g/ 8 oz spaghetti. Beat 3 to 4 eggs with 3 tablespoons cream or milk, seasoning and 2 tablespoons grated Parmesan cheese. Heat 50 g/2 oz butter add the strained spaghetti, bacon and egg mixture. Stir gently until the eggs have set and coated the pasta.

Tortiglioni with Beans

Spinach Lasagne

▲ ✿✿✿

SERVES 4

10 sheets of lasagne, see method

salt and freshly ground black pepper

1½ tablespoons olive oil

450 to 675 g/1 to 1½ lb fresh spinach or 350 g/12 oz pack frozen leaf spinach

2 medium onions

2 garlic cloves

For the cheese sauce:

50 g/2 oz butter or margarine

50 g/2 oz flour

750 ml/1¼ pints milk

1 or 2 eggs (optional)

175 g/6 oz Gruyère or Cheddar cheese

1 teaspoon made English mustard

2 or 3 tablespoons grated Parmesan cheese

If you are using lasagne that requires precooking, lower the sheets of pasta into boiling salted water, to which 1 teaspoon of the oil should be added. This helps to prevent the sheets sticking together. Put them into the water one by one, rather than all at once, as this also helps prevent them sticking.

Cook steadily until 'al dente', then drain well and allow to dry while preparing the other ingredients.

Lasagne that does not need precooking saves a lot of trouble. If you are using it straight from the packet, increase the amount of liquid in the sauce by adding an extra 150 ml/¼ pint milk. This prevents the dish being over-stiff. You improve the texture of this lasagne somewhat if it is placed into a dish of boiling water for 1 minute, then drained well before using.

Prepare the spinach by removing the stalks, then washing it in several lots of cold water. Cook in the water adhering to the leaves; add seasoning to taste. Strain very thoroughly, then chop finely. Cook frozen spinach as instructed on the packet.

Peel and finely chop the onions and garlic. Heat the remaining oil, add the onions and garlic and cook until tender. Mix with the spinach.

To make the cheese sauce, heat the butter or margarine in a saucepan, stir in the flour, then gradually add the milk. Bring to the boil, then stir or whisk until a smooth sauce. If adding the eggs, beat them well, then whisk into the hot, but not boiling sauce. Do not reheat it. Grate the cheese, stir most of it into the sauce, with the mustard and seasoning.

Place layers of lasagne, spinach and sauce in an ovenproof dish, beginning with lasagne and ending with lasagne and a coating of sauce. Sprinkle the last of the Gruyère or Cheddar cheese and the Parmesan cheese over the top of the sauce and bake for 25 to 30 minutes in a preheated oven, set to 190°C/375°F, Gas Mark 5.

OTHER LASAGNE DISHES:

Lasagna alla piemontese:

If making your own pasta, as on page 127, add a little grated Parmesan cheese to the dough or use ordinary lasagne. Layer the cooked sheets with Italian meat sauce, made by substituting a mixture of pork, veal and beef in the Bolognese sauce, page 128, and layers of grated cheese, then bake as recipe on left.

Seafood lasagne:

Layer the lasagne with seafood in a Béchamel sauce, see page 159, and sliced Mozzarella cheese. Top with grated Parmesan cheese, then bake as recipe on left.

Lasagne verde marchigiana:

Layer cooked lasagne verdi with Bolognese sauce, page 128, to which should be added cooked mushrooms or a chopped truffle and cooked diced chicken livers. Add layers of grated Parmesan cheese, spoonfuls of ricotta (cream cheese) and sliced Mozzarella cheese. Bake as recipe on left.

Macaroni Cheese

▲ ✪ to ✪✪

SERVES 4
75 g/3 oz macaroni
salt
Cheese sauce, as page 158
    made with 300 to 450 ml/¹/₂
    to ³/₄ pint milk etc., as
    explained in method
For the topping:
25 g/1 oz crisp breadcrumbs
3 to 4 tablespoons grated
    Cheddar or other cheese

Cook the macaroni in boiling salted water for the time given on the packet. Strain.

Make the sauce, as on page 158. If serving the dish at once and browning it under the grill, you can use 300 ml/¹/₂ pint sauce. If you are preparing ahead, so the dish is ready to reheat, you need the larger amount of sauce, as the pasta absorbs this during standing.

If cooking under the grill, use a flameproof dish. Mix the hot macaroni and hot sauce, put into the dish, top with the breadcrumbs and cheese and brown under a preheated grill.

If cooking in the oven, make the larger amount of sauce and mix with the macaroni. Put into an ovenproof dish, top with the breadcrumbs and cheese. Cook in a preheated oven set to 190°C/375°F, Gas Mark 5 for 25 to 30 minutes.

FLAVOURINGS TO ADD:
For a crisper topping, add a little melted margarine to the breadcrumbs and cheese.

Garnish with cooked tomato slices. Add cooked, sliced mushrooms and/or cooked sweetcorn, or broccoli spears, or chopped, cooked onions to the sauce.

Bucatini del Buongustaio

▲ ✪✪

SERVES 4
For the sauce:
1 aubergine
1 large onion
2 garlic cloves
100 g/4 oz mushrooms
2 tablespoons olive oil
1 × 425 g/15 oz can chopped
    plum tomatoes
sprig of sage
salt and ground black pepper

225 to 350 g/8 to 12 oz
    bucatini

Bucatini is a long pasta, not unlike spaghetti. This could be substituted if desired.

Peel and dice the aubergine. Peel and finely chop the onion and garlic. Wipe and slice the mushrooms. Heat the oil in a pan and cook the onion, garlic and aubergine for 5 minutes, then add the mushrooms, tomatoes, plus the liquid from the can. Add the sage and a little seasoning. Cover the pan and cook gently for 15 minutes. Remove the sage.

Meanwhile cook the pasta in boiling salted water until 'al dente', strain and add to the sauce ingredients. Heat for a short time, stirring gently to blend the sauce with the pasta.

Serve with bowls of grated Parmesan or other cheese.

PASTA FOR SLIMMERS:
Pasta itself is not a high-calorie food. The amount varies somewhat, according to the type of pasta; on average, 25 g/1 oz uncooked pasta contains 95 to 102 calories.

If you are anxious to lose weight, choose the foods served with pasta carefully. Most sauces can be made with less fat and still be enjoyable. Low-fat cheese can be used.

Spaghetti Pepperoni

▲ ✪✪

SERVES 4
For the sauce:
3 medium onions
2 garlic cloves
1 green pepper
1 red pepper
2 tablespoons olive oil
1 × 425 g/15 oz can chopped
    plum tomatoes
1 tablespoon tomato purée
1 tablespoon chopped oregano
2 fresh bay leaves or 1 dried
    bay leaf
salt and ground black pepper

300 to 350 g/10 to 12 oz
    spaghetti

To make the sauce, peel and finely chop the onions and garlic and deseed and dice the peppers. Heat the oil and cook the onions and garlic for 5 minutes. Add the tomatoes, with any liquid from the can, the tomato purée, herbs and seasoning. Simmer for 10 minutes, then add the diced peppers. Continue cooking for 10 minutes, or until the peppers are just soft. Remove the bay leaves or leaf before serving.

Meanwhile cook the spaghetti in plenty of salted water until 'al dente'. Strain and pile on to a heated dish or individual plates. Top with the sauce and serve with bowls of grated Parmesan or other cheese.

Pasta is spoiled by being kept waiting, so always cook the sauce, or any accompaniments that take longer to cook before the pasta.

TOMATO SAUCE:
The ingredients in the sauce on the left make an excellent tomato sauce if the peppers are omitted.

Use chopped basil in place of the oregano.

To make a slightly sweeter sauce, add 1 to 2 teaspoons brown sugar.

Fusilli with Ham and Ginger

Fusilli with Ham and Ginger ▲ ✪

SERVES 4

225 g/8 oz fusilli

salt and freshly ground black
    pepper

225 g/8 oz cooked ham

150 ml/¼ pint white wine or
    chicken stock

3 tablespoons double cream
    or thick yogurt

2 teaspoons grated fresh
    ginger, or to taste

Cook the fusilli in boiling salted water until 'al dente', then
strain. Meanwhile slice the ham and heat in the well-seasoned
wine or stock. Add the cream or yogurt and ginger and heat,
without boiling. Mix with the pasta and serve.

   Instead of cooked ham you can use cooked tongue and/or
chicken. Flaked white fish blends well with this sauce too.

   Vegetarians could use diced tofu.

TO ENHANCE THE FLAVOUR:
Garnish with chopped or
sliced preserved ginger.

CRISPY FRIED NOODLES:
Buy the very fine chow mein
noodles. Fry slowly in oil in a
frying-pan, turning and
flattening as you do so.

Tagliatelli Sicilienne ▲ ✪✪

SERVES 4

2 medium or 1 large aubergine

salt and freshly ground black
    pepper

2 medium onions

2 garlic cloves

2 tablespoons olive oil

1 x 425 g/15 oz can chopped
    plum tomatoes

2 teaspoons chopped basil or
    ½ teaspoon dried basil

3.6 litres/6 pints water

350 g/12 oz fresh tagliatelli

Wipe the aubergine(s) and cut into small dice, sprinkle with
salt and leave for 30 minutes. Drain, rinse in cold water and
dry well on absorbent paper.

   Peel and chop the onions and garlic. Heat the oil in a pan,
add the onion, garlic and aubergine(s) and cook for a few
minutes. Tip in the tomatoes, any liquid from the can, together
with the basil, and season to taste. Simmer steadily for 15 to
20 minutes.

   Meanwhile bring the water to the boil, add approximately
2 level teaspoons salt. Put in the pasta and cook until just
'al dente', i.e. about 3 to 4 minutes.

   Strain and top with the aubergine mixture and serve with
grated Parmesan cheese.

PASTA FOR VEGETARIANS:
Many pasta recipes are ideal
for vegetarians.

   Pasta adds protein to the
diet and can be given infinite
variety with new sauces and
accompaniments. Blend diced
tofu or nuts with the sauces
for extra protein.

RICE DISHES

Rice is the staple food of many countries and one that is the basis for a wide variety of dishes, both sweet and savoury. The best results in cooking are achieved by selecting the right type of rice. Whichever one is used, you know you are serving a very nutritious food.

Brown rice has more fibre than white, as the outer bran is retained. It gives a deliciously nutty taste to dishes but does, however, need longer cooking time, as shown in the table below.

PERFECTLY COOKED RICE

HERE ARE THE BASIC TYPES OF RICE:-
Short grain: Because of its excellent thickening properties this produces lovely creamy milk puddings. Also sold as 'pudding' or 'round' rice.
Medium grain: More correctly called 'arborio rice', this also thickens well. It is therefore ideal for risottos or similar dishes.
Long grain: This has a firmer texture when cooked and the grains should stay well separated. Some long grain rice is marked 'par-boiled', which means it has been treated to give better results.
Basmati: This is a long grain type of a particularly high standard.
Wild rice: This is really misnamed, as it is not a rice at all but comes from the seeds of a wild grass.
It is expensive, so it is often sold mixed with other types of rice.

In some cases, cooked rice is specified. If you are cooking it specially, you will need 25 g/1 oz uncooked rice to produce 75 g/3 oz rice when cooked.
Basic preparations: Most rice is sold as 'pre-washed', but if you do wash it – and Basmati rice needs plentiful washing – do so just before cooking.

COOKING RICE – METHOD 1
You can measure or weigh the rice.
If measuring allow the following liquid per cup of rice:
2 cups for long grain rice;
2$\frac{1}{2}$ cups for par-boiled rice or Basmati rice;
3 cups for brown and wild rice.
If weighing allow the following liquid per 28 g*/1 oz rice:
60 ml/2 fl oz for long grain rice;
75 ml/2$\frac{1}{2}$ fl oz for par-boiled and Basmati rice; 90 ml/3 fl oz for brown and wild rice.
* slightly over the usual metrication
Put the rice, cold liquid and a pinch of salt into a pan, bring to boiling point and stir briskly with a fork. Cover tightly, lower the heat so the liquid simmers and allow 15 minutes for long grain and Basmati rice; 20 minutes for par-boiled rice; 30 to 35 minutes for brown and wild rice.
The way to tell if rice is cooked is to press a few grains between the thumb and finger. It should feel just soft.
There should be no need to drain or rinse the rice. The first time you use this method, check carefully during cooking, so the pan does not boil dry; you may have the heat too high. Remember also that rice varies; one brand may need longer cooking than another so it is better to check early. Over-cooked rice is not pleasant.
When the rice is cooked, fluff it up with a fork, cover the pan with a folded cloth and stand for 2 or 3 minutes.

COOKING RICE – METHOD 2
Allow 1 litre/1$\frac{3}{4}$ pints water to each 100 g/4 oz rice. Add $\frac{1}{2}$ to 1 teaspoon salt; do not use too much at this stage, you can add more after cooking. Bring the water to the boil. Add the rice and cook for 1 or 2 minutes less than the time given in Method 1 for each type of rice. Test as before.
Strain the rice through a fine-meshed sieve. You can pour boiling water through the rice to whiten it. Return to the hot pan, cover with a cloth and leave for 2 or 3 minutes. Alternatively, spread the rice over a cloth on a baking tray, cover and leave in a slow oven for a few minutes. This not only keeps the rice hot and dries it, but helps it to fluff.

Rice Cutlets

SERVES 4 TO 8

300 g/10 oz short grain rice
600 ml/1 pint milk or stock, according to the type of dish with which these are to be served
25 g/1 oz butter or margarine
salt and freshly ground black pepper
2 eggs

For coating:
1 tablespoon flour
1 egg
50 g/2 oz crisp breadcrumbs

For frying:
25 g/1 oz butter
2 tablespoons sunflower oil

These rice cutlets make an excellent light supper dish served with a cheese or other savoury sauce, or as an accompaniment to fish, meat or vegetarian main dishes. With slight adjustments, they can be made into an interesting dessert, see right-hand column.

Put the rice, milk or stock and the butter or margarine into the top of a double saucepan or in a basin over a pan of boiling water. Cover and cook steadily, stirring from time to time, for about 40 minutes or until the rice is tender and all the liquid has been absorbed. Remove from the heat, add a little seasoning and the well-beaten eggs. Remove the mixture on to a plate, divide into 8 small portions, cover and allow to become quite cold and firm. Chill well if the portions are still soft.

Form into 8 cutlet shapes, coat in seasoned flour, then in the beaten egg and crisp breadcrumbs. Heat the butter and oil and fry the cutlets on either side until crisp and golden brown. Drain on absorbent paper and serve hot.

TO GIVE EXTRA FLAVOUR:
Add finely shopped mixed herbs or finely chopped fried onions and mushrooms to the rice towards the end of the cooking period.

SWEET RICE CUTLETS:
Cook the rice in milk, with a little vanilla essence, or a good pinch of nutmeg, or 1 to 2 teaspoons grated lemon rind. Add 2 tablespoons sugar, instead of the seasoning. Shape, coat and fry, as the recipe.

Serve with hot jam or fruit purée.

Kedgeree

SERVES 4

450 g/1 lb smoked haddock
2 eggs
50 g/2 oz butter or margarine
350 g/12 oz cooked long grain rice*
2 or 3 tablespoons milk or single cream
salt and freshly ground black pepper

To garnish:
chopped parsley
sliced egg

*110 g/4 oz before cooking.

While this is an excellent way of using left-over cooked smoked haddock or other fish, it is such a satisfying dish that it is worthwhile cooking the haddock specially. The fillet is better than a whole fish in this particular case.

Poach the haddock in a little water for 10 minutes, drain and break the fish into large flakes. Meanwhile, hard-boil the eggs, shell, slice half an egg for garnish and chop the remaining whites and yolks separately.

Heat the butter or margarine in a large pan, add the fish and the cooked rice and just enough milk or cream to moisten. Heat gently, stirring carefully, so the flakes of fish are not broken. Add the chopped egg whites to the mixture and season to taste. Spoon on to a heated dish and top with the egg yolks and parsley and garnish with the egg slices.

FREEZING COOKED RICE:
It is useful to have ready-cooked rice available to make dishes such as Kedgeree. Lightly freeze the rice, then carefully fork the grains to separate them and continue freezing.

MICROWAVE COOKING:
Rice can be cooked successfully in a microwave; you do not save much time but there is less likelihood of it sticking as in Method 1 or of it boiling over as in Method 2. I find the most successful result is achieved by cooking for the first half of the time on FULL POWER and the rest of the time on DEFROST. Check on specific instructions for your oven.

Kedgeree

Risotto con Peoci (Risotto with Mussels) ▲ ✪✪

SERVES 4
To cook the mussels:
I small onion
I garlic clove
I kg/2¼ lbs mussels in their
   shells
I teaspoon oil
150 ml/¼ pint fish stock or
   white wine
For the risotto:
2 small onions
I to 2 garlic cloves
I tablespoon olive oil
75 g/3 oz butter
350 g/12 oz arborio rice,
   see method and right
I litre/1¾ pints fish stock,
   made as below, also see
   right
salt and freshly ground black
   pepper

A risotto should have a deliciously soft creamy texture and be pleasantly moist. This is achieved by using the right kind of rice and adding the liquid gradually during the cooking process. Different brands of rice vary in the amount of liquid they absorb, so you may find you need slightly less than specified in the list of ingredients, or even slightly more.

The type of rice that produces a good risotto is easily available today but if you are shopping in Italy or in shops that specialize in Italian foods, you will find the real Italian rice that has a much larger grain.

To enjoy a risotto at its best, it must be served immediately after cooking.

To cook the mussels, peel and roughly chop the onion and garlic. Wash the mussels in plenty of cold water; discard any that do not close when tapped sharply. Heat the oil in a large pan, add the onion and garlic and cook for several minutes. Put in the fish stock or wine and the mussels. Heat briskly until the mussels open. Strain the liquid, keep this and remove the fish from both their shells. Do not try to force open any mussels where the shells do not open properly; discard them.

To make the risotto, peel and finely chop the onions and garlic. Heat the oil with 25 g/1 oz of the butter and cook the onions and garlic gently for 5 minutes. Add the rice and turn around in the buttery mixture over a low heat. Meanwhile, heat the fish stock. Add the liquid from opening the mussels, plus enough hot fish stock to cover the rice. Cook steadily until the rice has absorbed the liquid, then add a little seasoning and spoon over more of the stock. Continue adding liquid until the rice is almost tender, then gently stir in the rest of the butter, the mussels and enough of the hot stock needed to produce the correct texture. Adjust the seasoning and heat for the last few minutes. Serve with a generous amount of grated Parmesan or other cheese.

TO REPLACE ARBORIO RICE:
Use short grain – the type used to make milk puddings.

To replace fish stock:
Use water plus 1½ fish or chicken stock cubes.

OTHER RISOTTOS:
The risotto, left, goes with most ingredients. As there will be no liquid from the mussels, use 1·2 litres/2 pints stock.

Add a mixture of cooked shellfish, or cooked diced vegetables, or cooked diced chicken and ham, or savoury sausages instead of mussels.

Risotto alla Finanziera:
Omit the garlic and cook 100 g/4 oz sliced mushrooms and 8 chicken livers with the onions. Add a chopped red pepper with the rice. Use chicken stock.

Risotto alla Milanese:
Use beef stock plus a pinch of saffron. Omit the garlic. The classic recipe adds 50 g/2 oz beef marrow (from the bone) to the onions.

This is often served as an accompaniment to dishes.

Plaice Pilau ▲ ▲ ✪✪

SERVES 4 TO 6
I large plaice
salt and freshly ground black
   pepper
25 g/1 oz flour
For the fish stock:
I small onion
fish skin and bones
900 ml/1½ pints water
I teaspoon lemon juice
2 fresh bay leaves or I dried
   leaf
For the pilau:
2 small onions
I red pepper
75 g/3 oz butter
175 g/6 oz long grain brown
   or white rice
100 g/4 oz button mushrooms
2 tablespoons chopped fennel
   leaves or chopped parsley

Fillet and skin the whole plaice, following the directions on page 82. Cut the plaice across the fillets into 2.5 cm/1 inch strips and dust with the seasoned flour. Place in the refrigerator while preparing the fish stock and rice mixture.

Slice the onion for the stock, put into a saucepan with the fish skins and bones and the rest of the ingredients for the stock and season lightly. Boil fairly steadily for 15 minutes, then strain the stock; you need 600 ml/1 pint.

Chop the 2 onions finely and deseed and dice the pepper. Heat half the butter in a pan, add the onions and pepper, cook for 2 to 3 minutes, then add the rice and turn around in the onion mixture. Make sure all the grains are well-coated. Pour in the fish stock and cook steadily for 20 minutes, until the rice is tender. Add the mushrooms towards the end of the cooking time and adjust the seasoning.

Meanwhile heat the remaining butter in a frying pan, add the fish and cook quickly until golden brown and tender.

Mix the fish, plus any butter left in the pan, with the rice mixture, taking care not to break the fish strips. Fold in the fennel or parsley just before serving.

FISH STOCKS:
The stock in the recipe, left, is a simple one; no extra flavours are needed, as the rice mixture is interesting.

Adapt stock according to the dish; use some wine if you feel the recipe needs this. Do not use too high a proportion of herbs, onion, or garlic as most fish has a delicate flavour which is easily overwhelmed.

Use fish bones, whenever possible; these add a great deal of flavour to the stock.

Paella

Paella   ▲ ▲ ▲   ✿ ✿ ✿

SERVES 4
1 small chicken
100 g/4 oz fat pork or bacon
1 large Spanish onion
2 to 3 garlic cloves
450 g/1 lb tomatoes
1 red pepper
12 mussels, prepared as on
    page 134
12 large prawns
2 tablespoons olive oil
225 to 300 g/8 to 10 oz
    arborio rice
600 ml/1 pint water
¼ teaspoon saffron powder or
    strands
salt and freshly ground black
    pepper
75 g/3 oz chorizo (Spanish
    spiced sausage)

Cut the chicken into 8 portions and dice the pork or bacon. Peel and chop the onion and garlic. Skin and chop the tomatoes and deseed and dice the pepper. The mussels can be left on half their shells and the prawns peeled or left in their shells.

Heat the oil and fry the chicken and pork or bacon until golden and nearly tender. Remove from the pan, add the onion and garlic and cook for 5 minutes. Put in the tomatoes and cook for 2 to 3 minutes, then add the red pepper and rice.

Continue to stir over a gentle heat for 1 to 2 minutes, mixing the rice with the onion mixture. Boil the water, add the saffron and pour over the rice. Season lightly. Cook steadily until the rice is almost tender. Stir from time to time and check the amount of liquid.

Return the chicken and pork or bacon to the mixture and continue cooking until almost ready to serve. Thinly slice the chorizo, add to the pan with the mussels and prawns and any extra seasoning required. Heat for 2 to 3 minutes.

Serve straight from the paella pan.

NOTE: It is essential to check the amount of liquid during cooking; if necessary add more boiling water.

MAKING A PAELLA
The ingredients vary in different parts of Spain. The recipe left gives a typical mixture. You could add cooked peas, sliced squid and/or clams.

Some recipes are made with short grain rice, which gives a stickier texture; others with long grain rice, which keeps the grains separate.

The name paella comes from the pan in which it is cooked.

Sweetcorn Risotto   ▲   ✿ ✿

SERVES 4
2 onions
1 tablespoon olive oil
50 g/2 oz butter
225 g/8 oz arborio rice
750 ml/1¼ pints vegetable or
    chicken stock
pinch saffron powder or a few
    strands of saffron
salt and freshly ground black
    pepper
2 tablespoons chopped parsley
1 teaspoon chopped marjoram
225 g/8 oz canned or cooked
    sweetcorn

The quantity of rice in this risotto is smaller than in the one on page 134, for this is the type of risotto that makes an excellent accompaniment to main dishes.

Peel and finely chop the onions. Heat the oil with 25 g/1 oz of the butter and cook the onions for 5 minutes. Add the rice and turn in the buttery mixture. Heat the stock and saffron and strain if desired, see right-hand column. Moisten the rice with a little of the hot stock. Cook steadily, adding the liquid gradually, as described in the risotto recipe on page 134. Towards the end of the cooking period, add the seasoning, herbs and sweetcorn. Blend in the remaining butter just before serving the risotto.

USING SAFFRON:
Saffron comes from the stamens of a very special crocus. It is thought to be the most expensive spice in the world, but only a little is needed to give colour and flavour to food.

The strands can be heated in the liquid for a few minutes, then this can be strained but they do tend to dissolve in cooking.

EGG DISHES

Eggs are not only an essential ingredient in a great many dishes, but, as an important source of protein and vitamins, they can be used to provide nutritious light and main dishes. They also contain significant amounts of iron.

There have been worries about the safety of using eggs. The facts, as known today, are these: the number of eggs containing salmonella are very few; even so, it is wise to buy eggs from a reliable source, preferably where the date of laying and/or 'sell by' are given. Use the eggs as soon as possible after purchase and store them in the refrigerator. Certain people may be more easily affected by salmonella — they are the elderly, the very young, pregnant women, and the unfit. It is wise, therefore, for these people to avoid eating dishes containing uncooked or very lightly set eggs. Cooking to a high temperature destroys the salmonella bacteria and makes eggs safe eating for everyone.

BASIC WAYS OF COOKING EGGS

Boiled: Lower eggs into boiling water. Cook for 4 to 4¹/₂ minutes for a soft-boiled egg, and 8 to 10 minutes for a hard-boiled egg, depending upon the size and freshness of the egg. If putting in cold water and bringing to boiling point, allow 1 minute less cooking time. Crack the shells and cool hard-boiled eggs in cold water quickly to avoid a dark line around the yolk.

Fried: Heat a little fat in the pan – a non-stick pan requires only a few drops of oil. Break the egg on to a saucer and slide into the pan, or break it straight into the pan. Cook steadily. If you dislike the look of the yolk spoon a little fat over the top.

Poached: Bring water in a pan to boiling point, add a pinch of salt and a few drops of vinegar if desired – this helps to coagulate the white. Slide the egg into the water, make sure this keeps just at boiling point. Swirl the water around the egg with a spoon to make sure the white sets into a neat shape. If preferred, heat a small knob of butter or margarine in an egg-poacher, over hot water. Slide the egg in, cover and cook.

Scrambled: Beat the egg with seasoning and a little milk or single cream; allow 1 tablespoon to 1 or 2 eggs. Heat a small knob of butter or margarine in a pan, add the eggs and cook slowly, stirring only occasionally.

DISHES BASED ON BOILED EGGS

Egg cutlets: Hard-boil and chop 4 eggs. Make a sauce with 25 g/1 oz margarine, 25 g/1 oz flour, 150 ml/¹/₄ pint milk. Add the eggs, 25 g/1 oz soft breadcrumbs, 1 tablespoon chopped parsley and 2 teaspoons chopped capers. Form into cutlet shapes, coat in seasoned flour, beaten egg and crisp breadcrumbs and fry in a little hot oil until crisp and brown on either side. Drain on absorbent paper and serve hot or cold.

The mixture can be flavoured with 50 to 100 g/2 to 4 oz chopped cooked ham, or grated cheese, or chopped cooked mushrooms.

Eggs mornay: Hard-boil and shell eggs and put into an ovenproof dish. These can be served on a bed of creamed spinach, or creamed potatoes or mixed vegetables, to make a more substantial meal. Top with a Mornay sauce, made as on page 159, then with grated cheese. Heat under the grill or for 25 minutes in a preheated oven set to 190°C/375°F, Gas Mark 5.

Eggs Milanese: Put shelled hard-boiled eggs on a bed of cooked macaroni, tossed in a little butter and chopped parsley. Cover with Cheese sauce, made as on page 158, and

Piperade; Florence-Style Eggs
(see page 138)

with grated cheese and breadcrumbs. Bake as Eggs mornay, left.

Stuffed eggs: Hard-boil and shell the eggs, halve and carefully remove the yolks. Mash these and blend with a little butter or margarine or mayonnaise, then flavour with anchovy essence or chopped canned anchovies; grated cheese and chopped asparagus tips; flaked cooked or canned salmon or tuna or chopped prawns or other seafood.

The eggs can be served cold in salad or coated with a Cheese, or Tomato, or Mushroom sauce, recipes on pages 158 and 160. Bake as Eggs mornay, left.

DISHES BASED ON POACHED EGGS

Poached eggs are excellent on vegetable dishes, such as ratatouille or creamed spinach.

Poached eggs Hollandaise: This is a real luxury dish. Make Hollandaise sauce as page 160. Poach the egg(s), place on rounds of toast and coat with the sauce.

DISHES BASED ON SCRAMBLED EGGS

One really popular luxury dish is to serve the eggs with slices of smoked salmon. The scrambled eggs are equally good – whether hot or cold – served with smoked mackerel and smoked eel.

Cook sliced mushrooms in the butter or margarine, or heat minced or diced ham or chicken or mixed cooked vegetables. Add the beaten eggs and scramble.

Piperade: This is one of the most famous of all scrambled egg dishes. Peel and finely chop 1 medium onion and a clove of garlic. Skin and chop 2 medium tomatoes. Deseed and finely dice 1 red or green pepper (or use half of each). Heat 50 g/2 oz butter or margarine in a pan and cook the vegetables slowly until soft. Beat and season 4 eggs, pour over the mixture in the pan and scramble in the usual way. Garnish with parsley. This can be served with slices of fried ham.

MICROWAVE COOKING OF EGGS:
Never try to 'boil' eggs in a microwave. If poaching or 'frying' eggs, prick the yolks, as instructed in microwave books. Scrambled eggs are particularly good cooked in the microwave.

FREEZING EGGS:
Most of the dishes that include eggs as an ingredient can be frozen; those that are unsuitable are indicated. Never freeze any dishes containing whole cooked eggs – they become tough and leathery.

EGG DISHES IN MINUTES ▲ to ▲▲ ✿

Baked eggs: These are generally cooked in individual ovenproof ramekins or cocotte dishes, but several eggs can be cooked in an ovenproof serving dish. Use a preheated oven set to 190°C/375°F, Gas Mark 5. Bake for 10 to 15 minutes.

Crabmeat cocottes: Put flaked crabmeat and peeled prawns into a buttered cocotte dish and top with a spoonful of single cream or yogurt. Break an egg on top. Add more cream or yogurt and a few drops of melted butter. Bake for 12 to 15 minutes.

Florence-style eggs: Spoon a little creamed spinach into the bottom of each dish, break an egg on top and cover with a little double cream or thick yogurt, grated cheese and a few drops of melted butter. Bake for 15 minutes.

Valentine-style eggs: Mix sliced cooked mushrooms with a thick and well-seasoned tomato pulp. Spoon a little into cocotte dishes, top with an egg and a little grated cheese. Bake for 15 minutes.

Stuffed potatoes: Bake a jacket potato and cut off a lengthways slice. Scoop out the pulp and mash it with a little seasoning, butter or margarine. Spread this into the potato shell. Break an egg into it and top with grated cheese. Bake for 10 to 15 minutes.

Plain Omelette ▲ to ▲▲ ✿

SERVES 2
4 eggs
salt and freshly ground black
    pepper
water, see method
25 to 50 g/1 to 2 oz butter,
    see method

Beat the eggs lightly with the seasoning. If you add some water, it gives a lighter texture. Add up to 1 tablespoon water per egg. Do not over-beat this type of omelette.

Heat the butter in an omelette pan. If you use the full amount of butter, pour a little into the eggs just before cooking.

Pour the eggs into the omelette pan. Cook until just set at the bottom, then tilt the pan so the liquid egg runs to the sides. At the same time loosen the eggs from the sides of the pan. Continue like this until set to personal taste, then fold or roll away from the handle and tip on to a heated plate.

FLAVOURINGS FOR SAVOURY OMELETTES
Cheese: Add grated cheese to the beaten eggs or to the omelette just before folding. Fill with vegetables, or fish or chicken, in a cheese sauce, as in the picture.
Fish: Fill with shellfish or flaked white or smoked fish in a sauce, or add chopped prawns to the beaten eggs.
Meat: Add finely diced ham or crisp chopped bacon.

FOR A PERFECT OMELETTE: Never try to cook too many eggs at one time. The quantity given is ideal for a 12·5 to 15 cm/5 to 6 inch omelette pan.

Too large a pan means too thin an omelette, which could become dry in cooking.

Cook the omelette quickly. Do not 'work', i.e. tilt the pan etc., until the eggs have set on the bottom.

Soufflé Omelette ▲ to ▲▲ ✿

SERVES 2
4 eggs
water or other liquid, see
    method
sugar or seasoning, see
    method
25 to 50 g/1 to 2 oz butter

This type of omelette can be served as a savoury dish, with fillings as above, but usually it is a dessert.

Separate the eggs and beat the yolks with the sugar, see right, or seasoning. Add about $\frac{1}{2}$ tablespoon water or other liquid per egg, see right.

Whisk the egg whites until they stand in peaks and fold into the yolks just before cooking. Heat the butter and heat the grill on a medium setting before cooking the omelette.

Pour the eggs into the pan and cook until set on the bottom. It is very difficult to cook this type of omelette entirely on the top of the cooker, so place under the grill (take care the handle does not get too hot). Cook until set.

Cut the omelette lightly through the centre to make it easier to fold and add the filling, see right. Fold away from the handle and tip on to a heated plate.

FILLINGS AND FLAVOURINGS: Add 1 teaspoon sugar for each egg.

Add $\frac{1}{2}$ tablespoon cream or liqueur to each egg in place of water.

Fill with hot jam, or fruit purée, or poached fruit.

Top the folded omelette with a layer of sifted icing sugar, or brown sugar and flaked almonds. Place under the grill for a few minutes to caramelize.

Plain Omelette with a fish and cheese sauce filling

Chinese Pancakes

Pancakes ▲ ✪

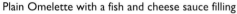

MAKES 10 TO 12
115* g/4 oz plain flour
pinch salt
1 egg with 280* ml/½ pint
   milk, or milk and water, or
   2 eggs with 250* ml/8 fl oz
   milk and water
1 tablespoon melted butter or
   olive or corn oil, optional,
   see method
For cooking:
few drops of oil

* use this metrication to give
   correct consistency.

Sift the flour and salt. Add the egg(s) and a little of the liquid and beat until a smooth batter. Gradually whisk in the rest of the liquid. Add the melted butter or oil just before cooking and whisk the batter. This fat improves the texture, stops the pancakes sticking and is invaluable when freezing them.

To cook the pancakes: If you have two pans, you can work more quickly to feed the family. Brush the base with a very little oil – this should be necessary for the first pancake only; after this you should be able to cook them, without adding any more oil.

Pour or spoon enough batter to give a wafer-thin layer over the base of the pan; tilt the pan to encourage the batter to flow to the sides. Cook steadily for 2 minutes, or until the pancake moves easily in the pan. Turn or toss and cook for the same time on the second side.

Keeping the pancakes hot: Place on a plate in a cool oven or over a pan of hot water. Cover with a 'hood' of foil.

FILLINGS FOR PANCAKES:
SAVOURY FILLINGS: These can be similar to those given for omelettes on page 138, or fill with cooked bacon, or roll around frankfurters or cooked sausages.

SWEET FILLINGS: Hot jam or marmalade, fruit purées, ice cream and fruit, ice cold yogurt and fruit.

You can serve the pancakes in the traditional way with lemon and sugar.

Chinese Pancakes ▲ ✪✪

MAKES 8 TO 10
175 g/6 oz plain flour
approximately 175 ml/6 fl oz
   boiling water
1 to 2 tablespoons sunflower
   oil

The Chinese pancakes used to wrap food, such as duck shown in the picture, are made quite differently from the batter mixture on this page.

Put the flour into a bowl and gradually add boiling water until you have a soft pliable dough that can be kneaded.

Knead for 5 to 6 minutes until smooth, cover and leave for 15 minutes, then form a long roll about 5 cm/2 inches in diameter. Cut 8 or 10 slices from this and flatten until each piece is 7·5 cm/3 inches in diameter. Brush the tops with oil, then place 2 together, with the oiled sides touching. Roll out until 15 cm/6 inches in diameter.

Heat a heavy frying-pan and rub it lightly with oil if you feel the pancakes might stick. Fry steadily on either side for 3 minutes. Cool slightly, then gently pull the two layers apart, so you have 8 to 10 thin pancakes. If cold, steam over boiling water before using.

PEKING DUCK:
It is essential that the duck is beautifully crisp for this dish. Hang in the air for several hours to dry well, before roasting as page 116. For extra crispness, brush the skin with a sugar syrup made by mixing 25 g/1 oz brown sugar with 5 tablespoons water, then cook.

To serve, cut the skin in long pieces, then slice the flesh neatly. Serve with strips of raw cucumber, spring onions and hoisin sauce.

Mushroom Quiche ▲▲ ✪✪✪

MAKES 4 TO 6
For the pastry:
175 g/6 oz plain flour
pinch salt
100 g/4 oz butter or margarine
cold water to bind
For the filling:
225 g/8 oz mushrooms
25 g/1 oz butter
75 g/3 oz Gruyère or Cheddar
  cheese
1 egg, size 1
2 egg yolks
225 ml/7½ fl oz single cream
  or milk
salt and freshly ground black
  pepper

Sift the flour and salt, rub in the butter or margarine and add enough water to make a firm rolling consistency. Roll out and line a 20 cm/8 inch flan tin or dish. Cover lightly and chill for 30 minutes.

Preheat the oven to 190°C/375°F, Gas Mark 5. Bake the pastry 'blind' for 15 minutes until firm and pale golden. It helps to crisp the base of the pastry if the baking tin or dish is placed on a preheated baking sheet.

While the pastry is cooking, prepare the filling. Wipe and slice the mushrooms. Heat the butter and cook the mushrooms for 2 or 3 minutes only. Place in the partially baked pastry case. Grate the cheese and add to the mushrooms.

Beat the egg and egg yolks, add the cream or milk and seasoning to taste. Spoon over the mushrooms and cheese. Reduce the oven heat to 160°C/325°F, Gas Mark 3 and continue cooking for a further 25 minutes, or until the filling is just set.

Serve hot or cold.

NEW FILLINGS FOR QUICHES:
Use cooked asparagus tips, a selection of cooked beans with cheese, chopped cooked ham and tongue, sliced chicken and a little chestnut stuffing or the suggestions below.
Onion and bacon: Peel and thinly slice 450 g/1 lb onions. Derind and chop 4 bacon rashers. Heat 2 tablespoons olive oil and fry the onions until tender. Fry the bacon separately until crisp. Add 1 teaspoon chopped sage and a good shake of black pepper. Put in the partially cooked pastry, add the eggs and cream. Cook as above.
Ratatouille: Fill the lightly baked pastry with 225 g/8 oz of well-drained ratatouille, as page 145. Top with thinly sliced cheese. Add the egg and cream mixture. Cook as above.

BAKING BLIND:
Use a sheet of greaseproof paper in the flan, topped with baking beans or crusts of bread. This holds the pastry base down.
  You can use foil instead.

CHANGING THE PASTRY:
If you are making the flan for a picnic, use slightly less fat in the pastry, i.e. to 175 g/6 oz flour use 85 g/3 oz fat.

Cheese pastry: Use the amount of fat above, plus 50 g/2 oz grated Parmesan or mature Cheddar cheese.

Wholemeal pastry: Use all wholemeal flour or half wholemeal and half white flour.

GOOD SOUFFLÉS

There is a belief that soufflés are difficult to make. That is far from true. If you analyse the ingredients, they are extremely simple.

It is important to whisk the whites until they stand in peaks, but do not let them become too stiff and dry. The method of adding these to the mixture is important. Take 1 tablespoon and beat it hard into the mixture, so making a softer texture. Then fold in the remaining egg whites gently but thoroughly. A higher proportion of egg whites than egg yolks gives a lighter soufflé.

Do not bake a soufflé too slowly or for too long; if you do it becomes dry. It should be beautifully golden in colour and slightly soft in the centre.

It is possible to prepare the mixture up to an hour before baking if the dish is completely covered with a mixing bowl to exclude the air. Serve as soon as it is baked.

The lobster soufflé, page 141, gives the standard proportions for a savoury soufflé, with the exception of the 3 tablespoons cream, which are important with lobster. You can use a little extra cream in other soufflés, but see the advice under the individual recipes.

Cheese soufflé: Make the panada as in the Lobster soufflé, add the egg yolks with 100 g/4 oz grated Cheddar or other cheese. You can add 1 tablespoon cream. Season well, including a little mustard.

Chicken soufflé: Make the panada as in the Lobster soufflé, but use chicken stock. Then add 2 tablespoons double cream. Add the egg yolks with 150 g/5 oz minced or finely chopped cooked chicken. Flavour with a little chopped thyme or rosemary.

Uncooked minced liver makes an excellent soufflé.

Fish soufflés: Use flaked, lightly cooked white fish or smoked haddock, or cooked or canned salmon, or tuna, or cooked prawns or crabmeat. Use fish stock in the panada, plus 1 tablespoon cream. Add the egg yolks, plus 150 to 175 g/5 to 6 oz of the fish.

Vegetable soufflés: There are several vegetables that make excellent soufflés, particularly asparagus, Jerusalem artichokes, carrots and spinach. Cook and pureé the vegetables. Use 225 ml/7 $^1/_2$ fl oz pureé instead of the stock or milk. Heat 25 g/1 oz butter or margarine, stir in 15 g/$^1/_2$ oz flour, then the vegetable purée. Cook until thickened, then proceed as Lobster soufflé.

Lobster Soufflé
▲ ▲ ▲   ✿ ✿

SERVES 2 TO 4
150 g/5 oz lobster flesh
3 tablespoons single cream*
For the panada:
25 g/1 oz butter
25 g/1 oz flour
150 ml/$^1/_4$ pint lobster stock, see right-hand column, or fish stock or milk
4 eggs or 3 to 4 eggs and 1 extra egg white
salt and freshly ground black pepper

* the cream softens the very firm lobster flesh

Preheat the oven at 190°C/375°C, Gas Mark 5. Grease an 18 cm/7 inch soufflé dish or 4 individual dishes.

Cut the lobster flesh into pieces, then mix with the cream.

Heat the butter in a pan, stir in the flour and gradually blend in the stock or milk. Bring to the boil and stir briskly as the sauce thickens to a binding consistency (a panada). Remove the pan from the heat and blend in the lobster flesh.

Separate the eggs and beat the yolks into the other ingredients. Season to taste. Whisk the egg whites until they stand in soft peaks and fold into the other ingredients.

Spoon the mixture into the soufflé dish or dishes. Bake for approximately 30 minutes if using the large dish and 15 to 18 minutes with individual dishes. The mixture should have risen well but be slightly soft in the middle. Serve at once.

This serves 2 people as a light main dish or 4 as an hors d'oeuvre.

MAKE LOBSTER STOCK:
Most fish stock is made by simmering fish bones and skin in water or water and white wine, see page 134.

Lobster stock is made by simmering the shell of the lobster in water or water and white wine, after removing all the flesh. Simmer for 15 to 20 minutes, then strain. This produces a pink stock. Boil rapidly to reduce the amount to that given in the recipe and to produce a stronger taste.

Cheese Soufflé

142

CHEESE DISHES

There is an almost bewildering selection of cheese available today, both home-produced and from many other countries. Make a point of trying some of the lesser-known kinds from time to time.

Cheese is undoubtedly one of the most popular 'convenience foods', for a meal of cheese, bread and pickles – known as a Ploughman's lunch – is eaten by many people. Add a good salad and you have a very appetizing and perfectly balanced meal nutritionally. Remember cheese is not only an important source of protein, but also of calcium. This is an essential mineral for people of all ages.

There are suggestions for quickly prepared snacks using cheese below and these are followed by a more ambitious dish. Never over-cook cheese; it becomes tough.

Microwave cooking of cheese dishes: Cheese melts very quickly in a microwave, so check cooking times.

Freezing cheese: Cheese freezes very well. If you have frozen a selection of cheeses, it is sensible to use creamy types first, as these tend to lose flavour more quickly than the hard type.

Cottage Cheese Eclairs ▲ ✪✪

MAKES 12 TO 18
Choux pastry, as Savoury
    profiteroles, page 50
sesame seeds
For the filling:
25 g/1 oz butter or margarine
350 g/12 oz cottage cheese
1 tablespoon chopped chives
1 tablespoon chopped parsley
salt and ground black pepper
watercress to garnish

Make the choux pastry as the recipe on page 50. Pipe or spoon into finger shapes, sprinkle with sesame seeds, if liked, and bake as the profiteroles, but allow a further 10 to 15 minutes, as the éclairs are larger. When cooked, slit the sides to allow the steam to escape and cool away from a draught.

Cream the butter or margarine and blend with the rest of the ingredients for the filling. Do not put into the eclairs too early; as cottage cheese is rather soft, it could spoil the texture of the éclairs. Serve garnished with watercress.

FOR GOOD-SHAPED ECLAIRS:
Lightly flour the baking trays. With your finger, mark straight lines the length you want the éclairs to be. The lines show up well on the floured surface and you then can pipe or spoon the pastry perfectly. Alternatively, use special finger-shaped patty tins.

Cottage Cheese Eclairs

QUICK AND EASY CHEESE DISHES

Cheese can turn most ingredients into a satisfying dish within a very short time.

Top cooked vegetables with a cheese sauce or a layer of grated cheese and immediately you have a satisfying meal. There are good low-fat cheeses available and vegetarian cheeses, too. Many blue cheeses cook well.

Cheese kebabs: Cut squares of a firm cheese, such as Gouda or Edam. Put on to skewers with cubes of fruit, like canned pineapple, dessert apples dipped in lemon juice to keep them a good colour, or with very small tomatoes and button mushrooms. Brush these with a few drops of oil. Grill for 3 to 4 minutes. Serve with crusty rolls.

Cheese-stuffed peppers: Choose red, green or yellow peppers. Cut off the tops and remove the centre cores and seeds. To fill 4 peppers, mix together 350 g/12 oz grated or crumbled cheese – this can be all one kind of cheese or use a mixture of cheeses – 2 skinned and chopped tomatoes, 4 tablespoons peeled and grated cucumber, 4 tablespoons chopped walnuts or cashew nuts, 1 tablespoon chopped parsley and 4 tablespoons soured cream or yogurt to bind. Season well. Spoon into the peppers.

To serve cold, chill and cut into slices and serve on a bed of salad.

To serve hot, brush the outside of the peppers with a few drops of oil and bake for 20 minutes in a preheated oven set to 190°C/375°F, Gas Mark 5.

Toasted cheese: Top toasted bread with slices of lean ham or well-drained hot cooked celery hearts or sliced tomatoes. Cover with slices of cheese or a good layer of grated cheese. Heat under the grill or for a short time in the microwave.

MAKING A FONDUE

This is one of the easiest ways in which to entertain friends. A fondue, with a glass of wine, makes a very satisfying meal.

While the recipe uses the classic choice of cheeses, you can adapt this to the cheese you like best, providing it cooks well. Cheddar, Cheshire and the Dutch cheeses – Gouda and Edam – provide well-flavoured fondues. Low-fat cheeses are not good for this particular cheese dish. If you want to substitute this type of cheese, it is better to use them in a thick Cheese or Mornay sauce, such as the recipes on pages 158 and 159.

The dips can be cubes of fresh bread, toast or squares of French bread, etc.

While you can use a metal fondue pot, it is better to choose a ceramic one, for this gets less hot and it is important that the fondue mixture does not become over-heated.

The small amount of cornflour given in the recipe below is not essential, but it does assist in preventing the mixture from curdling (separating) during cooking.

Classic Fondue ▲ ▲ ✿

SERVES 4 TO 6
350 g/12 oz Emmenthal cheese
100 g/4 oz Gruyère cheese
1 garlic clove
150 ml/¼ pint dry white wine
1 teaspoon cornflour
   (optional, see above)
To flavour:
1 tablespoon lemon juice
   optional
pinch ground or freshly grated
   nutmeg
freshly ground black pepper

Grate the cheeses; the proportions of these two cheeses can be changed to suit personal tastes. Halve the garlic and rub it around the fondue pot, or bowl in which the fondue is to be cooked, or the saucepan, see below.

Pour almost all the wine into the container and warm gently. Add the cheese, together with the cornflour. This should be blended smoothly with the last of the wine. Melt slowly until the mixture starts to bubble. This stage can be done in an ordinary saucepan over a low heat and the mixture then transferred to a fondue pot over the heater or to the bowl on top of a pan of simmering, not boiling water.

Gradually add lemon juice, nutmeg and pepper.

When dipping into the fondue, use a swirling movement, this helps to keep the cheese mixture smooth.

DIPPERS:
Bread and toast and raw vegetables, such as cauliflower florets, slices of raw courgettes, cucumber and button mushrooms.

Have wedges of dessert apple, thickly sliced bananas dipped in lemon juice to preserve the colour and cubes of fresh or well-drained canned pineapple.

VEGETABLES

It is interesting how the role of vegetables has changed. Once they were regarded as the accompaniments to meat, fish or other foods. Nowadays, they are frequently the most important part of the meal.

We have a wonderful range of vegetables from which to choose, many of which are used in dishes in this book. Shop wisely for vegetables and store them carefully, see pages 24 to 26.

On pages 148 and 149 are suggestions for making everyday vegetables a little more interesting.

The golden rule is to cook vegetables for the shortest possible time so they retain the maximum colour, texture and flavour. Frozen vegetables retain much of the nutritional value of really fresh produce. As they are blanched before freezing, shorten the cooking period, otherwise they will taste badly over-cooked.

Do not chop or slice green vegetables, or soak them in water for a long time before cooking; if you do, they will lose precious vitamins.

PERFECTLY COOKED VEGETABLES

MICROWAVE COOKING OF VEGETABLES:
This is an excellent method, providing the vegetables are young and of an even size.

The amount of liquid needed is minimal and very little, if any, salt need be added, as the vegetables retain much of their natural flavour.

This describes any vegetable where you can taste all the true flavour, where the colour is good and where the original firm texture is retained as much as possible.

When boiling vegetables, use the minimum amount of water; this means you need only a little salt. Make sure the water is boiling when the vegetables are added. Keep the lid on the pan and cook for the shortest possible time. You retain more of the vitamin content if the vegetables are placed into boiling water. Root vegetables should be cooked steadily, not quickly.

Green vegetables should be cooked as quickly as possible, but take care the delicate tops of greens, like broccoli, are not broken. Do not add salt to sweetcorn until almost cooked; the salt toughens it.

Take care with garnishing the vegetables, so they look as good as they taste. Green vegetables can be topped with chopped almonds, to give a change of colour. White vegetables, like boiled potatoes, can be topped with lightly cooked tomatoes – this garnish gives them the name of Spanish potatoes – or with various herbs or other greenery. Salad ingredients can be combined with hot vegetables for contrast. Green rocket is not only good in salads but excellent as a garnish for root vegetables.

Mangetouts Grandmère ▲ ▲ ✿

SERVES 4
3 medium onions
100 g/4 oz cooked ham, cut in a thick slice
50 g/2 oz butter or margarine
1 x 227 g/8 oz can chopped plum tomatoes
2 tablespoons chopped parsley
salt and freshly ground black pepper
300 g/10 oz mangetout peas

Peel the onions and cut into wafer-thin slices. Cut the ham into narrow strips. Heat the butter or margarine in a pan, add the onions and cook gently for 10 minutes, then tip in the tomatoes and liquid from the can. Heat for 2 or 3 minutes with the parsley and seasoning.

Meanwhile, bring a little water to the boil, add a pinch of salt, then the peas. Cook for 1 to 2 minutes only, then strain.

Add the ham and peas to the tomato mixture and heat for 2 to 3 minutes only. Serve as a light main dish with hot French bread or, to make a more substantial meal, with vegetables and pasta.

MANGETOUT PEAS:
Simply trim the ends before using. To retain the crisp texture, cook for only a very few minutes. They can be used raw in salads or be added to stir-fry dishes.

Ratatouille

Ratatouille

▲ ▲ ✪ ✪

SERVES 6 TO 8
3 onions
3 garlic cloves
675 g/1 ½ lb tomatoes
5 medium courgettes
2 large aubergines
4 tablespoons olive oil
salt and freshly ground black
   pepper
2 tablespoons chopped parsley

Peel and finely chop the onions and garlic. Skin and chop the tomatoes. Wipe and slice the courgettes and aubergines, see note right. Heat the oil and cook the onions and garlic gently for 5 minutes. Add the tomatoes and cook for a few minutes until the juice starts to flow. Put in the courgettes and aubergines and stir to mix. Add a little seasoning. Cover the pan and simmer for about 30 minutes, or until the vegetables are softened. Taste and add extra seasoning, then stir in the parsley. Sprinkling some on the top.

This is equally good hot or cold. It freezes well for 1 year.

COOKING AUBERGINES:
If you dislike the slightly bitter taste of aubergine skin, either peel them or score the skin, sprinkle with salt and leave for 30 minutes. Then drain, rinse in cold water and slice.

Turkish Beans

▲ ✪

SERVES 4
450 g/1 lb haricots verts
2 medium onions
3 garlic cloves
3 medium tomatoes
1 green pepper
salt and ground black pepper
2 tablespoons olive oil
1 tablespoon chopped mixed
   herbs, see right

Trim the ends of the beans. Peel and finely chop the onions and garlic. Skin and slice the tomatoes. Deseed and dice the pepper.

Cook the beans in well-seasoned water for 10 minutes.

Meanwhile, heat the oil in a large pan, add the onions and garlic and cook gently for 10 minutes; take care they do not brown. Add the tomatoes and pepper. Cook for 3 to 4 minutes only, as both these ingredients should keep firm.

Strain the beans. Mix with the other ingredients. Top with herbs and serve.

OTHER BEANS TO USE:
Substitute sliced runner or diced French beans. This is an excellent way to serve drained cooked or canned dried beans.

HERBS TO USE:
Include chopped chervil, sage and savory, as well as parsley and chives.

Potatoes Forestière   ▲ ✿✿✿

SERVES 4
450 g/1 lb potatoes
100 g/4 oz mushrooms
100 g/4 oz cooked lean ham
150 ml/¼ pint milk
salt and freshly ground black
    pepper
25 g/1 oz butter or margarine
To garnish:
chopped parsley, optional

Preheat the oven to 160°C/325°F, Gas Mark 3. Peel or scrape the potatoes and cut into slices about 5 to 8 mm/¼ to ⅓ inch in thickness. Keep in cold water until ready to cook, then drain and dry well. Cut the mushrooms and ham into small pieces and mix together.

Arrange layers of sliced potatoes, mushrooms and ham in a casserole, beginning and ending with potatoes.

Warm the milk, add a fairly generous amount of seasoning and pour over the ingredients in the dish. Melt the butter or margarine and spread over the potato topping. Bake for 1¼ hours, top with the parsley, if using and serve.

This makes a good light supper dish or an excellent accompaniment to cooked poultry.

POTATOES ANNA:
Cut the potatoes into wafer thin slices. Pack in layers in a dish or tin with a little seasoned melted butter between each layer. Bake as the recipe left.

SCALLOPED POTATOES:
Cut the potatoes as in the recipe left, arrange in layers in the dish. Cover with seasoned milk, top with butter or margarine; bake as recipe, left.

Latke   ▲ ✿

SERVES 4
450 g/1 lb old potatoes, weight
    when peeled
225 g/8 oz onions, weight
    when peeled
2 tablespoons finely chopped
    parsley
2 small eggs
salt and freshly ground black
    pepper
For frying:
2 tablespoons oil or 50 g/2 oz
    fat

Latke are interesting savoury pancakes. It is essential to press out the surplus moisture before blending the potatoes with the rest of the ingredients.

Use the coarse side of the grater and grate the potatoes. Place in a nylon sieve or strainer and stand this over a basin. Press gently with a wooden spoon to extract the surplus moisture; discard this liquid.

Finely grate the onions and mix with the grated potatoes and the rest of the ingredients.

Heat the oil or fat in a frying-pan or wok. Take spoonfuls of the potato mixture and drop into the oil or fat. Cook steadily for 5 minutes, or until golden brown and firm on the underside, then turn over and cook for the same time on the second side. Drain on absorbent paper and serve.

These are delicious with hot or cold meat or poultry dishes, or they make an excellent vegetarian dish if topped with sliced or grated cheese and grilled for 1 or 2 minutes.

ROSTI:
Scrub old potatoes and par-boil for 10 minutes. Drain, peel and coarsely grate.

To each 450 g/1 lb potatoes, you need about 50 g/2 oz butter.

Heat the butter in a frying-pan, add the potatoes, season lightly. Pat into a flat cake.

Cook steadily for 10 minutes. Place a plate over the pan, invert the pan so the rosti is on the plate. Slide back into the pan, with the browned side uppermost.

Cook for the same time on the second side.

Bean-Stuffed Peppers   ▲ ✿✿

SERVES 4
4 green peppers
1 red pepper
salt and freshly ground black
    pepper
For the filling:
2 medium onions
2 tablespoons sunflower oil
1 x 227 g/8 oz can chopped
    plum tomatoes
1 x 227 g/8 oz can red kidney
    beans
2 tablespoons chopped parsley
1 teaspoon chopped thyme
25 g/1 oz breadcrumbs
1 egg
For the topping:
4 tablespoons chopped
    walnuts

Cut a slice lengthways from each of the green peppers. Deseed the peppers, then dice the 4 slices removed. Deseed and dice the red pepper. Peel and finely chop the onions.

Put the green pepper cases into a very little boiling seasoned water and cook steadily for 3 minutes only, then drain and place in an ovenproof dish. Heat almost all the oil in a pan and add the onions. Cook for 5 minutes, then tip in the tomatoes, plus liquid from the can, the diced green and red peppers, the well-drained beans and herbs. Cook rapidly for 5 minutes, so any excess liquid evaporates.

Remove from the heat and add the breadcrumbs, well-beaten egg and seasoning to taste. Spoon the bean mixture into the pepper cases. Brush the sides of these with the last of the oil, top with the chopped nuts and bake for 20 minutes in a preheated oven, set to 200°C/400°F, Gas Mark 6.

These are equally good served hot or cold.

TO SERVE:
A green salad and roast potatoes make excellent accompaniments. The potatoes need to be put into the oven earlier than the peppers.

TO ROAST POTATOES WITH LITTLE FAT:
Peel and dry the potatoes. Do not put into hot fat but brush each potato with a little melted fat or oil. They roast perfectly and become beautifully crisp. Allow 1 hour for medium potatoes at the setting given in the recipe.

Vegetable Moussaka   ▲ ✪ ✪ ✪

SERVES 4

2 medium aubergines

salt and freshly ground black
   pepper

3 large onions

2 garlic cloves (optional)

3 large tomatoes

4 medium potatoes

50 g/2 oz margarine

3 tablespoons sunflower or
   corn oil

For the sauce:

225 g/8 oz cheese*

50 g/2 oz margarine

40 g/1½ oz wholemeal flour

600 ml/1 pint milk

½ to 1 teaspoon mixed spice
   or grated nutmeg

1 teaspoon French mustard

To garnish:

chopped parsley

* Use Cheddar or any good
   cooking cheese.

Wipe and thinly slice the aubergines; discard the stalk ends. Sprinkle the slices with salt and leave for 20 to 30 minutes if you dislike the slightly bitter taste. Drain, rinse the aubergines in cold water and dry on absorbent paper.

Peel and chop the onions and garlic. Skin and slice the tomatoes. Peel and thinly slice the potatoes. Heat half the margarine and oil in a pan, add the aubergines and potato slices and cook steadily for 10 minutes, turning over once or twice. Remove from the pan. Heat the rest of the margarine and oil, add the onions, garlic and tomatoes and cook for 10 minutes; make sure they do not brown. Mix half the aubergines and potatoes with the tomato mixture and season to taste. Keep the rest of the aubergines and potatoes to make the topping.

To make the sauce, grate the cheese. Heat the margarine, add the flour and stir over the heat for 1 or 2 minutes, then gradually blend in the milk. Stir until a smooth sauce is formed. Remove from the heat, add approximately 175 g/6 oz of cheese and season with salt, pepper, spice and mustard.

Spoon half the mixed vegetables into a casserole, add half the sauce and the remainder of the mixed vegetables. Top with a neat layer of aubergines and potatoes, then sauce. Cover the casserole with a lid or foil; make sure this does not touch the sauce. Bake for 1¼ hours in a preheated oven, set to 160°C/325°F, Gas Mark 3. Remove the lid, add the last of the cheese, return to the oven, raising the heat slightly, and cook for a further 10 minutes, or until the cheese topping has melted. Garnish with the parsley.

USING YOGURT:
Instead of making the sauce, you can use 450 to 600 ml/ ¾ to 1 pint thick Greek yogurt. Blend the cheese with this. Use in the same way as the sauce, see recipe left.

COOKING IN THE MICROWAVE:
The vegetables can be cooked in a large bowl instead of in the pan. Use FULL POWER and stir from time to time until they are just tender. Keep the bowl covered during this time. Use only half the amount of oil given left.

The completed dish can be cooked in the microwave or for 30 minutes only in the oven, as the vegetables are tender.

Vegetable Moussaka

NEW WAYS WITH FAMILIAR VEGETABLES

Although there are many unusual vegetables available, most families rely on the everyday varieties for the majority of their meals.

It is surprising how these can be given a completely different taste, with a different method of cooking or the addition of a few extra ingredients.

Asparagus: When this is in season and at its cheapest, turn it into a main dish. Place the cooked asparagus on a hot dish. Top with hot browned almonds or cashew nuts, wholemeal crumbs, fried until crisp, and a good layer of grated cheese.

Beetroot: This makes a delicious hot vegetable. Coarsely grate peeled, cooked beetroot. Peel and finely chop 1 or more onions. Cook gently in a little oil. When they are soft, add the beetroot and heat for 2 or 3 minutes. Add plenty of chopped parsley and a little chopped lemon balm

Cabbage or other green vegetables: Cook lightly, so they retain their firm texture. Heat in a little soured cream or fromage frais, plus a squeeze of lemon juice and a light sprinkling of caraway seeds.

Swedish cabbage: Ideally this is made with red cabbage, but a green one could be used. Shred the cabbage finely, put into boiling salted water for 2 minutes only, then drain. Peel and thinly slice 2 large onions and separate into rings. Core and slice 2 unpeeled dessert apples. Heat 1 tablespoon oil and gently cook the onions until nearly soft, add the apples and cabbage with enough vegetable stock to cover, plus 3 tablespoons red wine and any extra seasoning required. Cover the pan tightly and cook for 15 minutes. Lift the lid and boil quickly until any excess liquid evaporates.

Chopped cooked bacon can be added to this to make a light main dish.

Carrots: Scrape new carrots, peel older ones, and cook for a minimum amount of time to retain their firm texture.

Carrots Lyonnaise: Cook sliced carrots with neatly diced onions, plus a squeeze of lemon juice and 1 or 2 teaspoons sugar in the water. This is particularly good when cooking older carrots.

If you have a pressure cooker, use it for cooking older vegetables, see page 45.

Cauliflower and broccoli: Divide into small sprigs (florets) and cook lightly. Top with the nuts, etc., as mentioned under asparagus, above.

Give the familiar Cauliflower cheese a new taste by adding finely chopped cooked bacon or ham, or prawns, or red kidney beans to the cheese sauce.

Celeriac: Peel and slice. Keep in cold water with a good squeeze of lemon juice or few drops of white vinegar during preparation, so the vegetable does not discolour. There are many ways of serving this celery-flavoured root. Cook in boiling salted water until just tender, strain and heat gently in soured cream or fromage frais with a little lemon juice and lots of chopped parsley and chives.

Celeriac and tomato bake: Cook the sliced vegetable lightly, i.e. for 5 minutes only, in boiling seasoned water. Strain and arrange in layers with sliced tomatoes, grated cheese and finely chopped chives. Top with crisp breadcrumbs and grated cheese. Bake for 30 minutes in a preheated oven set to 190°C/375°F, Gas Mark 5.

Celery: Celery heart is excellent diced and cooked in well-seasoned brown stock. When it is cooked, mix with sliced cooked mushrooms. Another way to add flavour is to cook it in tomato purée or tomato juice, flavoured with a very little chopped basil and thyme.

Cucumber: Cucumber is an excellent hot vegetable. Slice and coat in seasoned flour and fry in a little hot oil.

Spiced cucumber: Cut peeled or unpeeled cucumber into 5 cm/2 inch slices, then divide each slice into 4 finger shapes. Cook for 5 to 6 minutes only in a little white wine vinegar, to which is added crushed garlic, a good pinch of mixed allspice and a few drops of olive oil. Strain, if necessary, although the surplus liquid should evaporate during cooking. This is excellent with most dishes, particularly fish.

Leeks: Chop several rashers of bacon and fry in the pan until crisp. Add several skinned and chopped tomatoes and 1 teaspoon chopped tarragon. Clean and thinly slice 450 g/1 lb young leeks. Cook gently in the bacon and tomato mixture in a covered pan for about 10 minutes, so the leeks retain their crunchy texture. Season to taste.

Lettuce: If you grow these and have an abundance, use them as a cooked vegetable, like cabbage – see the recipes on the previous page. Lettuce may develop a slightly bitter taste, so add a good teaspoon or two of sugar.

Marrow: When very young, this can be cut into thin slices, without peeling, and then each slice divided into quarters. The vegetable can be coated in seasoned flour and fried like courgettes.

Steam rather than boil marrow, so it retains its texture. Season lightly before cooking and when cooked, toss in heated butter or margarine with a generous amount of chopped parsley and chives.

Bean-stuffed marrow: Peel the marrow, cut into 7·5 cm/3 inch slices, halve the slices and scoop out the seeds. Steam as above — take care not to over-cook the vegetable. Fill with the stuffing suggested for peppers on page 150. Cover the dish and bake as timing and temperature given for peppers, below.

Mushrooms: Look for the wonderful variety of mushrooms available today — not only the large flat, cup and button types, but you can obtain oyster mushrooms, ceps, chanterelles, oyster and shiitake from time to time. Cook these together to make super light dishes.

Sesame mushrooms: Cook one type of mushroom, or better still, a selection in sunflower oil to which is added 1 to 2 teaspoons sesame oil. Top the mushrooms with a generous quantity of sesame seeds before serving.

Onions: These are an invaluable ingredient in many dishes, but they can be served as a main dish, see page 150.

ONION AND POTATO BAKE: Peel and coarsely chop 2 large onions, melt 50 g/2 oz of margarine in a frying pan, and cook them for 5 minutes. Peel and slice 6 large potatoes and fill an ovenproof dish with alternate layers of potato and onion. Season each layer with salt and pepper to taste and finish with fried onion on the top. Preheat the oven to 190°C/375°F, Gas Mark 5 and cook for 1 hour or until potatoes are tender.

Rosti (see page 146); Potatoes Forestière (see page 146); Onion and Potato Bake

USING DRIED BEANS:
The recipe on page 146 is an ideal method of using left-over cooked beans or giving a good flavour to the canned variety.

If cooking dried beans, take care to give the adequate amount of fast boiling before cooking slowly. This ensures that harmful enzymes are destroyed.

PEPPERONATA:
Deseed and chop 450 g/1 lb mixed red, green and yellow peppers. Peel and chop 2 garlic cloves and 2 onions. Skin and chop 450 g/1 lb tomatoes. Cook steadily in 2 tablespoons olive oil, until just tender. Season to taste.

Sweet and sour onions: Peel 4 large onions, slice and separate into rings.

Heat 2 tablespoons sunflower oil in a wok or large frying-pan and cook the onions for 10 minutes, stirring most of the time. Make sure they do not discolour. Add 1 tablespoon soy sauce, 2 tablespoons orange juice, 1 tablespoon honey, 3 tablespoons white wine vinegar and a little seasoning. Continue cooking gently until the onions are just softened. Serve with cooked rice and green beans.

Peppers: These are used in many recipes, but they are delicious for a main meal, see page 146, and in Pepperonata, left.

Rice-stuffed peppers: This is enough to stuff 8 peppers.

Choose red, green and yellow peppers. Cut a slice from the top of each and scoop out the cores and seeds. Blanch for 3 minutes in boiling salted water and strain.

Mix 225 g/8 oz cooked rice with 3 tablespoons melted margarine, 3 tablespoons chopped spring onions, 225 g/8 oz coarsely chopped nuts, 1 1/2 tablespoons chopped parsley, 1 teaspoon chopped rosemary, 3 tablespoons finely chopped fennel bulb or celery and seasoning to taste.

Spoon into the pepper cases and top with the slices removed. Brush the outsides with melted margarine or a few drops of oil. Cover the dish.

Bake in a preheated oven set to 180°C/350°F, Gas Mark 4 for 30 minutes.

Zucchini Ripieni (Stuffed Courgettes)   ▲▲ ✪✪

SERVES 4
4 large or 8 medium courgettes
2 small onions
175 g/6 oz mushrooms
25 g/1 oz butter
2 tablespoons olive oil
50 g/2 oz soft breadcrumbs
1 teaspoon chopped parsley
1 teaspoon chopped oregano
1/2 teaspoon chopped rosemary
50 g/2 oz Mozzarella cheese
salt and freshly ground black pepper
2 tablespoons grated Parmesan cheese
To garnish:
black and/or green olives

This Italian dish is equally good as an hors d'oeuvre or for a main meal.

Preheat the oven to 200°C/400°F, Gas Mark 6. Wash and dry the courgettes and remove the hard ends. Put into a steamer over a pan of boiling water and cook for approximately 10 minutes, or until just tender. Do not over-cook. Split the courgettes lengthways and carefully scoop out the centre pulp, chop this finely.

Peel the onions and wipe the mushrooms. Chop both very finely. Heat the butter and oil and cook the onions and mushrooms until tender. Add the breadcrumbs, courgette pulp and herbs and mix together. Grate or crumble the Mozzarella cheese and stir this into the mixture in the pan, but do not cook. Season to taste.

Arrange the courgettes on an ovenproof dish, press the filling into the centres, top with the Parmesan cheese and bake for 20 minutes. Garnish with the olives.

TO PREPARE AHEAD:
The stuffed courgettes can be refrigerated. Add the Parmesan cheese just before cooking.

USING THE MICROWAVE:
Cook the onions and mushrooms in just 1 tablespoon oil in a basin. Arrange the stuffed courgettes like spokes of a wheel on a flat dish; do not cover. Allow about 6 minutes on FULL POWER.

Creole Courgettes   ▲▲ ✪

SERVES 4
450 g/1 lb courgettes
2 medium onions
4 medium tomatoes
1 large red pepper
2 tablespoons sunflower or olive oil
few drops Tabasco sauce
salt and freshly ground black pepper
2 tablespoons chopped parsley

Wipe the courgettes and cut into 1·5 cm/1/2 inch slices. Peel and finely chop the onions. Skin and chop the tomatoes. Deseed and dice the pepper. Heat the oil in a pan, add the onions and cook gently for 5 minutes. Put in the tomatoes, cover the pan and simmer until a soft purée is formed, then add the courgettes and diced pepper, together with the Tabasco sauce and seasoning.

Stir well to blend the ingredients. Cover the pan and simmer for 15 minutes. Add the parsley and serve.

TO TURN THIS INTO A COMPLETE MEAL:
Serve topped with cheese or add diced tofu to the mixture.

Creole Courgettes; Stuffed Mushrooms; Zucchini Ripieni

Stuffed Mushrooms   ▲ ✪

SERVES 4

8 large or 12 medium open-
   type (flat) mushrooms
For the filling:
1 medium onion
1 to 2 garlic cloves
1 tablespoon sunflower oil
25 g/1 oz butter
50 g/2 oz feta or soft cream
   cheese
50 g/2 oz soft white or
   wholemeal breadcrumbs
2 tablespoons chopped parsley
1 teaspoon chopped oregano
1 teaspoon finely grated lemon
   rind
2 teaspoons lemon juice
salt and freshly ground black
   pepper

Wipe the mushrooms or wash them in cold water; do not peel them, as much of the flavour is lost by doing this. Remove the stalks from the mushrooms and chop them; leave the caps whole. Peel and finely chop the onion and garlic. Heat the oil with the butter and cook the onion and garlic with the mushroom stalks for 5 minutes. Remove from the heat and add the rest of the ingredients for the stuffing. Mix well, season to taste.

Spoon over the dark side of the mushrooms. Place these in a greased dish and bake for 15 minutes in a preheated oven, set to 190°C/375°F, Gas Mark 5. If preferred, you can cover the dish and bake for approximately 5 to 6 minutes in the microwave on FULL POWER. Serve as an hors d'oeuvre, a snack or an accompaniment to main dishes.

TO MAKE A CHANGE:
Use grated hard cheese and increase the quantity.

Use chopped cooked ham or other meats.

PÂTÉ-STUFFED MUSHROOMS:
Use only 25 g/1 oz breadcrumbs and 100 g/4 oz soft liver pâté or diced liver sausage in the filling.

SIMPLE SALADS

The value of uncooked vegetables and fruit is stressed nowadays and there is no better way to combine these colourful, crunchy and nutritious foods, together with other ingredients, than in a salad. Serve salads with hot as well as cold dishes. Often its crisp texture is just right to complement a cooked main dish.

Buy salad ingredients with a critical eye; nothing is worse than wilting lettuce. Advice about judging quality and storing salad ingredients is on pages 24 and 26.

Be adventurous in the mixture of foods you combine in salads. There are no 'rules' about what is right or wrong, so your imagination can run riot. Choose the ingredients to give contrasting colours, textures and flavours. Select unusual as well as classic salad dressings, see page 156.

QUICK AND EASY SALADS

PREPARING SALAD INGREDIENTS
Wash lettuce and other salad greens gently and carefully in cold water. Shake dry in a salad shaker or a clean teacloth, or pat very gently with absorbent paper and allow time for the vegetables to become crisp again. When lettuce is expensive and not at its best, use shredded cabbage, Brussels sprouts, young raw spinach leaves and Chinese cabbage (also known as Chinese leaves, bok choy and po tsai). Ring the changes by using more than one kind of lettuce, or mix lettuce with curly endive.

Cut tomatoes, cucumber and other vegetables neatly or dice them, according to the recipe. Separate the white heads of chicory into individual leaves, these make an attractive shape around the edge of a salad bowl.

If making cheese salad, either grate or dice the cheese neatly or spoon softer cheeses into a pleasing shape.

Do not add the dressing too early to the salad; it spoils its crispness.

Keep the salad covered in the refrigerator until ready to serve.

Each of the salads that follow is a complete dish; but a selection of these would be excellent for a buffet meal.

Celery salad: Neatly chop the tender stalks of celery and mix with oil and vinegar dressing, page 156. Add a generous amount of chopped parsley and chopped chives and a little chopped tarragon. Garnish with strips of red pepper.

Green salad: In France, this generally means a salad of crisp lettuce only in an oil and vinegar dressing or with these ingredients offered to you to mix the dressing to your own taste.

It can, however, be a mixed salad if you consider the choice of green ingredients available. You could have lettuce of various kinds, cucumber, chopped green-tinged celery, green pepper, green grapes, watercress and mustard and cress, with chopped green herbs. This salad is generally dressed with oil and vinegar or lemon juice.

Mixed salad: There can be no standard recipe for this salad, as it means you mix together a number of ingredients to form a pleasing contrast of flavour, colour and texture. Make sure you have some crisp ingredients like celery, apples or radishes. Give the salad colour with red, green or yellow peppers, as well as tomatoes. Have refreshing cucumber and segments of citrus fruit, for a change.

This salad should have some surprise ingredients, so it does not always look and taste the same.

Potato salad: The golden rule is that this salad should be mixed, whenever possible, with freshly cooked, hot potatoes. Dice them and mix with mayonnaise or other dressing. It gives a good flavour if you use a little oil and vinegar dressing and then add the required amount of mayonnaise. Mix the potatoes with chopped parsley, chopped chives or finely chopped spring onions, gherkins and capers. Give it a crisp texture by adding chopped celery when the potatoes have become cold. Add chopped mint to a salad made with new potatoes.

Russian salad: Mix together a variety of diced cooked root vegetables, such as carrots, swede, turnip and sweet or ordinary potatoes. Add cooked peas and sliced green beans, too. Mix with mayonnaise, preferably while the vegetables are hot, so they absorb the flavour. Garnish with chopped parsley.

Cooked frozen mixed vegetables make an excellent alternative to the traditional blend of ingredients.

Sweet and Sour Bean Salad

▲ ✪

SERVES 4
225 g/8 oz cooked or canned
    flageolet beans
225 g/8 oz cooked or canned
    red kidney or adzuki beans
100 g/4 oz cooked or canned
    soya, haricot or butter
    beans
1 dessert apple
$^1/_2$ celery heart
small bunch spring onions

Drain all the beans well and mix together. The choice of beans gives a blend of green, red and white colours. Core and dice the apple. Chop the celery and the spring onions. Mix with the beans.

Put the mustard into a basin, blend in the oils, then add the rest of the ingredients. Spoon over the beans.

A crisp green salad makes this into an excellent and very nutritious meal.

FOR THE DRESSING:
1 to 2 teaspoons Dijon
    mustard
4 tablespoons olive or corn oil
1 teaspoon sesame oil
2 tablespoons lemon juice
1 tablespoon orange juice
2 tablespoons thin honey
1 to 2 tablespoons grated root
    ginger
1 tablespoon sesame seeds
salt and freshly ground black
    pepper

Tomatoes Provençale

▲ ✪

SERVES 4
4 large tomatoes
salt and freshly ground black
    pepper
1 x 227 g/8 oz can tuna in oil
1 garlic clove
4 tablespoons mayonnaise, see
    page 157
1 teaspoon lemon juice
2 tablespoons diced cucumber
2 tablespoons chopped green
    olives
few lettuce leaves

Cut a slice from each tomato; if this is done at the stalk end, the tomatoes stand upright more easily. Carefully scoop out the centre pulp, leaving the cases intact. Drain them and season lightly. The right-hand column gives suggestions for using the tomato pulp removed.

Drain the tuna and keep the oil. Break the fish into flakes. Peel and crush the garlic and blend with the mayonnaise, together with a little of the oil from the tuna and the lemon juice. Mix with the tuna, cucumber and olives. Spoon into the tomato cases and top with the slices removed. Serve on a bed of lettuce.

Any tuna oil left can be used in an oil and lemon dressing to serve with a fish salad.

TO USE THE TOMATO PULP:
This can be liquidized and made into an uncooked or cooked sauce for pasta salads or hot pasta or rice.

Use for filling pancakes or omelettes.

It makes an excellent alternative to tomato purée from a tube, mixed with mayonnaise as a dressing for a prawn cocktail.

Tomatoes Provençale

Spiced Coleslaw   ▲ ✿

SERVES 4

For the spiced dressing:

3 tablespoons mayonnaise, see
    page 157

$1/2$ teaspoon curry powder

$1/2$ teaspoon ground nutmeg

$1/2$ teaspoon paprika

I teaspoon made mustard

I tablespoon olive oil

I tablespoon lemon juice

salt and ground black pepper

$1/4$ to $1/2$ white cabbage or
    cabbage heart

I dessert apple

2 medium carrots

2 tablespoons diced gherkins

2 teaspoons capers

2 tablespoons chopped parsley

Make the dressing before cutting the cabbage and other
ingredients so they do not become dry.

To make the dressing: Blend ingredients together.

Finely shred the cabbage by hand or with the attachment on
the food processor or mixer. Core, but do not peel the apple;
cut this into neat dice. Peel and grate the carrots. Add these
ingredients to the dressing, together with the gherkins, capers
and parsley. Mix thoroughly. Do not make this too far ahead,
as the cabbage and other ingredients should remain crisp.

This is the kind of salad children will enjoy. You can omit
some of the spices if serving it to younger children. Other
salads that are likely to be popular are the melon and celery
and the waldorf.

CRUNCHY COLESLAW:
Omit the spices from the
dressing. You can use yogurt,
instead of mayonnaise, for a
lighter dressing. Season well.

Add chopped celery,
chopped nuts, more apple and
diced fresh pineapple.

Melon and Celery Salad

SERVES 4 TO 6

I small or $1/2$ large melon

I celery heart

3 tablespoon oil and vinegar
    dressing, see page 156

2 teaspoons grated fresh
    ginger or $1/2$ teaspoon
    ground ginger

lettuce or endive

2 or 3 tablespoons chopped
    walnuts

Remove the seeds from the melon and cut the pulp into neat
balls, using a vegetable scoop, as shown on the right. Neatly
dice the celery. Blend the dressing with the ginger and leave
the celery in this until ready to serve the salad. Arrange the
melon and celery on the lettuce or endive and top with nuts.

To make a change use diced dessert apples with the celery
and melon. Put the apple into the dressing immediately it is
prepared to keep the colour.

Alternatively, mix one avocado with the melon and half the
amount of celery used in the recipe above. Add one diced
avocado to the dressing, plus a little lemon juice to stop the
flesh discolouring. The ginger is optional

USING A VEGETABLE SCOOP:
Insert the bowl into the melon
and slowly turn the stem of
the scoop in the fruit until you
can see you have cut out a
neat ball shape.

Avocado and Grapefruit Salad;
Melon and Celery Salad.

Waldorf Salad   ▲ ✿

SERVES 4 TO 6

4 dessert apples

I celery head

small bunch of grapes (optional)

mayonnaise, see page 157
    or salad dressing as
    described in right-hand
    column

50 g/2 oz walnuts or pecan
    nuts

Core, but do not peel the apples. Cut into neat dice. Chop the tender sticks of celery into small equal-sized pieces; retain a few leaves for garnish. Do not use the tougher pieces of celery. Halve the grapes and remove any seeds. Mix the ingredients with the mayonnaise or dressing. Coarsely chop the nuts and mix most of them with the other ingredients. Spoon into a bowl, arrange a few celery leaves around the edge and top with the last of the nuts.

COOKED SALAD DRESSING:
Make Béchamel sauce, page 159. When thickened remove from heat. Whisk 2 egg yolks with 2 tablespoons white wine vinegar. Add to sauce. Cook slowly until thickened again. Season and cover to prevent a skin forming.

Avocado and Grapefruit Salad   ▲ ▲ ✿

SERVES 4 TO 6

I ordinary grapefruit

I pink grapefruit

2 small avocados

2 tablespoons sunflower oil

2 teaspoons lemon juice, or to
    taste

2 teaspoons sugar, or to taste

salt and freshly ground black
    pepper

Cut away the peel from the grapefruit, then cut out the segments; do this over a basin so the juice can form part of the dressing. Skin, stone and slice the avocados.

Add the oil, lemon juice, sugar and seasoning to the grapefruit juice. Keep the avocado in this until just before serving the salad. Arrange alternate slices of the fruits on a plate and serve with a garnish of lettuce leaves and parsley.

CITRUS SALAD:
Arrange segments of pink and ordinary grapefruit and oranges on watercress. Add Citrus-Sherry Dressing and nuts.

DRESSING:
Blend the juice of the fruits, which flows when peel is removed with a little olive oil, seasoning, sherry and sugar.

NEW LOOK SALADS

ENCOURAGING CHILDREN TO
EAT VEGETABLES
Quite often a child who does not enjoy cooked vegetables will be more inclined to eat them raw in a salad.

Let the child help you make the salad and suggest what could be added to improve the colour and flavour, so he or she takes an interest in what is to be eaten. Add the child's favourite kind of fresh and dried fruits, including nuts, plus the vegetable ingredients that form the basics of the particular salad. The choice of ingredients will depend upon the age of the child; small children should not be given nuts to eat as they could choke on them.

Serve a side salad with or instead of a cooked vegetable with some hot main meals such as pasta dishes. The crisp texture often makes a pleasing accompaniment.

The following salads are easy to make, yet each of them has an unusual and interesting flavour. Serve as light snacks, starters to a meal, or with meat or other proteins to make a main dish. Each salad serves 4.

Herbed green coleslaw: Shred 100g/4 oz young spinach leaves and 100 g/4 oz Brussels sprouts or cabbage. Mix with 1 tablespoon chopped parsley, 1 tablespoon chopped chives, 1 diced green pepper, 6 tablespoons diced cucumber, 1 teaspoon chopped tarragon and 1 teaspoon chopped mint. Toss in Spiced dressing, page 154.

To make a main meal, serve with cheese or eggs.

Indonesian-style salad: Cook 225 g/8 oz green beans and 100 g/4 oz mangetout or shelled peas; make sure they keep their crunchy texture. Prepare the dressing while the vegetables are being cooked.

To make peanut dressing, peel and crush 2 garlic cloves and finely chop 1 small red chilli pepper – include the seeds for a really hot taste. Blend 2 tablespoons peanut butter, 2 tablespoons peanut or sunflower oil, 1 tablespoon lemon juice, 1 tablespoon soy sauce, 1 teaspoon sugar and seasoning. Stir the well-drained, but still hot beans and peas into the dressing. Cool, then add 100 g/4 oz peanuts. Spoon on to shredded Chinese leaves and top with bean sprouts and peanuts.

To make a main meal, increase the quantity of nuts and add some heated red kidney beans to the green beans, peas and dressing.

Orange and celery salad: Cut away the peel from 4 large oranges: do this over a basin so no juice is wasted. Blend the orange juice with 6 tablespoons yogurt, 3 tablespoons mayonnaise, made as page 157, 1 tablespoon lemon juice, 2 tablespoons chopped spring onions, 1 tablespoon chopped fennel leaves and 1 tablespoon chopped chives. Add salt and freshly ground black pepper to taste.

Cut the segments from the oranges, discarding all pips and skin. Blend with a diced celery heart, a finely chopped fennel root and 3 tablespoons chopped cashew nuts.

Spoon on to shredded lettuce leaves; use a selection of different types of lettuce. Pour the dressing on top and garnish with whole cashew nuts.

To make a main meal, serve with sliced cold or hot duckling. For a vegetarian meal, serve with cottage cheese.

Rice salad: Cook 175 g/6 oz mixed long grain and wild rice, drain well and, while hot, toss in Lemon sesame dressing, see below. Allow to cool. Dice ¹/₄ small celery heart, coarsely chop 100 to 175 g/4 to 6 oz walnuts. Blend with the rice and a generous amount of chopped parsley.

To make a main meal add nuts and some finely diced tofu to the hot rice and dressing.

Bulgar wheat salad: This wheat, also known as cracked wheat, gives salads, as well as other dishes, a most interesting flavour. To obtain its particular texture, the wheat has been partially cooked by boiling, then dried and cracked into small pieces. Like all wheat products, it is an excellent source of protein and fibre.

Place 100 to 150 g/4 to 5 oz of bulgar wheat in a bowl. Cover with boiling water and leave for 25 minutes. Drain well and place on absorbent paper to dry. Put into a bowl with Lemon and oil dressing, see below. Add diced cucumber, sliced spring onions, sliced tomatoes, cooked peas, sweetcorn, chopped chives and chopped mint.

To make a main meal, serve with a mixture of cheeses, such as Brie, Danish Blue and Lancashire.

SALAD DRESSINGS

Even the most appetizing salad can be spoiled if it is served with an indifferent dressing, so make these carefully and be prepared to adjust the flavourings to suit the particular ingredients of the salad. Buy the best quality oils possible and use really fresh herbs when these are needed.

If you are worried about using uncooked eggs in a mayonnaise, then try the recipes with hard-boiled eggs or tofu; both make an excellent change.

Oil and Vinegar Dressing   ▲ ✿

SERVES 4
salt and freshly ground black
    or white pepper
¹/₂ teaspoon Dijon mustard
6 tablespoons virgin olive oil,
    or see method
1¹/₂ to 2 tablespoons wine
    vinegar, see method
little sugar or honey, see
    method

This is also known as a vinaigrette or French dressing. Lemon juice can be used instead of the vinegar. It is important to buy the best quality of oil and vinegar for this. You can use white or red wine vinegar – this is better than a malt vinegar. If you like to add a few drops of a flavoured vinegar, such as raspberry, tarragon etc., it adds a subtle taste.

Olive oil is generally chosen for this dressing, but you can use part olive and part other oil, such as corn oil, to give a lighter dressing. The sugar or honey is not essential, but there are times when a slightly sweetened dressing is needed.

The proportions of oil and vinegar or lemon juice are purely a matter of personal taste. As today's health advisors suggest we eat less fat, it is a good idea to accustom your palate to a sharper dressing, using a higher proportion of vinegar or lemon juice. Try other fruit juices, such as apple or orange.

Put a good pinch of salt and a shake of pepper into a bowl or a jar with the mustard. Stir in the oil, then add the vinegar and taste the dressing. Adjust the seasoning to taste and blend in a little sugar or honey if required.

The ingredients can be blended in a liquidizer.

CURRY DRESSING:
Blend a little curry paste with the mayonnaise opposite, or add a pinch of curry powder or ¹/₂ teaspoon curry paste to the ingredients on the left.

MUSTARD DRESSING:
Add an extra 1 teaspoon French or made English mustard to the ingredients left, or blend enough made mustard to give a definite taste to mayonnaise. Add a little sugar or honey to balance the flavour.

LEMON AND OIL DRESSING:
Use lemon juice instead of vinegar in the dressing on the left.

Oil and Vinegar Dressing; Mayonnaise

Mayonnaise ▲ ▲ ✪

SERVES 4 TO 6

2 egg yolks

1 teaspoon Dijon mustard

salt and freshly ground white* pepper

up to 300 ml/¹/₂ pint virgin olive oil or use a mixture of olive and sunflower or corn oils for a lighter textured dressing; this quantity of oil(s) is the maximum the egg yolks will absorb, see the method

3 teaspoons white wine vinegar or lemon juice, or a mixture of these

1 tablespoon very hot water, optional

*this gives a better colour

Make sure the egg yolks and the oil(s) are at room temperature; often the cause of the sauce's curdling during mixing is because one or both are too cold.

To make by hand: Put the egg yolks into a mixing bowl and add the seasonings. Whisk to blend. Hold the container of oil or mixture of oils in one hand, and leave your 'working' hand free to whisk continually. Add the oil(s) in a very slow trickle, whisking all the time. If by any chance there is the slightest sign of the mixture curdling, stop adding the oil and whisk very hard. If that does not help, you will need to add another egg yolk. Beat this in and start adding the oil once again.

The 2 egg yolks should absorb the quantity of oil specified but for many people that gives too oily a dressing, so stop when sufficient has been incorporated. Add the vinegar or vinegar and lemon juice. The hot water lightens the dressing.

Use at once or cover and refrigerate for 2 to 3 days only.

To make in a liquidizer or food processor: You can use whole eggs if desired. This makes a much lighter dressing than one made with just the yolks, but it means you cannot add as much oil. Put the eggs into the goblet or bowl with seasonings. Keep the motor running at the lowest speed possible. Gradually trickle in the oil through the feeding funnel, or space in the lid, or with the lid at a slight angle. When this has been incorporated, add the vinegar or lemon juice and hot water.

WITH HARD-BOILED EGGS: Hard-boil, shell and remove the yolks. Cream these with 2 tablespoons single cream or yogurt and seasonings as in recipe left. Then gradually blend in up to 150 ml/¹/₄ pint oil. Flavour with lemon juice or vinegar.

TOFU MAYONNAISE: Liquidize 175 g/6 oz tofu, a little salt and pepper, 1 teaspoon Dijon mustard and 1 tablespoon wine or lemon juice.

Gradually beat in 3 to 5 tablespoons oil.

YOGURT DRESSING: Season thick Greek yogurt, add lemon juice or white wine vinegar to taste with a little Dijon mustard and sugar. To enrich this, beat in 1 to 2 tablespoons olive oil.

SAUCES & STUFFINGS

Nowadays foods are less likely to be coated with a sauce; rather the sauce is poured on to the dish or plates and the food is then arranged on top of it. This allows you to see and admire the appearance of both the basic dish and its accompanying sauce.

The consistency of sauces has changed; you will find the classic white sauce plus some variations, but you will be very up-to-the-minute if you reduce the amount of flour slightly, so you have a less cloying mixture. Of course, if the sauce is being used to bind ingredients together, then the proportions should not be changed.

A new word has become familiar. This is 'coulis'. It describes the unthickened, clear purée or even liquid made from the juices of fruits, tomatoes, etc. It makes a most refreshing sauce. You will find suggestions for making this on pages 117 and 160. Often, vegetables are cooked with the main ingredient. They make a splendid sauce if liquidized, see page 95.

The emphasis on modern stuffings is to make use of interesting mixtures of ingredients, such as fruit with vegetables, plenty of herbs, nuts and rice.

Most of the recipes for sauces and stuffings are found beside the recipes, where they are an essential part of that particular dish.

SAUCES MADE WITH A ROUX

The term 'roux' is used to describe the fat and flour used in the first stage of making many sauces.

The traditional method is to cook the roux well first, then add the liquid slowly, stirring all the time. It is possible to make the sauce more rapidly, adding the liquid quickly, then whisking or stirring briskly when it comes to the boil. Whichever method you choose, it is essential that the sauce is adequately cooked, otherwise you will have the rather unpleasant taste of uncooked flour and the sauce will not thicken to the correct consistency.

EASY-TO-MAKE SAUCES

Cheese sauce: This is one of the most popular sauces. Any good cooking cheese can be added to a Béchamel or White sauce, on page 159. It is a good way of using up odd pieces of cheese. Never over-cook cheese in a sauce.

A delicious cold cheese sauce is made by mixing cream or curd or sieved cottage cheese with fromage frais or yogurt. Season well and add a little French mustard.

Cucumber sauce: Add about 175 g/6 oz grated raw cucumber to either the Béchamel sauce or White sauce. Heat for a few minutes only, then add a good squeeze of lemon juice. A little chopped mint can be added.

Cucumber can be blended with Hollandaise sauce, on page 160, or with cold fromage frais or yogurt.

Mushroom sauce: It is better to cook the mushrooms separately to give the sauce a better colour. To the amount of Béchamel or White sauce on page 159, allow 100 to 175 g/4 oz to 6 oz mushrooms. Wipe and slice, then poach in a little milk or stock, or cook in butter or margarine. Blend with the sauce and heat for 1 to 2 minutes.

Mushroom Sauce; Cucumber Sauce; Béchamel Sauce

Béchamel Sauce ▲ ✪✪

SERVES 4

300 ml/¹/₂ pint milk plus any extra required, see method
1 small onion
piece of celery, optional
1 bay leaf, optional
25 g/1 oz butter or margarine low-fat spread can be used, see right-hand column
25 g/1 oz flour, see right-hand column
salt and freshly ground black or white pepper

Pour the milk into a saucepan. Peel the onion, chop the celery and add to the milk, with the bay leaf. Bring the milk just to boiling point, remove from the heat, cover and leave to infuse for 30 minutes. Strain and measure the milk. If necessary add more, to give 300 ml/¹/₂ pint again.

Heat the butter or margarine in the pan, stir in the flour, then blend in the milk. This can be done very slowly stirring all the time, but you can pour in all the milk, bring the sauce to the boil and whisk vigorously to produce a smooth sauce — but see right-hand column. Add seasoning to taste.

Thinner consistency: The recipe above produces the standard coating consistency, but today's sauces are usually thinner. You can use slightly more milk or add a little single cream for richness. Alternatively, whisk in a small amount of fromage frais or yogurt at the end of the cooking time.

Using vegetable, meat or fish stocks: When the sauce is to be served with any of these foods, it is a good idea to use some of the stock in which the vegetables have been cooked, instead of using all milk. This gives a more interesting flavour.

Mornay sauce: This is a classic sauce based upon a Bechamel, not a white sauce.

White sauce: Omit the onion and celery and simply make the sauce with the 300 ml/¹/₂ pint milk.

Brown sauce: The method of making the sauce is similar to that above, but use a good brown stock instead of milk.

Blending method: Blend the flour and milk and add to the pan with the fat. Stir or whisk until smooth and thickened.

Using low-fat spread: This produces a less rich sauce and care must be taken that the mixture does not burn because of the lower fat content.

USING THE MICROWAVE:
Blend the flour or cornflour with the liquid, in a good-sized jug or basin – you must have room to whisk or stir the sauce.

Heat for a few seconds, open the door, whisk or stir. Continue like this, heating and whisking, until the sauce is completed.

The butter, margarine or low-fat spread is added to the sauce in the usual manner. It is sensible to choose the microwave when making a sauce with low-fat spread, as mixtures do not stick to a basin, as they may do in a saucepan.

CORRECTING LUMPY SAUCES:
If brisk whisking does not remove small lumps, then liquidize the sauce. It will become smooth but appear less thickened.

Return it to a pan and cook for a short time to restore it to the desired consistency.

SAVOURY SAUCES

These can cover a wide range of flavours and be made in a number of ways. The Onion sauce, right, is made by the more traditional method and the Five-minute sauce typifies today's simplified way of producing an interesting sauce quickly and easily — and without using fat and flour.

Experiment with adding new flavours to established sauces, such as when making a gravy. Consider the food with which it is to be served and whether the gravy will enhance that flavour. It may be a good idea to add a little wine or fruit juice to sharpen the taste. If you feel the dish will be too bland, then add herbs, such as garlic, tarragon or rosemary. Shredded and lightly cooked sorrel gives a piquant flavour to either a brown sauce, a gravy or white sauce; add 100 g/4 oz to each 300 ml/½ pint of sauce.

Sometimes familiar sauces can become boring. If you have made a Bolognese sauce on many occasions, vary it. Follow the recipe on page 128, but instead of using all minced beef, use equal quantities of minced beef and pork.

Hollandaise Sauce ▲▲ ✿

SERVES 4 TO 6
100 to 175 g/4 oz to 6 oz
    butter, see method
3 egg yolks
2 to 3 tablespoons lemon juice
    or white wine vinegar, or to
    taste
pinch cayenne pepper,
    optional
salt and freshly ground white*
    pepper

*this gives a better colour than
    black pepper

This sauce which is delicious with a wide range of foods is the best-known of all those made by the whisking method. It is very important when making whisked sauces that the water under the basin does not boil. If it becomes too hot, the egg yolks will set and the sauce will lose its smooth texture.

Bring the butter out of the refrigerator and stand in a warm place; do not allow it to become oily. If you are making the sauce in the classic manner, it should be a spreading consistency.

You can reduce the butter content of this sauce to 75 g/3 oz, but really it is better not to make it with a lesser amount. 100 g/4 oz butter produces a sauce with the right flavour.

Put the yolks and some of the lemon juice or vinegar into a basin; you can add the rest later when you assess the taste. Stand over a pan of simmering, not boiling water. Add the seasonings. Whisk briskly until the eggs become thick and creamy. Gradually whisk in the butter. This means adding a piece about the size of a large hazelnut; when that is blended, add the next piece. Continue like this until all the butter is absorbed. Taste during this process and add more lemon juice or vinegar if required.

Serve hot or cold with fish and vegetable dishes and eggs.

QUICK METHOD OF MAKING:
Put all the ingredients except the butter into the goblet of a liquidizer or bowl of a food processor. Switch on to blend. Heat the butter to boiling point. Keep the machine running – choose a low speed if possible. Pour the very hot butter slowly on to the whisked egg yolk mixture. The sauce will thicken.

BASED ON HOLLANDAISE SAUCE:
TARTARE SAUCE: Add chopped gherkins, parsley and capers to the cold Hollandaise sauce. Serve with fish.

Five-Minute Tomato Sauce ▲ ✿

SERVES 4 TO 6
450 g/1 lb ripe tomatoes
few spring onions
2 or 3 basil leaves or pinch
    dried basil
1 teaspoon brown sugar
salt and freshly ground black
    pepper
1 tablespoon tomato purée

Halve the tomatoes and wash the spring onions. Put all the ingredients into the liquidizer and switch on until a smooth mixture is formed. Heat for a few minutes.

This sauce has the fresh flavour of uncooked tomatoes. It is typical of the thin sauce that is so popular today. For a more usual tomato sauce, see page 130. Do not use an ordinary onion with this short cooking time – its flavour is too harsh.

TOMATO COULIS:
Either rub ripe uncooked tomatoes through a fine sieve and flavour with seasoning and chopped fresh basil, or other herbs, or heat the mixture as in the recipe, left, then sieve this. A little lemon juice gives a sharper coulis.

Onion Sauce ▲ ✪

SERVES 4 TO 6
3 medium onions
1 garlic clove (optional)
50 g/2 oz butter or margarine
25 g/1 oz flour
300 ml/¹/₂ pint stock, see right
4 tablespoons red or white
   wine, see right
salt and cayenne pepper
1 tablespoon finely chopped
   chives
1 tablespoon finely chopped
   parsley

Peel the onions and chop them very finely and evenly, for this version of the sauce is not sieved. Peel and crush the garlic. Heat the butter or margarine and cook the onions and garlic until very soft; do not allow to brown.

Blend in the flour, then stir in the stock and continue stirring as the sauce comes to the boil and thickens to a coating consistency. Blend in the rest of the ingredients and heat for a few minutes before serving.

STOCK AND WINE TO USE:
Use a brown stock and a robust red wine with meat, a white stock, with red or white wine with poultry, and fish stock with white wine with a fish dish.

SMOOTH SAUCE:
Put ingredients into a liquidizer or through a sieve. Add the herbs, then reheat.

Cranberry Sauce ▲ ✪✪

SERVES 8
450 g/1 lb fresh or frozen
   cranberries
4 tablespoons water
175 g/6 oz caster sugar
4 tablespoons port wine

Wash fresh cranberries. The frozen kind can be cooked without defrosting, but the sauce takes longer to cook. Put the water and sugar into a pan – make sure to choose one with a well-fitting lid. Stir until the sugar has dissolved, then add the cranberries, cover the pan and cook steadily for about 8 minutes, or until the 'popping' noise ceases. Remove the lid, add the port wine and cook gently, without a lid on the pan, until the sauce is the desired consistency.

FREEZING:
This sauce freezes well, so it is worthwhile making a good-sized batch.

CRANBERRY ORANGE SAUCE:
Use orange juice instead of water and port wine and add 2 teaspoons grated orange rind to the cranberries.

Onion Sauce; Five Minute Tomato Sauce; Hollandaise Sauce

Tangy Lemon Sauce   ▲ ✿

SERVES 4
1 teaspoon grated lemon rind
300 ml/¹/₂ pint chicken stock
2 eggs yolks
1¹/₂ tablespoons lemon juice
salt and freshly ground black
    pepper
lemon rind for garnish

Simmer the lemon rind and stock for 5 minutes. Beat the egg yolks and lemon juice in a bowl. Whisk in a little of the hot chicken stock. Return to the saucepan and whisk over a very low heat until a coating consistency; do not allow to boil. Season to taste and garnish with thinly pared lemon rind.

Serve with poultry, veal or fish (you can use fish stock instead of the chicken stock), or mixed vegetables (use vegetable stock if preferred).

CITRUS SAUCE:
Add 2 teaspoons grated orange zest; use just 1 tablespoon lemon juice and 2 tablespoons orange juice. This is excellent with duck or pork.

Cumberland Sauce   ▲ ✿✿

SERVES 4 TO 6
2 large oranges
300 ml/¹/₂ pint water
2 level teaspoons arrowroot
2 tablespoons port wine
1 tablespoon lemon juice
4 tablespoons redcurrant jelly
salt and freshly ground black
    pepper
1 teaspoon made English
    mustard
sugar to taste

Cut the top zest from the oranges, then cut this into narrow matchstick pieces. Soak in the water for 30 minutes, then simmer in an open pan for 10 to 15 minutes, or until the liquid is reduced to 150 ml/¹/₄ pint and the zest is tender. Halve the oranges and squeeze out the juice. You need 150 ml/¹/₄ pint; if there is not enough, dilute with a little water or use another orange. Blend the juice with the arrowroot.

Pour into the pan with the orange zest and add the rest of the ingredients. Stir over a moderate heat until a clear, thickened sauce is formed. Serve hot or cold.

This is an excellent sauce in which to heat slices of ham or tongue. It blends well with liver pâté or poultry.

USING CORNFLOUR:
If you have no arrowroot, use cornflour instead. This does not give quite such a clear sauce as arrowroot.

MAKING STUFFINGS

Many stuffings in this book are given with the particular dish to which they are especially well suited. The stuffings below are extremely popular and can be served with a number of different foods, as stated in the recipes.

Choose a refreshing stuffing that contains fruit for serving with richer meats or poultry, such as duck or goose.

Parsley and Thyme Stuffing   ▲ ✿ to ✿✿

SERVES 4 TO 6
100 g/4 oz soft breadcrumbs
50 g/2 oz butter, margarine or
    shredded suet
1 to 2 tablespoons chopped
    parsley
1 teaspoon chopped fresh
    thyme or ¹/₂ teaspoon dried
    thyme
1 teaspoon grated lemon rind
1 egg
salt and freshly ground black
    pepper

Put the breadcrumbs into a basin. If using butter or margarine, melt them. Add the fat and all the other ingredients to the breadcrumbs.

This is the accepted stuffing with chicken and turkey, but it goes well with veal and is good for stuffing large tomatoes, peppers and other vegetables. If you are cooking it separately, allow 40 minutes in a preheated oven, set to 190°C/375°F, Gas Mark 5, or adjust the cooking time to the temperature of the oven.

Cover the baking dish tightly, so the stuffing does not dry.

If using a processor: Put the pieces of bread, sprigs of herbs and a small piece of lemon rind into the bowl. Switch on until they are chopped, then add the unmelted fat, egg and seasoning. Switch on for a few seconds.

Cooking in the microwave: This stuffing retains all the fresh flavour of the herbs. Allow about 10 minutes in a covered dish on FULL POWER.

BACON STUFFING:
Use the recipe, left, with the addition of 2 to 3 finely chopped uncooked bacon rashers. You could reduce the fat to 25 g/1 oz.

LIVER STUFFING:
Add the diced uncooked liver from the chicken or turkey to the ingredients, left. Obviously you have a stronger liver taste when using the larger turkey liver, but the flavour is excellent.

Crunchy Rice Stuffing; Tangy Lemon Sauce; Cumberland Sauce

Crunchy Rice Stuffing

▲   ✿ to ✿ ✿

SERVES 6 TO 8

225 g/8 oz cooked long grain rice
100 g/4 oz walnuts or pecan nuts
100 g/4 oz tenderized dried apricots
100 g/4 oz celery
1 red pepper
1 green pepper
2 tablespoons chopped parsley
1 teaspoon chopped rosemary or ½ teaspoon dried rosemary
2 tablespoons sunflower oil
salt and freshly ground black pepper

Put the rice into a bowl. Chop the nuts, apricots and celery fairly finely. Deseed and dice the peppers.

Mix all the ingredients together. To retain the crunchy texture, cook for 25 to 30 minutes only in a covered dish in a preheated oven set to 200°C/400°F, Gas Mark 6 or for 8 to 10 minutes in the microwave cooker.

This stuffing is suitable for all kinds of poultry or meat – lamb in particular. It is very good hot or cold.

This is an excellent basic recipe. The proportions of nuts can be increased, so it becomes an ideal main dish for vegetarians if they are participating in a meal where meat or poultry is being served. You can choose a mixture of wild and ordinary long grain rice.

RICE AND LIVER STUFFING:
Omit the apricots in the recipe left.

Add the diced uncooked liver from a chicken, turkey or other bird, or 100 g/4 oz lambs' liver.

The stuffing then has an entirely different texture and flavour; the liver softens the other ingredients. It does have an excellent flavour.

CRANBERRY RICE STUFFING:
Add 100 g/4 oz cooked sweetened cranberries to the ingredients, left.

Chestnut Stuffing

▲   ✿ ✿

SERVES 4 TO 6

450 g/1 lb chestnuts
300 ml/½ pint chicken or turkey or bacon stock
50 g/2 oz hazelnuts or walnuts, optional
100 g/4 oz bacon rashers
2 tablespoons chopped parsley
25 g/1 oz butter or margarine
salt and freshly ground black pepper

Wash and slit the chestnuts. Put into a pan of boiling water and simmer for 10 minutes – no longer, otherwise it is difficult to peel the nuts and keep them whole. Cool sufficiently to handle, but while they are still warm, remove the shells and inner brown skins. Put into the stock, cover and cook steadily for 20 minutes. Strain the chestnuts and keep the stock.

Chop all the nuts and bacon rashers and mix with the parsley. Melt the butter or margarine and add to the chestnut mixture with enough stock to make a soft consistency. Season to taste.

Cook as the stuffing above.

This is an excellent stuffing for all kinds of poultry and for vegetables, too. If serving with duck or goose, add 2 chopped and lightly cooked onions to the rest of the ingredients.

VEGETARIAN STUFFING:
Omit the bacon in the recipe left and increase the butter or margarine to 50 g/2 oz. Chop most of the chestnuts until very fine, but leave some coarsely chopped.

USING CHESTNUT PURÉE:
Canned unsweetened chestnut purée makes an excellent stuffing. Follow directions on the left or above. Use 300 g/10 oz canned purée to the proportions given.

EATING OUTDOORS

Food eaten in the open air gives the greatest pleasure to so many people. The recipes that follow are for these occasions, but the development of insulated cold bags and insulated boxes allows one to take a whole range of hot or cold dishes. Obviously, they cannot be carried in the same container. The word 'picnic' covers a great many different meals, ranging from a few sandwiches to a beautifully laid out buffet with an elaborate menu.

A meal of sandwiches: Do not feel that sandwiches are an apology for a good spread. Bread is one of the most important foods and the fillings, if chosen carefully, can be as sustaining and nutritious as a hot main dish.

Make sure sandwich fillings are not too dry – that would make them unappetizing – or so moist that they soften and break the bread. As well as the usual wholemeal, brown or white breads, consider filling pitta bread. These neat little 'pockets' enable you to pack the most satisfying mixtures, as shown in the picture on page 165. Many of the salads on pages 152 to 156 would make excellent fillings for pitta bread.

Other picnic foods: Cold meats, cooked fish, such as salmon, salads, a quiche or pizza (recipes on pages 140 and 180) are easy to transport, so too are the special moulds on these pages.

Choose refreshing fruits rather than sweet desserts. Check on the facilities for obtaining beverages or carry them in flasks. Few things can spoil a picnic more than being thirsty and not being able to obtain a drink of any kind.

Turkey and Ham Cream ▲▲ ✿✿✿✿

SERVES 6 TO 8
550g/1¼ lb cooked turkey,
    preferably breast
225 g/8 oz cooked ham
5 tablespoons white vermouth
    or dry sherry
1 teaspoon Dijon mustard
1 tablespoon tomato purée
1 teaspoon light soy sauce
salt and freshly ground black
    pepper
1 sachet (1 level tablespoon)
    gelatine
4 tablespoons mayonnaise, see
    page 157
2 tablespoons chopped capers
2 tablespoons chopped chives
1 teaspoon chopped lemon
    thyme
225 ml/7½ fl oz whipping or
    double cream
1 tablespoon lemon juice
To garnish:
gherkin 'leaves', see right
sliced cherry tomatoes or
    radishes

Marinating the cooked turkey adds extra flavour to the meat and produces a more succulent texture.

Lightly oil a 1·35 kg/3 lb loaf tin or oval mould or line it with baking parchment.

Mince the turkey and ham separately, or chop the meats very finely. Pour 2 tablespoons of the vermouth or sherry into a dish and add the mustard, tomato purée, soy sauce and a little seasoning. Place the turkey in this mixture, stir well to mix, then cover and leave in the refrigerator for one hour. Stir several times to make sure the turkey absorbs all the various flavours.

Pour the remaining vermouth or sherry into a good-sized basin, add the gelatine, allow to stand for 2 or 3 minutes, then dissolve over a pan of very hot water or in the microwave cooker. Cool, then add the mayonnaise, the turkey with any liquid remaining in the dish, the ham, capers, chives and thyme.

Whip the cream until it stands in peaks and fold into the turkey mixture, with a little lemon juice and any extra seasoning required. Add the latter 2 ingredients slowly so you can assess the flavour.

Spoon into the prepared tin or dish and allow to set.

Turn out and garnish the top of the cream with gherkin 'leaves' and small rounds of tomato or radish. Serve with bread and various salads.

ADAPTING THE RECIPE:
Use thick yogurt instead of whipped cream; this gives a sharper flavour so sherry is better than vermouth. You may like to omit the lemon juice.

Use cooked tongue in place of ham or a mixture of ham and tongue.

Chicken, pheasant or veal could be used instead of turkey.

GHERKIN LEAVES, ETC:
Choose small gherkins. Drain well, then cut out diagonal shapes to resemble leaves. Serrate the edges of the small rounds of tomato or radish to give the effect of a flower. Pieces of gherkin should be cut into fine strips to make the stalks.

Turkey and Ham Cream;
Chestnut Terrine

Chestnut Terrine

▲▲ ✿✿✿

SERVES 4 TO 6

ingredients as the Chestnut
  loaf, below, but omit the
  walnuts or other nuts

For the stuffing:

100 g/4 oz walnuts

100 g/4 oz cashew nuts

50 g/2 oz wholemeal bread

1 red pepper

1 tablespoon sunflower oil

2 tablespoons chopped parsley

Prepare the Chestnut loaf, below, then prepare the stuffing. To make this, chop the nuts and make the bread into crumbs. Deseed and finely dice the pepper. Mix the stuffing ingredients together and season lightly.

Put one third of the chestnut mixture into the prepared tin, add half the stuffing, then another third of the chestnut mixture, the last of the stuffing and then the final layer of chestnut mixture.

Bake as the loaf below. Serve hot or cold.

LENTIL TERRINE:
Use 450 ml/³/₄ pint thick lentil purée, made by cooking split golden lentils, instead of chestnut purée in this recipe, or in the Chestnut loaf, below.

Chestnut Loaf

▲▲ ✿✿✿

SERVES 4

To coat the tin:

little butter or margarine

40 g/1¹/₂ oz crisp breadcrumbs

For the loaf:

1 x 425 to 453 g/15 to 16 oz
  can unsweetened chestnut
  purée or use fresh
  chestnuts, see right

50 to 100 g/2 to 4 oz walnuts

25 g/1 oz butter or margarine

4 tablespoons chopped spring
  onions

2 tablespoons chopped chives

2 tablespoons chopped parsley

1 tablespoon tomato purée

25 g/1 oz rolled oats or soft
  wholemeal breadcrumbs

2 eggs

salt and freshly ground black
  pepper

Grease the base and sides of a 900 g/2 lb loaf tin, or line it with baking parchment, or grease and coat with the crisp breadcrumbs. This coating helps to make the outside of the loaf a firmer texture. Preheat the oven to 160°C/325°F, Gas Mark 3. Spoon the chestnut purée into a bowl, chop the nuts fairly coarsely, so they add more texture to the mixture.

Melt the butter or margarine. Blend the nuts, butter or margarine and the remaining ingredients with the chestnut purée.

Spoon the mixture into the tin and bake for 1 hour. Do not cover the tin; the mixture becomes firm on top which makes it easier to turn out.

To serve hot, allow to stand for 5 minutes in the tin then turn out carefully. Serve with salad or mixed vegetables.

To serve cold, leave in the tin until quite cold. Serve with mixed salad.

USING FRESH CHESTNUTS:
You will need about 675 g/ 1¹/₂ lb fresh chestnuts to give a comparable amount of purée. Slit the chestnut skins, heat in the oven or in simmering water for 10 minutes, or until soft enough to remove both outer shells and inner skins. Do this while they are hot.

Simmer shelled nuts in lightly seasoned water for 20 to 25 minutes, then sieve or liquidize to make a purée.

TO ADD FLAVOUR:
Celery salt could be included in addition to seasoning.

Use hazel or cashew nuts in place of walnuts.

BARBECUES

COCONUT PEACHES:
Halve ripe peaches, remove the stones. Blend equal amounts of butter, brown sugar and desiccated coconut. Spread over the peaches, then put the two halves together. Wrap in foil and cook for 15 minutes.

The filled halved peaches can be heated under a grill for 5 minutes. Do not put the halves together when cooked in this way.

JAMAICAN ORANGES:
Cut away the skin from large oranges. Place on a double thickness of foil, sprinkle with brown sugar and a little rum. Enclose in the foil.

Bake for 10 minutes over the barbecue fire or in a preheated oven, set to 200°C/400°F, Gas Mark 6.

Open the foil carefully so no rum is spilled.

Whatever method of heating the barbecue is chosen, do take the greatest precautions to see that young children are carefully supervised, so there is no possibility of their being burned.

Traditional barbecued food should be highly flavoured, but make sure some of the meat and fish is cooked with a milder flavour, for anyone whose tastes differ.

If you do not own a barbecue, you can still enjoy the same kind of food. Cook it under a preheated grill, then carry it into the garden.

FOODS FOR THE BARBECUE
Choose fairly robust foods that do not break easily.
Fish: Herrings, mackerel, cutlets of cod and salmon or whole fish; shark is ideal, see page 79. The Seafood kebabs on page 79 would be a good choice.
Meats: Chops, steaks, joints, spare ribs, sausages, hamburgers.
Poultry: Joints of chicken or turkey or whole chickens.
Vegetables: Jacket potatoes are the prime favourite. Other vegetables, such as sliced young carrots and sliced onions, can be cooked in buttered foil parcels over the fire. Mushrooms and tomatoes can be cooked in a frying-pan.
Desserts: Jamaican oranges and Coconut peaches can be cooked on foil over the barbecue fire, see recipes left.

SUCCESSFUL BARBECUE COOKING
Make sure the barbecue is sufficiently hot before starting to cook; charcoal should be glowing red.

Keep the food well basted with seasoned oil or a barbecue sauce, see below, or protected from the fierce heat on a double thickness of foil.

Use strong pans with long handles; make sure these are not pointing in such a way that they could be knocked over. Use long forks, tongs or spoons when handling the food, so your hands are not too near the fierce heat.
Cooking time for barbecued foods: The time for cooking steaks, chops, etc. is similar to that required when cooking the food under a preheated grill set to high.

If cooking joints or whole poultry, allow the same time as if they were being cooked in an oven heated to at least 190 to 200°C/375 to 400°F, Gas Mark 5 to 6.

If food is becoming too well-cooked too early, move it to the edge of the barbecue.

Barbecue Sauce   ▲ ✿

SERVES 4
1 medium onion
1 to 2 garlic cloves
2 tablespoons olive oil
2 tablespoons brown malt vinegar, or to taste
2 tablespoons tomato ketchup
1 tablespoon soy sauce
1 teaspoon Worcestershire sauce, or to taste
1 tablespoon brown sugar
5 tablespoons white wine or cider or stock
salt and freshly ground black pepper

Peel and finely chop the onion and garlic. Heat the olive oil and add the onion and garlic. Cook for a few minutes – this could be done on the cooker indoors. Add the rest of the ingredients and stir to mix. Cover the pan and keep hot on the edge of the barbecue. Use it to brush over meat, poultry and fish as these cook. Any left can be spooned over the food.

FOR A MORE DELICATE FLAVOUR:
Use only half the amount of ketchup and choose white wine vinegar.

Omit the garlic and Worcestershire sauce.

FOR A HOTTER FLAVOUR:
Add a little curry powder and/or grated fresh ginger.

FOR A SWEETER FLAVOUR:
Add 1 tablespoon plum jam or honey or extra sugar.

Orange Barbecued Pork   ▲▲ ✪✪

SERVES 4

4 pork chops or slices of pork
   fillet

For the marinade:

1 garlic clove

2 teaspoons finely grated
   orange rind

150 ml/¼ pint orange juice

1 teaspoon grated ginger

2 tablespoons sweet sherry

2 tablespoons olive oil

Cut away any surplus fat from the pork chops. Peel and finely chop the garlic clove and put into a dish with the rest of the marinade ingredients. Put the meat into this mixture and leave for just 15 minutes. Remove the pork from the marinade and place over the hot barbecue. Turn the meat over several times while it is being barbecued to make sure it is thoroughly cooked. Allow about 20 minutes' cooking time.

Brush the chops with the marinade during the cooking process.

Serve with a crisp green salad to which you can add segments of fresh orange, to enhance the orange flavour.

TO MAKE A CHANGE:
For a sweet marinade add 1 or 2 tablespoons jelly-type orange marmalade.

This dish can be served for a more formal meal with a garnish of orange slices and cooked broccoli spears as shown in the picture.

Devilled Chicken   ▲ ✪✪

SERVES 4

4 chicken drumsticks

4 chicken wings

For the basting sauce:

2 teaspoons chopped
   rosemary

2 teaspoons chopped parsley

1 teaspoon chopped thyme

2 tablespoons sunflower oil

2 tablespoons white wine

1 tablespoon soy sauce

2 teaspoons French mustard

few drops Tabasco sauce

freshly ground black pepper

Dry the chicken joints well, then cut away the tips from the wing joints – these are excellent for flavouring stock. Make very light cuts in the chicken portions, so the basting sauce penetrates and imparts a good flavour to the flesh.

Blend the ingredients for the basting sauce together. Put the chicken joints in this and turn around until well coated.

Place the chicken joints over the barbecue; they are easier to handle if on a thick piece of oiled foil.

Cook for about 15 minutes, brushing with the basting sauce during this time.

Serve topped with the last of the sauce and with jacket potatoes and a green salad or the Spiced coleslaw on page 154.

TO MAKE A CHANGE:
Coat the chicken joints with the Barbecue sauce on the opposite page and brush with this during the cooking period.

Devilled Chicken

PUDDINGS & DESSERTS

The emphasis today is on quickly and easily made desserts, with a special liking for ice cream, sorbets and fruit-flavoured yogurts. Old-fashioned puddings, one of the most popular being a Bread and butter pudding, have their place too; you will find the recipe on page 175, with suggestions on how this may be varied from time to time.

Fresh fruit forms the basis of many of today's light and healthy desserts; a selection of recipes based on fruit follows.

Lemon and Avocado Creams ▲▲ ✪✪

SERVES 4
1 sachet (1 level tablespoon) gelatine
150 ml/¼ pint water plus extra liquid, see method
50 g/2 oz caster sugar
3 tablespoons lemon juice
2 small or 1 large avocado(s)
150 ml/¼ pint whipping or double cream
To decorate:
4 crystallized lemon slices

Sprinkle the gelatine on the 150 ml/¼ pint cold water, stand for 2 to 3 minutes to soften the gelatine, then dissolve over a pan of very hot water or in the microwave cooker. Add the sugar to the hot mixture so it dissolves completely.

Put the lemon juice into a basin. Halve the avocado(s), scoop out the pulp and mash or liquidize this with the lemon juice. Blend with the dissolved gelatine. Measure the mixture and add sufficient water to make a generous 450 ml/¾ pint. Allow to cool and begin to stiffen. Whip the cream until it stands in soft peaks and fold most of it into the avocado mixture.

Spoon into 4 glasses. When set, top with the rest of the cream and decorate with the lemon slices.

KEEPING AVOCADOS A GOOD COLOUR:
Lemon juice or other acid ingredients help to keep avocado pulp a good colour.

Prepare the lemon juice or dressing before cutting the avocado.

Exposure to the air also discolours avocado pulp, so, if possible, cover mixtures containing this fruit.

Macaroon Apples ▲ ✪✪

SERVES 4
4 large cooking apples
3 tablespoons apricot jam
25 g/1 oz ground almonds
2 large macaroon biscuits
4 blanched almonds

Preheat the oven to 190°C/375°F, Gas Mark 5. Slit the apple skins around the centre and remove the cores. Put half the jam into a basin and mix with the ground almonds. Press this mixture into the centre of the apples. Place in an ovenproof dish and cook for 50 minutes to 1 hour, or until tender. Carefully remove the skins, keeping the apples in a good shape.

Crush the macaroon biscuits to make fine crumbs. Warm the remaining jam, brush or spread it over the fruit and coat with the biscuit crumbs. Return to the oven for a further 5 minutes. Top each apple with an almond and serve.

USING THE MICROWAVE:
This is ideal for baking apples, especially when the skins are removed, as in the recipe on the left. Follow the instructions given in your particular microwave cookery book as to timing.

Melon and Raspberries ▲▲ ✪

SERVES 4 TO 6
2 or 3 small melons
225 g/8 oz raspberries
75 g/3 oz cream cheese
150 ml/¼ pint crème fraîche
50 g/2 oz caster sugar
1 to 2 tablespoons Curaçao or brandy or sweet sherry
To decorate:
50 g/2 oz raspberries
little sugar
mint or raspberry leaves

This simple but very delicious dessert originates from the south of France, where small melons and raspberries are plentiful in the summer.

Although given as a dessert, it can be served as an unusual hors d'oeuvre. There is plenty of filling for the 3 melons.

Halve the melons and scoop out the seeds. Chill the fruit while you prepare the raspberry filling. Crush or sieve the raspberries, blend with the cream cheese, then gradually whip in the crème fraîche. Add the sugar and the alcohol and spoon into the melon. Chill, or even freeze very slightly, until just before serving, then spoon into the melon halves. Top with whole raspberries, a little more sugar and the leaves; these could be frosted as described on the right.

FROSTED LEAVES:
Wipe or wash and dry the leaves. Brush with a little lightly whisked egg white, then coat on both sides with sifted icing sugar or caster sugar. Leave in the air to dry.

INSTEAD OF CREME FRAICHE:
Use fresh whipping or double cream. Whip, then add a few drops of lemon juice, before adding a little port wine.

Cherry Clafouti

▲ ▲ ✿ ✿

SERVES 4

450 g/1 lb ripe dessert
    cherries
15 g/¹/₂ oz butter
For the batter:
75 g/3 oz plain flour
25 g/1 oz caster sugar
3 eggs, size 1
225 ml/7¹/₂ fl oz milk
few drops vanilla essence
For the topping:
little icing sugar

Stone the cherries, as described on page 117. Do this over a basin to make sure no juice is wasted.

Blend together the ingredients for the batter. Preheat the oven to 200°C/400°F, Gas Mark 6. Grease a 1·5 to 1·8 litre/ 2¹/₂ to 3 pint pie or soufflé dish with butter. Heat for a few minutes then add the cherries and any juice. Cover with the batter.

Bake for 30 minutes, or until well risen. Sift with icing sugar and serve at once.

In the Kentish pudding, right, the hot ingredients are topped with batter, as in Yorkshire pudding. Bake at the temperature for Yorkshire pudding.

KENTISH PUDDING:
Peel and slice 4 or 5 dessert apples and coarsely chop about 50 g/2 oz nuts.

Heat 25 g/1 oz butter in a pie dish, add the apples, nuts and 50 g/2 oz sultanas, with 25 g/1 oz brown sugar and 1 tablespoon lemon juice. Heat for 5 minutes. Add the batter and bake for 25 to 30 minutes. Top with sugar and serve.

Summer Pudding

▲ ✿ ✿ ✿ ✿

SERVES 6

350 g/12 oz bread, weight with
    crusts
900 g/2 lb fruit, this can be any
    mixture of soft fruits, but
    some should be red in
    colour, like raspberries and
    loganberries, to colour the
    bread
2 to 3 tablespoons water
sugar to taste

Cut the crusts from the bread, then thinly slice it – if you have not bought ready-sliced bread. Cook the fruit in the water; use the larger quantity if the fruit is firm. Add sugar to taste. Allow the fruit to become cool, if it is too hot, it is inclined to break the bread.

Line the bottom and sides of a 1·2 litre/2 pint basin with most of the bread; leave sufficient for the covering.

Add the fruit and juice. Cover with the last of the bread. Put a layer of greaseproof paper over the top, then a plate and light weight. Stand the basin on a plate, as some of the juice may come out with the weight on top. Leave overnight and turn out on to the serving dish, baste any white patches with the reserved juices and if there is any surplus serve as a sauce. This is a surprising pudding; it does not taste or look as though it is based upon bread.

Serve with cream, ice cream, fromage frais or yogurt. The dessert can be decorated with whipped cream and a few whole berries, but that is not essential.

LUXURY SUMMER PUDDING:
Instead of bread use thinly sliced plain cake.

ALL THE YEAR PUDDING:
This is equally suitable for other times in the year.

Autumn: Use blackberries and apples.

Winter: Use imported plums or canned fruit.

Spring: Use early rhubarb. Do not add any water with this; a little grated orange rind added during cooking gives it an interesting taste.

Summer Pudding

Apricot and Raisin Mould

▲ ▲ ✿ ✿ ✿ ✿

SERVES 4 TO 6

175 g/6 oz dried apricots
600 ml/1 pint water
25 to 50 g/1 to 2 oz caster
    sugar
1 tablespoon lemon juice
1 sachet (1 level tablespoon)
    gelatine
25 g/1 oz seedless raisins
150 ml/¹/₄ pint double cream
To decorate:
25 g/1 oz blanched almonds

Soak the apricots in the water for several hours, unless using
the tenderized type, when this stage can be omitted. Tip into
a saucepan, add the sugar and lemon juice, cover the pan and
simmer gently until tender. This takes about 45 minutes.

Take out 2 or 3 apricots for decoration. Allow the gelatine
to soak for 2 minutes in 3 tablespoons of the apricot syrup,
then dissolve over hot water or in the microwave cooker.

Liquidize the apricots and the syrup and add the dissolved
gelatine. Stir well to blend, you should have barely 600 ml/
1 pint of apricot purée. Allow to cool and become slightly
syrupy, then add the raisins.

Whip the cream and fold all but 2 tablespoons of it into the
mixture. Spoon into a mould rinsed in cold water and allow to
set. Cut the reserved apricots into narrow strips.

Turn the mould out on to the serving dish and top with the
cream, apricot strips and the almonds.

OMITTING THE SUGAR:
This dessert could be made
without additional sugar, just
depending upon the natural
sweetness of the dried fruit.

CHANGING THE FLAVOUR:
Use half water and half sweet
cider or orange juice.

Harvest Cheesecake

▲ ▲ ✿ ✿ ✿ ✿

SERVES 6

For the base:
150 g/5 oz digestive or
    wheatmeal biscuits
40 g/1¹/₂ oz walnuts
75 g/3 oz butter
pinch ground ginger
For the topping:
450 g/1 lb dessert apples
150 ml/¹/₄ pint sweet cider or
    apple juice, plus extra, if
    required, see method
5 cm/2 inch cinnamon stick or
    good pinch ground
    cinnamon
1 sachet (1 level tablespoon)
    gelatine
225 g/8 oz curd or cream
    cheese
225 ml/7¹/₂ fl oz thick Greek
    yogurt
25 to 50 g/1 to 2 oz caster or
    light brown sugar
To decorate:
1 or 2 dessert apples
    preferably with a red skin
1 tablespoon lemon juice
few walnut halves

Grease a 20 cm/8 inch cake tin with a loose base or line it with
baking parchment. You can use a spring-form tin, described
on page 42.

Crush the biscuits to make fine crumbs. Chop the walnuts
and mix with the crumbs. Melt the butter and add to the
walnut mixture with the ginger. Press into the base of the tin
and place in the refrigerator while you prepare the filling.

Peel, core and thinly slice the apples. Put the cider or apple
juice into a pan, with the cinnamon, and gently poach the
apples for 5 to 10 minutes, until tender but still retaining their
shape. Strain the liquid and cool slightly.

Measure this and, if necessary, add a little more cider or
apple juice to make 150 ml/¹/₄ pint again. Sprinkle the gelatine
on it, stand for 2 or 3 minutes, then dissolve over hot water or
in the microwave cooker. When it is cold and syrupy, mix with
the cheese and yogurt, the poached apples and sugar to taste.
Do this carefully, so the apple slices do not break.

Spoon over the biscuit base and leave until set. Core and
slice, but do not peel the raw apple(s). Dip into lemon juice so
they do not discolour, then arrange in a spiral effect on top of
the jellied filling and add the walnut halves.

This cheesecake is an excellent basic one. Instead of apples
and/or pears, you could substitute well-drained canned
pineapple or apricots or mangoes.

Use the syrup from the can instead of cider or apple juice.

TO TURN OUT OF THE TIN:
Wrap a warm teacloth round
the sides of the tin to soften
the jelly slightly. Leave for only
a few seconds.

Place a tin with a loose base
on a jam jar, then push this
upwards. The tin sides drop
away leaving the cheesecake
on its base. This can be
removed.

If using a spring-form tin,
simply unhook it and remove
the dessert.

VANILLA FLAVOURINGS:
Use essence sparingly or
insert halved vanilla pod into a
jar of sugar to flavour this,
then use the sugar in cooking.

Harvest Cheesecake; Tiramisu

Tiramisu

▲ ▲   ✿ ✿

SERVES 4 TO 6

12 to 14 savoiardi* or boudoir
    biscuits or 4 to 6 trifle
    sponge cakes
3 tablespoons brandy
6 to 8 tablespoons strong cold
    coffee
2 eggs, size 1
50 g/2 oz caster or icing sugar
225 to 300 g/8 to 10 oz
    Mascarpone cheese
2 to 4 oz bitter or plain
    chocolate

* Italian sponge fingers. You
    will probably need the
    larger quantities if making
    this in layers in a dish.

This dessert has become popular because so many Italian
restaurants include it on the menu. The recipes vary a great
deal, so alternative suggestions are given on the right. Soft
Italian Mascarpone cheese is an essential ingredient.

Place the biscuits in a serving dish; if using trifle sponges,
cut each of these into 4 pieces. Blend the brandy and coffee
together and spoon over the biscuits or sponges, making sure
they are evenly moistened.

Separate the eggs, add the caster or sifted icing sugar to
the yolks and whisk until thick and creamy. Blend with the
cheese. Whisk the egg whites until stiff, fold into the cheese
mixture. Spread this over the base of the biscuits or sponges.
Coarsely grate the chocolate and cover the dessert with it.
Chill well before serving.

TO VARY THE DISH:
Omit the uncooked eggs; whip
150 ml/$^1/_4$ pint double cream
and blend with the sugar and
cheese or use half whipped
cream and half thick yogurt,
plus a squeeze of lemon juice.

Many recipes mix 225 g/
8 oz well-drained canned fruit
salad into the cheese mixture.
You could use diced ripe fruit.

Use half brandy and half
rum.

ICED DESSERTS

The recipes for ice creams, iced desserts and sorbets on this and the following pages will enable you to make a wide range of dishes. The first selection of ice creams are unusual and luxurious; they would be ideal for special occasions, especially if served in almond, brandy or fruit baskets. These desserts have a high percentage of cream and can be stored in your freezer or freezing compartment of the refrigerator for several weeks, without losing either taste or texture.

Iced desserts are not all luxury foods, some of these are based upon low-fat yogurt and fromage frais – ideal if you are on a slimming diet. There are nutritious, but inexpensive, ices that will be great favourites with children too. When you freeze low-fat mixtures, it is better to store them for only a limited time, as indicated in the specific recipes.

Ice cream mixtures are satisfactory whether frozen in an ice cream maker, a freezer or the freezing compartment of a domestic refrigerator, but sorbets have a better texture if you use an ice cream maker. The advantages of this appliance are given on page 46.

YOGURT ICE CREAMS

The inclusion of yogurt in an ice cream adds a delicious and piquant flavour. To achieve a perfectly smooth texture, without the use of gelatine, you must use equal quantities of full-cream yogurt and whipped cream.

If you use low-fat yogurt and no cream, it is advisable to eat the ice soon after it is frozen. The alternative is to add gelatine, as in the low-fat yogurt ice cream. This prevents the mixture becoming so hard that it is not pleasant to eat. Ices made with low-fat yogurts are excellent if you are slimming; they are also ideal for children.

Lemon Honey Granita   ▲ ▲   ✿ ✿ ✿

SERVES 4 TO 6
4 large or 6 medium lemons
4 tablespoons water, you may
    need a little more, see
    method
2 tablespoons thin honey
50 g/2 oz caster sugar
1 fresh bay leaf or a sprig of
    lemon balm
450 ml/³/₄ pint low-fat yogurt
    or fromage frais

A granita is the name given to the type of ice in which the mixture forms small granules. It is very refreshing.

Cut a slice from each lemon; check that you leave the side of the fruit, which enables it to stand upright, intact.

Carefully scoop out all the pulp and juice with a teaspoon; do this over a basin, so no juice is wasted. Discard any white pith, skin and pips from the fruit removed. Sieve or liquidize the pulp and juice. You need 150 ml/¹/₄ pint. If there is less than this, dilute with extra water. Cut out extra pith from the lemon cases and from the slices removed. Cover.

Put the 4 tablespoons water into a pan with the honey, sugar and bay leaf or balm. Stir over a low heat until the sugar has dissolved, then allow to become quite cold. Blend with the lemon purée and the yogurt or fromage frais. Do not remove the herb at this stage.

Pour into a freezing tray or shallow dish and leave until lightly frozen, then gently fork the mixture and remove the herb. Freeze again for a short time, until sufficiently firm to spoon into the lemon cases. Decorate with the slices of lemon and place the fruit in the freezer.

Always remove from the freezer about 20 minutes before required and keep in the refrigerator.

ORANGE GRANITA:
Use 4 to 6 oranges instead of lemons. Honey is less good with oranges, so omit it and use just the sugar. Use half orange purée and half yogurt or fromage frais.

COFFEE GRANITA:
This can be made by just freezing sweetened coffee.

Make sure the coffee is of an excellent flavour. It can be flavoured with a little Tía Maria or Kahlua (coffee liqueurs), or use equal amounts of sweetened coffee and yogurt or fromage frais.

Coconut and Orange Ice Cream

Mango and Passion Fruit Sorbet

Coconut and Orange Ice Cream ▲▲▲ ✪✪✪

SERVES 6 TO 8

zest from 2 oranges
75 g/3 oz creamed coconut
150 ml/¹/₄ pint orange juice
2 eggs
75 g/3 oz caster sugar
50 g/2 oz desiccated coconut
50 g/2 oz candied orange peel
450 ml/³/₄ pint whipping or
  double cream
2 tablespoons Curaçao
  (optional)

Cut the zest from the oranges into very narrow strips and blanch for 5 minutes, see right. Cut the creamed coconut into small pieces and put into a saucepan with the orange juice. Heat gently until the coconut has melted. Separate the eggs, blend the yolks with 25 g/1 oz of the sugar and the orange mixture. Cook in the top of a double saucepan or in a basin over hot but not boiling water until the mixture coats the back of a wooden spoon. Stir in the desiccated coconut. Chop the candied peel very finely, add to the warm orange-custard, then allow this to become quite cold.

Whip the cream until it stands up in soft peaks and stir into the coconut mixture, together with the Curaçao. Whisk the egg whites until stiff, fold in the rest of the sugar, then blend this into the ingredients. Spoon into the container and freeze.

To serve, scoop into balls. Top with the orange zest.

TO PREPARE ZEST:
Pare the top coloured part of the rind from the fruit with a potato peeler. Avoid any white pith.

TO BLANCH FRUIT RINDS:
Put into cold water, bring to the boil and simmer for 5 minutes, or until softened. Keep the zest in the liquid until ready to use, then drain and dry.

Mango and Passion Fruit Sorbet ▲▲ ✪✪✪

SERVES 4

2 ripe mangoes
4 passion fruit
1 tablespoon lemon juice
75 g/3 oz caster sugar
150 ml/¹/₄ pint water

Cut the skin from the mangoes and cut the pulp from the stones. Halve the passion fruit and scoop out all the pulp. The two fruits can be sieved or liquidized. Heat the lemon juice with the sugar and water only until the sugar has dissolved. Add to the fruit purée and allow to cool.

Freeze until firm. If using the freezer, stir once or twice during freezing. This sorbet is beautifully light if frozen in an ice cream maker.

Using egg whites: You can whisk 1 or 2 egg whites until stiff, then fold these into the fruit purée when it is slightly frozen. This extends the purée and gives a greater volume, but the egg whites do take away some of the natural fruit flavour.

Using other fruit purées: Many other fruit purées can be made into sorbets and water ices. Adjust the amount of lemon juice and sugar to personal taste, but remember that too much sugar hinders – and can even prevent – the mixture freezing.

The combination of melon and passion fruit is delicious.

WATER ICES:
Use 300 ml/¹/₂ pint water with the lemon juice and sugar instead of the 150 ml/¹/₄ pint in the recipe for the sorbet.

WATERMELON WATER ICE:
Scoop out and sieve the pulp. To each 300 ml/¹/₂ pint melon purée, allow 300 ml/¹/₂ pint of the lemon flavoured syrup. Blend with the purée and freeze as for a sorbet, stirring from time to time.

Water ices make splendid 'lollies' for children and have the goodness of fresh fruit.

Christmas Pudding

Christmas Pudding   ▲ ▲ ✪ ✪ ✪ ✪

SERVES 8
50 g/2 oz plain flour
$^1/_2$ level teaspoon mixed spice
$^1/_2$ level teaspoon cinnamon
$^1/_2$ to 1 level teaspoon nutmeg
110* g/4 oz soft breadcrumbs
110* g/4 oz brown sugar
110* g/4 oz mixed candied
    peel
110* g/4 oz blanched almonds
110* g/4 oz grated apple
1 small carrot
1 lemon
450 g/1 lb mixed dried fruit –
    225 g/8 oz raisins,
    110* g/4 oz sultanas,
    110* g/4 oz currants
110* g/4 oz butter or suet
2 eggs
1 tablespoon golden syrup or
    black treacle
150 ml/$^1/_4$ pint stout, ale or
    beer
$^1/_2$ to 1 level teaspoon
    cinnamon

* use this Metrication

Mix together the flour, spices, breadcrumbs and sugar. Chop the peel and almonds. Peel and grate the apple and carrot. Grate the rind and squeeze out the juice of the lemon.

Mix all these ingredients together with the dried fruits. If using butter, melt it; otherwise, grate the suet, unless using already shredded. Add the fat to the other ingredients.

Beat the eggs and stir into the rest of the ingredients with the syrup or treacle and stout or other liquid.

Stir well; let all the family stir for good luck. If possible, allow to stand overnight so the flavours mature.

Spoon into a 1·5 litre/2$^1/_2$ pint basin and cover with greased greaseproof paper and foil.

Steam or boil for 6 to 8 hours. Remove the damp covers and when the pudding is cold, put on dry paper.

On Christmas Day, steam for a further 2 hours before serving. Serve with Brandy butter, see recipe, right.

If you would like a change from the traditional pudding use diced dried apricots instead of the mixture of dried fruits. Choose golden syrup and not black treacle and caster, instead of brown, sugar. This gives a golden-coloured pudding.

BRANDY BUTTER:
Cream together 100 g/4 oz unsalted butter with 100 g/4 oz sifted icing sugar and 50 g/2 oz soft brown sugar until soft.

Gradually beat in 2 tablespoons brandy – or to taste.

Pile or pipe into a serving dish. Decorate with almonds. Chill but do not freeze.

Bread and Butter Pudding

▲ ✿✿✿

SERVES 4

2 or 3 large slices of bread,
   according to personal taste
40 g/1 1/2 oz butter
2 eggs
2 egg yolks
40 g/1 1/2 oz caster or light
   brown sugar
600 ml/1 pint milk
50 g/2 oz sultanas

The crusts on the bread may be removed or left on; they give a change of colour to the pudding. Spread the bread with the butter, then cut into neat squares or triangles. Arrange neatly in a 1·2 litre/2 pint pie dish.

Beat the eggs and egg yolks with 25 g/1 oz of the sugar. Warm the milk, add to the eggs, beat well and then stir in the sultanas; this makes sure they are evenly distributed.

Pour over the bread and butter. Allow to stand, if time permits, for 30 minutes before baking, then sprinkle the remaining sugar over the top.

Preheat the oven to 150°C/300°F, Gas Mark 2. Bake for approximately 1 1/4 hours or until just firm.

MACAROON BREAD AND
BUTTER PUDDING:
Use 2 slices of bread and butter and 2 macaroon biscuits. Quarter the biscuits and arrange with the bread and butter.

ORANGE BREAD AND BUTTER
PUDDING:
Add the finely grated zest of 2 oranges to the milk, with 25 g/1 oz chopped candied peel. Top with marmalade.

Almond Cherry Pudding

▲ ▲ ✿✿✿

SERVES 4 TO 6

110* g/4 oz butter
110* g/4 oz caster sugar
2 large eggs
110* g/4 oz self-raising flour or
   plain flour sifted with 1
   teaspoon baking powder
50 g/2 oz ground almonds
50 g/2 oz breadcrumbs
50 g/2 oz glacé cherries
For the sauce:
25 g/1 oz glacé cherries
25 g/1 oz blanched almonds
15 g/1/2 oz cornflour
300 ml/1/2 pint milk
25 g/1 oz butter
40 g/1 1/2 oz caster sugar

* use this metrication

Grease a 1·2 to 1·5 litre/2 to 2 1/2 pint pudding basin well. Cream the butter and sugar until soft and light. Beat the eggs and gradually add to the creamed mixture. Sift the flour or flour and baking powder into the mixture, then mix this, together with the ground almonds and breadcrumbs, with the creamed mixture.

Cut the cherries into quarters and add to the pudding mixture. There is no need to add any extra liquid.

Spoon into the basin, cover with greased greaseproof paper and/or foil. Steam over boiling water for 1 1/2 hours, then turn out and serve with the sauce.

To make the sauce, finely chop the cherries and almonds. Blend the cornflour with the cold milk and butter. Put into a saucepan and stir over a moderate heat until thickened. Add the sugar, cherries and almonds. Heat for 2 minutes.

USING THE MICROWAVE:
The pudding can be cooked on the setting that gives two-thirds of the full output for approximately 9 minutes, see pages 44 to 45.

Allow to stand for 3 or 4 minutes before turning out.

The sauce can be cooked in a basin in the microwave, instead of in a saucepan. Stir several times during cooking to keep it smooth.

Chocolate-Coffee Pudding

▲ ✿✿✿

SERVES 4

225 ml/7 1/2 fl oz strong coffee
15 g/1/2 oz cocoa powder or
   25 g/1 oz chocolate powder
225 ml/7 1/2 fl oz milk
3 eggs or 2 eggs and 2 egg
   yolks
50 to 75 g/2 to 3 oz caster
   sugar, see method
50 g/2 oz fine cake crumbs or
   soft breadcrumbs
For the sauce:
15 g/1/2 oz cocoa powder or
   25 g/1 oz chocolate powder
1 level tablespoon cornflour
4 tablespoons strong coffee
300 ml/1/2 pint milk
25 to 40 g/1 to 1 1/2 oz caster
   sugar

Grease a 1·2 litre/2 pint pie dish and preheat the oven to 160°C/325°F, Gas Mark 3. Warm the coffee and dissolve the cocoa or chocolate powder in it. Add the milk. Beat the eggs and sugar together; you may need the larger amount of sugar if you are using cocoa powder and breadcrumbs. Add the milk mixture. Put the crumbs into the pie dish, strain the liquid over them and allow to stand for 15 minutes before cooking.

Bake for approximately 45 minutes, or until just firm and serve hot with the sauce.

To make the sauce, blend the cocoa or chocolate powder with the cornflour and add the coffee and milk. Pour into a saucepan, stir over a moderate heat until the sauce thickens, then add the sugar.

TO STEAM THE PUDDING:
Put into a greased 1·2 litre/ 2 pint basin, cover and steam over hot but not boiling water for approximately 1 1/4 hours.

ALMOND CHOCOLATE
PUDDING:
Use 25 g/1 oz crumbs and 25 g/1 oz ground almonds in the pudding. When it is baked, top with blanched flaked almonds. Return to the oven for a few minutes.

SUCCESSFUL BAKING

Many people find that baking is their favourite form of cooking. For other people, it is rather alarming; there are so many different things that can go wrong – the cake may sink, the bread may be heavy, etc. Those horrid events do happen – but rarely – if you understand the theory behind making dishes that are baked and cooking them correctly.

The way you handle the ingredients is far more important when you are making bread, a cake or biscuits than when stirring a soup. Each type requires a different technique. You will find certain words used in recipes and these are important.

If, in the recipe, it states you should **fold in the flour**, it means you use a gentle flicking and turning movement – not a vigorous one. If, on the other hand, you are advised to knead the ingredients, then the action is steady, firm and energetic. Creaming the ingredients together means a brisk beating movement, either by hand with a wooden spoon, or in a mixer. The object is not only to combine the ingredients together but to aerate them too.

Cooking times and temperatures are all important. Take the trouble to preheat the oven, so it is at the right temperature when the food is placed in it. If a size is given for the cake tin, do try to use a similar one, for this makes a difference to the cooking time. Ovens vary quite appreciably and you are the best judge of whether your oven is average, slightly fierce or more gentle than the usual, so follow recipes in the light of your specific knowledge of your own cooker.

Sweet Scones

Sweet Scones ▲ ✪

MAKES 10 TO 12
225 g/8 oz self-raising flour or plain flour sifted with 2 teaspoons baking powder or with ½ level teaspoon bicarbonate of soda and 1 level teaspoon cream of tartar
pinch salt
25 to 50 g/1 to 2 oz butter or margarine or low-fat spread
25 to 50 g/1 to 2 oz caster sugar
approximately 150 ml/¼ pint milk to mix

Preheat the oven to 220°C/425°F, Gas Mark 7. There is no need to grease the baking sheet or tray for plain scones like these. A little flour sifted on to the baking sheet or tray prevents the bottom of the scones becoming too brown.

Sift together the flour, raising agent and salt. Rub in the fat, add the sugar and gradually mix in enough milk to make a soft rolling consistency. That is one of the secrets of a good scone; the mixture must be soft. Also, the oven must be thoroughly preheated.

Mix the dough well, turn out on to a lightly floured surface and roll out until 2 cm/¾ inch thick. Cut into 10 to 12 rounds for average-sized scones or to 18 for very small ones.

Put on to the baking tray or sheet and cook for 10 minutes, or until firm when pressed on the side. Lift on to a wire cooling tray. Eat when fresh or reheat for a few minutes in the oven or a few seconds in the microwave cooker – using 50 per cent POWER, see right-hand column.

REHEATING SCONES AND ROLLS: Wrap in foil if you want them to keep soft and reheat for a few minutes at 200°C/400°F, Gas Mark 6.

FLAVOURING SCONES:
CHEESE: Omit sugar. Add seasoning and 50 to 75 g/2 to 3 oz grated cheese. Bake at 200°C/400°F, Gas Mark 6.

FRUIT: Add 50 to 75 g/2 to 3 oz mixed dried fruit, or chopped dates, or nuts.

ORANGE: Add a little grated orange rind. Bind with orange juice, not milk.

Date and Pecan Nut Teabread ▲▲ ✪✪

SERVES 6
225 g/8 oz cooking dates
100 g/4 oz pecan nuts
4 tablespoons water
25 g/1 oz margarine
175 g/6 oz self-raising flour or plain flour sifted with 1½ level teaspoons baking powder
25 g/1 oz light brown sugar
1 egg
2 tablespoons milk

Grease and flour or line a 675 g/1½ lb loaf tin. Preheat the oven to 180°C/350°F, Gas Mark 4.

Chop the dates and the nuts. Heat the water and pour over the dates. Allow to stand for 15 minutes. Rub the margarine into the flour or flour and baking powder and add the nuts, sugar, softened dates and liquid. Beat the egg and add to the mixture with the milk. Beat briskly to mix the ingredients. Spoon into the prepared tin and bake for 40 minutes or until firm.

When cold, slice and spread with butter.

ALTERING THE FLAVOUR:
Use walnuts instead of pecan nuts.

Use half white and half wholemeal flour with an extra ½ tablespoon milk.

Use all wholemeal flour with an extra 1 tablespoon milk.

Shortcrust Pastry

MAKES A 10 × 2·5 IN TART SHELL
225 g/8 oz plain flour, see method
pinch salt
110* g/4 oz fat, this can be all cooking fat or all lard or ordinary or polyunsaturated fat or margarine
water to bind, see method

* use this metrication to give correct balance between fat and flour

IF MAKING WITH HARD FAT: Sift the flour and salt into a mixing bowl, cut the fat into small pieces and drop into the flour. Rub in with the fingertips until the mixture forms fine crumbs. Gradually add water to make a firm rolling consistency.
IF MAKING WITH SOFTENED FAT: Sift the flour and salt. Put the fat into a mixing bowl, add a little flour (amount as given on the packet) plus the recommended amount of water. Cream with a fork, then gradually add the rest of the flour.
IF USING A FOOD PROCESSOR OR MIXER: Follow the methods above, but be careful that the dough is not over-handled. It may be better to add the liquid gradually by hand if using hard fat.
TO ROLL THE PASTRY: Sprinkle a little flour on the pastry board and rolling pin and roll out the pastry with short, sharp movements.
TO BAKE THE PASTRY: Shortcrust pastry is generally baked in a preheated moderate to moderately hot oven i.e. 190 to 200°C/ 375 to 400°F, Gas Mark 5 to 6, depending upon the dish.
TO BAKE BLIND: This term denotes that the pastry is baked without a filling, see page 140.

TO MAKE A FRUIT FLAN:
Make shortcrust pastry, see recipe left.

Roll out the pastry and line the flan dish or tin. Bake 'blind'.

Fill the cooked cold pastry with well-drained canned or cooked fruit or dessert fruit. Measure 150 ml/¼ pint syrup (this is enough for a 20 cm/ 8 inch flan), or use water and sugar with lemon juice to flavour. Blend with 1 teaspoon arrowroot and 2 tablespoons redcurrant jelly or sieved apricot jam. Heat until smooth, cool slightly, then brush or spread over the fruit.

HOME-MADE BREAD

Do not allow the thought of using yeast worry you; it is not difficult in any way. The important point is that you are dealing with an ingredient that can be 'killed' by using excessive heat. This is why it is essential to keep yeast doughs in a warm, but not hot position during the process of proving. The yeast has to be killed when the bread is baked, hence the hot oven.

Certain terms are used in bread-making.

Kneading: This means pushing the dough to and away from you. Use the base of the hand, called the 'heel'. The purpose is to distribute the yeast evenly to activate it.

Proving: The term used in yeast cookery to denote rising.

Knock back: After the dough has risen, it is kneaded again; this stage is known as 'knocking back' – it returns the dough to its original bulk.

Wholemeal Bread   ▲ ✪✪✪✪ or ✪✪✪

MAKES 2 LOAVES

Recipe No. 1

Follow proportions given for white bread, right, but substitute strong wholemeal flour

Recipe No. 2

Use the same proportions of flour, yeast, etc, as white bread but use 575* ml/ 1 pint water

* use this metrication

Recipe No. 1: Wholemeal flour absorbs more liquid than white flour, so you will need to add another 1 to 2 tablespoons of warm water to obtain a texture that can be kneaded. Proceed as for white bread, in the recipe right. This gives crusty wholemeal bread.

Recipe No. 2: The amount of liquid specified produces a soft sticky dough. Beat with a wooden spoon until the dough feels springy and leaves the sides of the bowl clean. This can be done with a dough hook or in a food processor.

Put into the greased and warmed loaf tins, see page 179, and allow to prove in the tins for about 25 minutes only.

Bake in a preheated oven set to 200°C/400°F, Gas Mark 6 for approximately 40 minutes if making the two loaves as in the recipe for white bread.

This recipe gives a soft and moist wholemeal bread.

BROWN BREAD:
Use equal quantities of white and wholemeal flour and follow the method for white bread.

STONEGROUND FLOUR:
This refers to the method of grinding the wheat.

TOPPINGS FOR THE DOUGH:
Put a good sprinkling of rolled oats, poppy or sesame seeds on the dough when in the tins or formed into loaves.

Wholemeal Bread; White Loaf; Cottage Loaf

White Bread

▲ ✿✿✿✿

MAKES 2 LOAVES
675 g/1½ lb strong flour
1 teaspoon salt
25 g/1 oz butter or lard or
    margarine or 1 tablespoon
    olive or other oil
20 g/¾ oz fresh yeast or 1
    sachet of the dried yeast
    sold to add to the flour, see
    right-hand column, too
450 ml/¾ pint water
1 tablespoon sugar, see
    method

If you have never made bread before this is a good amount with which to begin. You do not have too great a bulk for kneading and it is worthwhile making more than one loaf.

Sift the flour and salt into a large bowl. Rub in the fat or add the oil.

If using fresh yeast, put it into a separate basin. If using dried yeast, add it to the flour.

Heat the water to about 43°C/110°F (tepid); the easiest way is to boil half the quantity and make it up to 450 ml/¾ pint with cold water – this gives just about the right heat.

Cream the fresh yeast, add the water, top with a sprinkling of flour and leave for about 10 minutes, or until the surface is covered with bubbles. Blend with the flour.

If using dried yeast, mix the water with the sugar and add to the flour. Sugar is not essential with fresh yeast.

Turn the dough out on to a lightly floured working surface and knead thoroughly. To do this, fold the dough towards you, then push it away. Continue like this until the dough is firm and elastic and no longer feels sticky.

This stage can be done with the dough hook in an electric mixer or in a food processor; use a low speed.

To test if the dough is sufficiently kneaded, press firmly with a floured finger. This will leave an impression, but if it comes out the dough has been handled enough. Do not over-knead, as this spoils the bread. It is particularly easy to do this with a mixer or food processor, so test frequently.

The dough is then ready to 'prove'. Either return to the mixing bowl and cover with a teacloth or place in a very large saucepan and cover with a lid. Remember, it should rise to twice its original bulk – so allow plenty of space. It can be put into a lightly oiled large polythene bag. Put the dough in a warm place, such as the airing cupboard, or use the microwave cooker.

This amount of dough should take about 1 hour in a warm place and 2 to 2½ hours in a cooler room temperature. You can leave it for 12 hours in the refrigerator, then bring it out to room temperature.

Knock back (knead) the dough again and shape.

To make 2 tin loaves: Grease and warm two 450 g/1 lb loaf tins. Divide the dough into two halves and press out to neat oblongs, the same length and 3 times the width of the tins. Fold to fit the tins and place in the tins with the fold underneath.

To make 2 bloomer loaves: Form the dough into 2 large sausage shapes and place on lightly greased baking trays. Make equally-spaced shallow cuts along the top.

You could make one loaf and about 12 small rolls. Place rolls on a lightly greased baking sheet, allowing plenty of space between them.

Cover the dough lightly and leave until nearly double in size. This takes from 20 minutes. Meanwhile, preheat the oven to 220°C/425°F, Gas Mark 7.

Bake the loaves for approximately 35 minutes and the rolls for 12 to 15 minutes.

To test if cooked, knock on the bottom of the loaf; it should sound hollow. Turn out of the tin. If the sides are not as crusty as you like, simply place on a flat baking sheet and return to the oven for a few minutes.

USE OF SALT:
The amount of salt in these recipes is fairly low, in keeping with advice upon using less salt. You can increase it to 1½ level teaspoons.

DRIED YEAST:
The recipe, left, gives the method of using modern dried yeast. There is also the type in which the yeast, sugar and warm water are mixed, left to rise, then added to the flour, like fresh yeast.

FRUIT BREAD:
Mix up to 100 g/4 oz mixed dried fruit with the flour.

HERB BREAD:
Add 1 crushed garlic clove to the water and about 2 tablespoons finely chopped fresh mixed herbs to the flour.

MILK BREAD:
Use butter as the fat in the dough and mix with warm milk.

OATMEAL BREAD:
Omit 75 g/3 oz flour and add this weight of medium oatmeal or rolled oats. Top the dough with rolled oats when in the tins, before proving.

RYE BREAD:
Use half white flour and half rye flour – to give a light-textured bread.

TOMATO BREAD:
Cut 4 to 5 sun-dried tomatoes into very small pieces. Soak in a little boiling water for 2 to 3 minutes. Using the water as part of the liquid in the recipe along with the tomatoes. Sun-dried tomatoes have a very distinctive savoury taste.

TYPES OF YEAST:
Yeast is available in fresh or dried forms. The ways of using both varieties are given in the method, right.

USING THE MICROWAVE COOKER:
A microwave cooker can shorten the proving time of the dough. Check specific instructions in your manufacturer's book as to the setting to be used.

Do not exceed the recommended periods stated.

Bread bakes well in a combination cooker.

FREEZING YEAST DOUGHS:
Bread and other yeast products freeze well.

RECIPES BASED ON THE BREAD MIXTURE

MAKING BUNS

These are wonderfully economical cakes for children and they have a great deal of nutritional value. Their fat content is very low, especially if you use the bread mixture on page 179 without increasing the fat. You will need to add a little sugar.

If you take off about a quarter of the dough after proving and before forming it into loaves, you can knead 25 to 50 g/1 to 2 oz sugar into it. If icing the buns, as in Swiss buns below, then sugar in the dough could be omitted.

From the amount of dough suggested you can make 10 to 12 buns. If you decide to make a very large batch with all the dough, you can freeze the surplus very successfully.

Fruit buns: Knead in the sugar, as suggested above, plus 50 g/2 oz dried fruit. Form into rounds and allow to prove on lightly greased baking trays until nearly double in size. Bake for 12 to 15 minutes in a preheated oven set to 220°C/425°F, Gas Mark 7.

When the buns come out of the oven they can be given a sticky topping. Mix 1 level tablespoon sugar with 1 tablespoon boiling water. Brush over the buns.

Swiss buns: Knead the dough. Add a little extra sugar or omit it, see suggestion above. Form into finger shapes and allow to prove on lightly greased baking trays. Bake as instructions given above. When cold, cover the buns with icing.

Glacé icing to cover 10 to 12 buns: Sift 100 g/4 oz icing sugar into a basin and gradually add enough water or fruit juice to make a firm spreading consistency.

Spoon a little on each bun. Dip a palette knife into hot water, pat dry, but use while warm. Spread the icing neatly over the top of the buns. Allow to set.

MAKING A PIZZA

A pizza is an ideal dish for many occasions; children can take slices as part of a packed meal for school and it can be served for a picnic, main meal or light snack with a salad.

The basis of the pizza is a bread dough, so either make this, using 225 g/8 oz of flour and the other ingredients, given on page 179, in proportion, or take a quarter of the bread dough after proving and before it is formed into loaves.

Roll out the dough until 6 mm/¼ inch thick. Make one large or two small rounds.

The tomato topping has to be made, cooled, and put on the base for the final proving, so prepare it earlier.

To make the tomato topping: Peel and finely chop 1 medium onion and 1 to 2 garlic cloves. Skin and chop 450 g/1 lb tomatoes, preferably the plum type. Heat 1 to 2 tablespoons olive oil in a pan, add the onion and garlic and cook for 5 minutes. Put in the tomatoes and continue cooking until a thick purée forms. Add 1 teaspoon chopped fresh oregano or ½ teapoon dried oregano with salt and freshly ground black pepper. Taste the mixture and, if you want to emphasize the tomato flavour, add 1 tablespoon tomato purée or 4 or 5 finely chopped sun dried tomatoes that have been soaked for 3 minutes in boiling water, then drained.

Place the round(s) of dough on a lightly greased baking sheet, brush the top(s) with a little olive oil, then spread with the tomato mixture, plus the topping of your choice.

Sprinkle a good layer of grated Parmesan or other cheese over the pizza. Cover lightly and allow to prove for 25 to 30 minutes in a warm place.

Preheat the oven to 220°C/425°F, Gas Mark 7 and bake for 20 to 25 minutes. The topping can be protected with foil towards the end of the cooking time, so it does not dry. If your oven is inclined to be on the gentle side, preheat it to 230°C/450°F, Gas Mark 8, for a pizza should be cooked quickly.

If you prefer a moister topping, spread the tomato mixture over the dough before proving. Bake for a good 10 minutes then add the final topping.

TOPPINGS FOR PIZZAS: Many ingredients can be used as a topping for the pizza, over the tomato base.

Anchovy fillets and olives are the most usual but try strips of bacon or thick Bolognese sauce or the Chilli meat balls, recipes on pages 106 and 128.

Seafood, such as mussels, prawns and cockles, make a good topping and so do lightly cooked mixed vegetables.

Coconut Shortcake

Coconut Shortcake   ▲ ✿✿

MAKES 4

150 g/5 oz self-raising flour or plain flour sifted with 1¼ teaspoons baking powder
50 g/2 oz margarine or low-fat spread, see right
25 g/1 oz desiccated coconut
75 g/3 oz caster sugar
1 egg
milk to mix
fruit in season

There are many kinds of shortcake; this is typical of the low-fat type, rather like a scone. It must be eaten when freshly baked.

Grease a 20 cm/8 inch sandwich tin or a flat baking sheet. Preheat the oven to 190°C/375°F, Gas Mark 5. Put the flour or flour and baking powder into a mixing bowl and rub in the margarine or low-fat spread. Add the coconut and sugar.

Break the egg on to a saucer. Carefully spoon off 1 tablespoon of the white into a basin, see right. Add the yolk and any white left to the flour mixture, then blend in enough milk to make a soft rolling consistency. Pat or roll out and place into the tin or make into a neat round and place on the baking sheet. The latter method gives crisper edges.

Bake for 25 to 30 minutes or until firm. Cool or serve warm with cream and well-drained cooked or canned fruit or sliced fresh fruit.

USING LOW-FAT SPREAD: This cannot be used in ordinary recipes. It is quite satisfactory in a scone-like mixture, or a fruit crumble.

FOR A TOPPING: Brush the uncooked shortcake with lightly whisked egg white, sprinkle with 25 g/1 oz Demerara sugar and 25 g/1 oz desiccated coconut, then bake.

Passion Cake   ▲ ▲ ✿✿✿

SERVES 8

175 g/6 oz young carrots
75 g/3 oz walnuts
175 g/6 oz butter or margarine
175 g/6 oz soft brown sugar
3 large eggs
175 g/6 oz wholemeal self-raising flour or plain flour sifted with 1½ teaspoons baking powder
50 g/2 oz ground almonds
1 tablespoon milk

There are many recipes for carrot cake, or Passion cake as it is often called today. Spices can be added.

Grease and flour or line a 20 cm/8 inch cake tin. Preheat the oven to 180°C/350°F, Gas Mark 4.

Peel and finely grate the carrots just before making the cake. Do not soak them in water. Coarsely chop the walnuts.

Cream the butter or margarine and sugar until soft and light. Beat the eggs and gradually blend into the creamed mixture. Fold in the flour or flour and baking powder with the ground almonds. Add the carrots, walnuts and the milk. Mix thoroughly, then spoon into the prepared tin. Bake for 1 hour, or until firm to the touch. Cool for 5 minutes in the tin.

DECORATING THE CAKE: Quark, the slightly acid-flavoured, German soft cheese, makes an excellent filling and topping. Split the cold cake through the centre and spread with a good layer of Quark. Top with Quark and decorate with chopped or halved walnuts. Curd cheese could be used instead. You need about 350 g/12 oz.

Swiss Roll   ▲ ✪✪

SERVES 6
85*g/3 oz flour, see right
3 eggs, size 1 or 2
110*g/4 oz caster sugar
For the filling:
4 to 5 tablespoons jam
For rolling the sponge:
little caster sugar

*use this metrication

FLAVOURING THE SPONGE:
Add ¼ to ½ teaspoon vanilla
essence or use vanilla
flavoured sugar, see page 35.
Chocolate: Omit 15 g/½ oz
flour and add the same
amount of cocoa powder or
chocolate powder, depending
upon how strongly flavoured
you would like it to be.
Coffee: Add 1 to 2 teaspoons
coffee essence to the eggs or
blend the same amount of
instant coffee powder with a
very little boiling water.

ADDING WATER AND/OR
BUTTER:
If the eggs are small, you are
well advised to add 1
tablespoon hot water to the
mixture just before cooking.

25 g/1 oz melted butter can
be folded into the sponge
after adding the flour. This
should not be too hot.

Preheat the oven to 190 to 200°C/375 to 400°F, Gas Mark 5
to 6. Line a large Swiss roll tin, approximately 23 × 33 cm/
9 × 13 inches, with greased greaseproof paper or baking
parchment.

Sift the flour and keep in a warm place, while whisking the
eggs and sugar (this lightens it).

Whisk the eggs and sugar until really thick – you should be
able to see the trail of the whisk in the mixture. If you are
whisking by hand, rather than with an electric mixer, then you
will achieve a lighter result if you use a balloon, rather than a
rotary whisk. Fold the flour gently and carefully into the light
fluffy egg mixture, using a large metal spoon. Pour into the tin
and bake above the centre of the oven for 10 minutes, or until
firm to the touch.

Meanwhile, warm, but do not over-heat the jam. Sprinkle
the caster sugar over a sheet of greaseproof paper. Turn the
cooked sponge on to the sugared paper and strip away the
greaseproof or baking parchment used to line the tin. Spread
the sponge with the warmed jam.

To roll easily, make a light cut about 2·5 cm/1 inch from the
narrow end of the sponge nearest to you. Fold over firmly.
This first fold is the secret of easy rolling.

Lift the greaseproof paper and use it to help you roll the
sponge. Place the roll on a wire cooling tray away from a
draught.

If making a sponge sandwich: Grease and flour or line two
sandwich tins measuring 18 to 19 cm/7½ to 8 inches. Preheat
the oven to 190°C/375°F, Gas Mark 5.

Prepare the sponge as above, then spoon or pour the
mixture into the tins and bake for approximately 15 minutes,
or until firm to a gentle touch.

Invert each sponge in turn on to a folded teacloth held on
the palm of one hand, so they can be turned upside down
again on to the wire cooling tray.

When cold, sandwich together with jam and dust the top
with caster sugar.

KINDS OF FLOUR TO USE:
White flour gives a much
lighter sponge. As the eggs
and sugar are beaten so
vigorously in this type of
sponge, they provide the light
texture, so you can use plain
flour without a raising agent.
If, however, you are making
this sponge for the first time,
you may feel happier using
self-raising flour or plain flour
sifted with ½ teaspoon baking
powder.

MAKING A CREAM-FILLED
SWISS ROLL:
Make the sponge as the
recipe, left, and place on the
sugared paper. Remove the
cooking paper.

Roll with the sugared paper
inside the sponge. When cold,
unroll carefully. Fill with
whipped cream and jam, then
roll up again.

Swiss Roll

Chocolate Rum Gâteau ▲ ▲ ▲ ✿ ✿ ✿

SERVES 6 TO 8

For the walnut-crumb sponge:
40 g/1½ oz walnuts
40 g/1½ oz digestive biscuits
175 g/6 oz butter
175 g/6 oz caster sugar
3 eggs, size 1
1 tablespoon rum
100 g/4 oz self-raising flour sifted with ½ teaspoon baking powder or plain flour with 1½ teaspoons baking powder

For the filling and topping:
75 g/3 oz sultanas
3 tablespoons rum
175 g/6 oz plain or bitter chocolate
50 g/2 oz walnuts
150 g/5 oz icing sugar
150 g/5 oz butter

Line a 1·1 kg/2½ lb loaf tin with greased greaseproof paper or baking parchment. Preheat the oven to 180°C/350°F, Gas Mark 4.

Finely chop the walnuts and crush the biscuits. Cream the butter and sugar until soft and light. Beat the eggs with the rum. Gradually beat the eggs and rum into the creamed mixture, adding a little flour and baking powder if the mixture shows signs of curdling. When all the eggs and rum have been incorporated, add the rest of the flour, the nuts and crumbs.

Spoon into the prepared tin and bake for approximately 45 minutes, or until firm to the touch. Cool for about 10 minutes in the tin, then turn out and allow to cool. Split into 3 layers.

For the filling and topping, soak the sultanas in the rum while the sponge is cooking. Melt 150 g/5 oz of the chocolate and coarsely grate the remainder. Coarsely chop the walnuts. Sift the icing sugar and cream with the butter. Then add the melted chocolate and beat well until light in texture. Add the sultanas, rum and half the walnuts.

Sandwich the layers with some of the chocolate and rum mixture. Spread the remainder over the top, but not the sides of the gâteau. Sprinkle the last of the walnuts and the grated chocolate over the top icing. Chill well before serving.

This is equally good as a gâteau with tea or coffee or as a dessert. It goes well with fresh fruit salad.

BAKING PARCHMENT:
This is the modern material for lining tins. It does not need greasing, except in very exceptional circumstances, i e a very fragile mixture or one inclined to stick, such as meringues

In freezing, use when separating slices of meat, fish, etc.

ORANGE HAZELNUT GÂTEAU:
For the sponge, use Curaçao instead of rum and chopped hazelnuts instead of walnuts. Cream 1 teaspoon finely grated orange zest with the butter and sugar.
For the filling and topping, soak the sultanas in Curaçao or a mixture of orange juice and the liqueur. Use hazelnuts instead of walnuts.

CAKES WITHOUT EGGS

It is quite difficult to find cake recipes that do not use eggs, but the following are very popular with everyone, not just people who are allergic to eggs.

Moist fruit cake: Grease and flour or line a 20 cm/8 inch cake tin. Preheat the oven to 190°/375°F, Gas Mark 5.

Make 300 ml/½ pint moderately strong tea with a teabag; this will ensure it contains no leaves. Pour it into a saucepan, add 75 g/3 oz margarine and 100 g/4 oz moist brown sugar, together with 150 g/5 oz mixed dried fruit. Heat only until the margarine has melted, then allow to cool.

Sift 300 g/10 oz self-raising flour with ½ level teaspoon bicarbonate of soda, ½ teaspoon ground cinnamon and a pinch ground nutmeg. Blend the tea and fruit mixture with the dry ingredients. Spoon into the prepared cake tin and bake for 1 hour, or until firm.

Oaty fruit cake: Follow the recipe above, but use 200 g/7 oz self-raising flour and 75 g/3 oz rolled oats, together with ½ level teaspoon baking powder.

Citrus sponge: Grease and flour two 16·5 to 18 cm/6½ to 7 inch sandwich tins. Preheat the oven to 190°C/375°F, Gas Mark 5.

Cream 75 g/3 oz butter or margarine with 100 g/4 oz caster sugar, the grated rinds of 1 orange and 1 lemon and 1 level tablespoon golden syrup.

Sift together 175 g/6 oz self-raising flour and ½ level teaspoon baking powder. Mix 1 tablespoon lemon juice with 3 tablespoons orange juice.

Mix the flour and the fruit juices into the creamed ingredients, then stir in 4 tablespoons milk. Spoon into the two tins and bake for 15 to 18 minutes, or until firm to a gentle touch.

Turn out, allow to cool and sandwich together with jam or marmalade and top with caster sugar.

FREEZING CAKES:
Most cake freeze well. It is a good idea to cut the cake in slices before freezing. Separate the slices with pieces of waxed or greaseproof paper.

This means you can take just the required number of portions from the frozen cake and defrost these.

Open-freeze cakes, then wrap when frozen. This means the decorated or delicate surface of the cake is not spoiled by packaging.

Rich fruit cake

To ice the cake:
First brush away any loose crumbs from the surface of the cake. In order to help the marzipan adhere spread the cake with a little warmed and sieved apricot jam.

For the marzipan:
Blend together 225 g/8 oz ground almonds, 100 g/4 oz sifted icing sugar and 100 g/ 4 oz caster sugar. Add a few drops of almond essence and 2 egg yolks. Mix with a knife, then gently gather the mixture together with your fingers. It should be a firm rolling consistency. *If you do not want to use uncooked eggs*, then bind the mixture with sweet sherry.

Roll out the marzipan on a board coated with caster sugar to a size to cover the cake. Place over the cake and gently press to the top and sides so it adheres well.

Neaten the edges, then roll to give a flat surface.

Allow to dry out for 48 hours before adding the Royal icing.

For the royal icing:
Sift 450 g/1 lb icing sugar. Whisk 2 egg whites until just frothy – do not over-beat. Add the icing sugar gradually to the egg whites, then add $1/2$ to 1 tablespoon lemon juice plus 1 teaspoon glycerine.

Beat until the icing is white and glossy. Do not overbeat. *If you do not want to use uncooked egg whites*, buy the icing sugar which incorporates these, see page 35.

Spread the icing evenly over the cake, then neaten with a palette knife or icing ruler. Keep any excess icing covered with a damp cloth so it does not harden. Allow the coating to dry before using the rest of the icing for piping.

There always seems a very long list of ingredients needed for rich fruit cakes, but as you will see from the proportions given on the opposite page, these fall into four groups. If you prepare each group separately you will find that mixing the cake is 'child's play'.

Group A: This consists of the flour and spices. If you have not made a really rich fruit cake before, you may be surprised to see plain flour with no raising agent is specified. This is because you do not want the cake mixture to rise too much, for it cannot carry the weight of fruit and tends to sink. So do not use baking powder with plain flour or self-raising flour. Sift the flour and spices together; this makes them easier to mix.

Group B: The ingredients in this group should be creamed together until soft and light; do not overbeat. You can use an electric mixer quite happily. The measures of black treacle or golden syrup mean just level tablespoons.

Group C: The eggs and alcohol. There is not a lot of the latter, for I prefer to soak the cake during storage. If you do not want to use alcohol, substitute exactly the same amount of milk or orange juice.

Group D: The various fruits. Nowadays, most dried fruit is sold ready-cleaned, but if you want to clean it, then rub it in a floured cloth or rinse in cold water and allow it to dry on flat trays in the kitchen for 48 hours. Many cakes have been spoiled by using damp fruit. There is no need to wash or flour the cherries.

To make the cake:
Decide on the size cake required. Assemble the ingredients and divide them into groups **A**, **B**, **C** and **D**.

Line the selected cake tin carefully. Put brown paper, then greased greaseproof paper or baking parchment on the base of the tin. Place a band of greased greaseproof paper or baking parchment around the inside of the tin. Tie a deep band of brown paper around the outside of the tin; this should come well above the top of the tin.

Order of mixing:
Sift the flour and spices (**group A**).

Cream the ingredients until soft (**group B**).

Beat the eggs and alcohol together (**group C**) and beat gradually into the creamed mixture. If this shows signs of curdling, beat in a little of the flour mixture.

Stir in all the flour then all the fruit ingredients from **group D**. Blend well, but never over-beat this type of mixture.

Spoon into the prepared tin and spread level. Then press the mixture with damp, not wet knuckles; this helps to keep the top of the cake from becoming too hard.

Baking the cake:
Many people like to bake a rich fruit cake at a very low setting throughout the whole time. I prefer to use a very moderate heat at the beginning, given in the chart as Temperature A, then reduce this for the rest of the cooking period to Temperature B. I find this helps to keep the cake beautifully moist.

Temperature A: 160°C/325°F, Gas Mark 3.

Temperature B: 140 to 150°C/275 to 300°F, Gas Mark 1 to 2.

There is choice of temperatures under **B** because ovens vary. If your oven is inclined to be on the hot side, use the lower setting. There is, however, a very easy way to check on progress in baking this type of cake, as below.

TO CHECK ON BAKING:
At the end of the first third of baking time, the cake should have changed colour very slightly. If it is darkening too much, reduce heat immediately.

At the end of the second third of the cooking time, the cake should have darkened but still feel soft on top.

At the end of the baking time, the cake should feel firm and when you listen carefully there should be no humming sound. If there is a hum, it means the cake is not quite cooked and needs slightly longer. Test again a little later.

Always allow a rich fruit cake to cool in the baking tin.

PROPORTIONS

R means round tin; **S** means square tin. First measurement is cm; second is inches.
T means tablespoon and **t** means teaspoon.
In a few cases the metric measurements are not the familiar and standard ones. Those given ensure that you produce a similar sized cake to that made by imperial measures. These are based on the fact that 28.35 g is the true equivalent of 1 oz. Page 4 deals with weighing awkward amounts.

INGREDIENTS	R: 20/8 S: 18/7	R: 23/9 S: 20/8	R: 25/10 S: 23/9	R: 28/11 S: 25/10	R: 30/12 S: 28/11
plain flour	225 g/8 oz	340 g/12 oz	450 g/16 oz	570 g/20 oz	680 g/24 oz
ground cinnamon	³/₄ t	1 t	1¹/₄ t	1¹/₂ t	1³/₄ t
mixed spice	³/₄ t	1 t	1¹/₄ t	1¹/₂ t	1³/₄ t
butter	170 g/6 oz	280 g/10 oz	400 g/14 oz	510 g/18 oz	625 g/22 oz
moist brown sugar	170 g/6 oz	280 g/10 oz	400 g/14 oz	510 g/18 oz	625 g/22 oz
black treacle or syrup	³/₄ T	1 T	1¹/₄ T	1¹/₂ T	1³/₄ T
lemon zest	1 t	1¹/₂ t	1¹/₂ t	2 t	2¹/₂ t
eggs, size 2	4	6	8	10	12
sherry or rum or brandy	1¹/₂ T	2 T	2¹/₂ T	3 T	3¹/₂ T
candied peel, chopped	85 g/3 oz	140 g/5 oz	200 g/7 oz	255 g/9 oz	310 g/11 oz
blanched almonds, chopped	85 g/3 oz	140 g/5 oz	200 g/7 oz	255 g/9 oz	310 g/11 oz
glacé cherries, quartered	85 g/3 oz	140 g/5 oz	200 g/7 oz	255 g/9 oz	310 g/11 oz
currants	340 g/12 oz	450 g/16 oz	570 g/20 oz	680 g/24 oz	800 g/28 oz
sultanas	225 g/8 oz	280 g/10 oz	340 g/12 oz	400 g/14 oz	450 g/16 oz
seedless raisins	170 g/6 oz	225 g/8 oz	280 g/10 oz	340 g/12 oz	400 g/14 oz

BAKING TIMES

TEMPERATURE A:	1¹/₄ hours	1¹/₂ hours	1¹/₂ hours	1¹/₂ hours	1³/₄ hours
TEMPERATURE B:	1³/₄ hours	2 hours	2³/₄ hours	3¹/₂ hours	4¹/₂ hours

QUANTITIES OF ICINGS TO ALLOW:
The recipes are on the left column of the opposite page.

The amount of marzipan and Royal icing, or sugar paste is sufficient to cover the complete cake. There will be sufficient icing for piping and a small amount of decoration.

The quantities vary slightly depending upon how thick a layer of marzipan and icing is required.

Allow just under half the quantities if covering the top of the cake only.

For a 20 cm/8 inch round or an 18 cm /7 inch square cake: Marzipan made with 300 to 350 g/10 to 12 oz ground almonds, etc. Royal icing made with 675 to 750 g/1¹/₂ to 1³/₄ lb icing sugar, etc. or the same amount of sugar paste.

For a 23 cm/9 inch round or 20 cm /8 inch square cake: Marzipan made with 350 to 400 g/12 to 14 oz ground almonds, etc. Royal icing made with 750 to 900/1³/₄ to 2 lb icing sugar, etc. or the same amount of sugar paste.

For a 25 cm/10 inch round or 23 cm /9 inch square cake: Marzipan made with 400 to 450 g/14 oz to 1 lb ground almonds, etc. Royal icing made with 900 g to 1 kg/2 to 2¹/₄ lb icing sugar, etc. and the same amount of sugar paste.

For a 28 cm/11 inch round or 25 cm /10 inch square cake: Marzipan made with 450 to 550 g/1 to 1¹/₄ lb ground almonds, etc. Royal icing made with 1 to 1·12 kg/2¹/₄ to 2¹/₂ lb icing sugar, etc. or the same amount of sugar paste.

For a 30 cm/12 inch round or 28 cm /11 inch square cake: Marzipan made with 550 to 675 g/1¹/₄ to 1¹/₂ lb ground almonds, etc. Royal icing made with 1·12 to 1·35 kg/2¹/₂ to 3 lb icing sugar, etc. or the same amount of sugar paste.

MAKING PRESERVES

Even if you do not want to make a very large quantity of preserves, it is very satisfying to take advantage of produce which you grow yourself or can buy cheaply.

If you decide to make low-sugar jams, etc., you must take great care in storing them. Either sterilize, like bottled fruit, or freeze.

When you open a jar of a low-sugar preserve, keep it in the refrigerator and use the contents within 2 or 3 weeks. The jam will set, for it is the natural pectin in the fruit, not the sugar, that makes that happen. Sugar is the preservative. To be certain that correctly made jams and jellies keep well, without the added precautions mentioned above, you must use the full amount of sugar.

Choice of sugar: There is more about selecting sugar on page 35. Preserving sugar is a good choice, as less scum forms. If you do not use this, then choose granulated or caster sugar. The natural sugars, described on page 35, give a good flavour to preserves.

MAKING MARMALADE

PROPORTIONS OF FRUIT AND SUGAR

Sweet marmalade:
To 450 g/1 lb Seville oranges, allow 1·8 litres/3 pints water and 1·35 kg/3 lb sugar, plus 6 tablespoons lemon juice, or use special sugar with added pectin, plus 3 tablespoons lemon juice.

Semi-sweet marmalade:
To 450 g/1 lb Seville oranges, allow 1·5 litres/2½ pints water and 1·12 kg/2½ lb sugar, plus 3 tablespoons lemon juice, or use special sugar with added pectin.

Bitter orange, lemon or kumquat marmalade:
To 450 g/1 lb Seville oranges, lemons and kumquats allow 1.2 litres/2 pints water and 900 g/2 lb sugar.

Mixed fruit marmalade; tangerine marmalade:
Proportions as bitter orange marmalade, plus 3 table-spoons lemon juice or use special sugar with added pectin.

Marmalade is undoubtedly the most 'cost effective' of all preserves to make, for from a relatively small amount of fruit, you can produce a good amount of marmalade.

However, marmalade creates a problem in setting. It has the shortest period in which it will set of any preserves, so you must check frequently to ensure you do not pass this stage.

STAGES IN MAKING MARMALADE
A. Cut up the fruit. The pips and any pith should be tied in a muslin bag – never discard these, as they contain much of the pectin in the fruit and are therefore needed for setting.
B. Soak the fruit in the recommended amount of water overnight.
C. Simmer gently to soften the peel. This is most important, as the peel does not soften after the sugar has been added. See points about using a pressure cooker or microwave under **A** in jam-making, page 188.
D. Add the sugar, plus any lemon juice, if needed, or use the special sugar containing pectin.
E. Stir until the sugar has dissolved, then follow stages **C** to **E** under jam-making, page 188.

Mixed Fruit Marmalade

MAKING CONSERVES

These could be called luxury preserves as they have really large pieces of fruit in them. You can choose this method of preparation instead of the usual method of making jam with these fruits, or any others you choose.

Halved apricots and dessert plums, diced mangoes or fresh pineapple, whole strawberries or black (dessert) cherries.

Use it for diced marrow in marrow ginger, on this page.

STAGES IN MAKING CONSERVES

A. Prepare the fruit. Put it into a container with the sugar; use exactly the same amount and type of sugar as when making jam. See page 188.

B. Turn the fruit in the sugar until well-coated. If any fruit is inclined to discolour, such as fresh apricots, add lemon juice to the sugar. This will also help the conserve to set.

C. Gently simmer the fruit with the sugar. Stir carefully until the sugar has dissolved, but try not to break soft fruit, like strawberries.

D. When the sugar has dissolved boil rapidly, as for jam, and continue as stages **C** to **E** on page 188.

MAKING JAM

Use preserving sugar, granulated sugar or the special sugar mentioned in 3. below and on page 35.

PROPORTIONS OF FRUIT AND SUGAR FOR JAM

Group 1: Rich in pectin

blackcurrants, firm damsons, green gooseberries

To each 450 g/1 lb fruit add: 150 ml/¼ pint water and 500 g/1 lb 2 oz sugar

Group 2: Average amount of pectin

fruits not given in groups 1 and 3

To each 450 g/1 lb fruit add: 450 g/1 lb sugar. No water if soft and ripe, 2 tablespoons if firm

Group 3: Low in pectin

ripe apricots, blackberries, dessert cherries, strawberries

To each 500 g/1 lb 2oz fruit add: 450 g/1 lb sugar plus 1 tablespoon lemon juice or 2 tablespoons redcurrant juice or use special sugar with added pectin

To make good jam, you need first class fruit. It should be ripe, so you have the full flavour, but not over-ripe or damaged.

In the case of a few fruits, such as damsons and gooseberries, you can use either firmer, under-ripe fruit with a little more water to soften and slightly more sugar, or really ripe fruit.

Use preserving sugar, granulated sugar or the special sugar mentioned in 3. below and on page 35.

FRUITS CAN BE DIVIDED INTO THREE GROUPS

1. There are a few fruits, such as blackcurrants, which are very high in natural pectin. When making these into jam, use slightly less fruit than sugar.
2. The majority of fruits have a reasonable amount of natural Pectin. Use equal quantities of fruit and sugar.
3. When making jam with fruit like strawberries, which are low in natural pectin, it is important to use slightly more fruit than sugar and add extra pectin, in the form of lemon juice or redcurrant juice, or by using the special sugar that has pectin added.

STAGES IN JAM-MAKING

A. Soften the fruit to extract the pectin. This can be done in a large saucepan or preserving pan on top of the cooker, see point C, or in a pressure cooker or a bowl in the microwave. A pressure cooker is very good for this purpose, especially when dealing with fruits with a fairly tough skin, such as blackcurrants. A microwave is not so good for these fruits, but excellent for softer fruits.

If using an ordinary pan, soften the fruit slowly. Whichever method is used, do not over-cook the fruit at this stage, otherwise colour and flavour are lost. Nevertheless, the skins of fruit must be soft, for they do not soften once the sugar has been added.

B. Add the sugar and stir over a fairly low heat until it is thoroughly dissolved. This is very important.

If using a pressure cooker, treat it like an ordinary saucepan from this stage onwards. While you could continue making the preserve in a bowl in the microwave, it is easier to transfer the fruit to an ordinary pan, once it has been softened. If, however, you decide to continue using the microwave, you must open the door at intervals of a few seconds to stir the sugar and fruit and make sure it has dissolved. Add lemon juice or other pectin, if required, at this stage.

C. When the sugar has dissolved, it is very important that the jam boils rapidly. This is why the container must be sufficiently large for this to happen, without fear of the preserve boiling over. This is just as important when using a bowl in the microwave as in an open pan on top of the cooker.

D. Test early in the boiling process to see if the jam has reached setting point and continue to test at frequent intervals. If any preserve over-boils, you can destroy the setting qualities so it will never set and you will certainly lose both colour and flavour.

E. Ladle the hot jam carefully into heated jars, fill up to 6 mm/¼ inch of the top of the jar – the less space there is the better. Put on the waxed jam discs and then add the final cover.

If making jam with whole fruit in it, allow to cool slightly in the container, stir to distribute the fruit, then put into the jars. The whole fruit stays evenly distributed.

F. Store in a cool dry place.

FREEZING FRUITS AND PRESERVES

There may be fruit available but it is not always convenient for you to make the jam or marmalade at that time. This is a case for freezing the fruit.

While freezing does not impair the fruit, it does lessen its natural setting qualities, so always use lemon juice when making the jam or marmalade.

If the recipe already gives lemon juice, then use double the quantity. You can use the sugar containing pectin, even if this is not necessary when making preserves with the fresh fruit.

Freezing low-sugar preserves: Put into jars, as usual, but do not fill to the very top. Allow at least 2·5 cm/1 inch at the top. All fruits contain a lot of liquid which expands in freezing and the space allows this to happen. Seal the top well and cover with foil.

Lemon Curd   ▲ ▲   ✪ ✪

MAKES ABOUT 600 g/20 OZ
225 g/8 oz caster sugar
110 g/4 oz fresh butter
finely grated zest from 2 to 3
   lemons
juice from 2 large lemons
2 eggs, size 1 or 2

It is important that this is cooked slowly; the top of a double saucepan or a basin over hot, but not boiling water is ideal. The curd can be made in the microwave on DEFROST setting; whisk or stir frequently, just as when making this over hot water.

Put the sugar, butter, lemon rind and most of the juice into the container. Heat, stirring from time to time, until the butter melts. Beat the eggs and whisk into the other ingredients. Continue cooking, stirring very frequently, until the mixture coats the back of a wooden spoon. Taste the preserve and add the remainder of the lemon juice if you feel it will improve the flavour.

NOTE: If you find the mixture starts to curdle (separate) during the latter stage of cooking, immediately remove from the heat and whisk very hard. When the curd is smooth again, continue cooking.

REDUCING THE SUGAR:
You can use 175 g/6 oz.

USING LOAF SUGAR:
If using this, rub the lumps against the lemons to extract all the flavour.

OTHER FRUITS TO USE:
Oranges, grapefruit and mixed citrus fruits all make good curds. Use the equivalent amount of rind and about 4 tablespoons juice, or to taste.

Lemon Curd; Blackcurrant Jam
(see page 188)

Index

PHOTOGRAPHIC ACKNOWLEDGEMENTS

Special photography taken by Amanda Heywood: 1, 4/5, 60, 77, 85, 86, 89, 91, 93, 95, 104, 107, 110, 114L, 114C, 114R, 115, 117, 119, 121, 123, 124, 137, 145, 151, 154, 157, 159, 161, 163, 165, 171, 181;

Reed International Books Ltd/Howard Allman: 96, 98, 112; Sue Atkinson: 54; Bryce Attwell: 33; David Burch: 73, 78L, 78R, 80; Paul Bussell: 42; Nick Carman: 74; John Cook: 84L, 84CL, 84CR, 84R, 94L, 94CL, 94CR, 94R; Chris Crofton: 13L, 65L, 82L, 82C, 82R, 133, 135; Laurie Evans: 15, 48, 62, 142, 169; Robert Golden: 11; Paul Grater: 10, 13R; Melvin Grey: 53, 69, 71, 187; Christine Hanscomb: 25; James Jackson: 102, 109; David Johnson: 139R; David Jordan: 32; Sue Jorgensen: 30; Paul Moon: 127R, 131; Vernon Morgan: 7, 9A, 9B, 27, 52L, 55, 57L, 57R, 65R, 141, 153, 173L; James Murphy: 6BR, 67, 101, 129, 167, 173R; Ian O'Leary: 49, 51, 127L, 189; Roger Phillips: 8, 38, 41, 182; Reed Consumer Books Picture Library: 19, 21, 139L, 147, 149, 176, 178; Charlie Stebbings: 28; Clive Streeter: 6L, 22, 59, 83; Paul Webster: 37, 174;

Other Photographs reproduced courtesy of: Pam Bewley Publicity: 46B; Braun UK Ltd: 43; Moulinex Swan Holdings Ltd: 46A, Paragon Communications: 40, 45; Philips Whirlpool: 44, 47; J Sainsbury PLC: 17; The Tea Council : 34;